SIXTH EDITION

ESSENTIALS OF ACCOUNTING

ARTHUR E. CARLSON, PhD
Professor of Accounting
School of Business Administration
Washington University, St. Louis

JAMES A. HEINTZ, DBA, CPA
Professor of Accounting
Indiana University
Bloomington, Indiana

MARY E. BURNET, MBA, CPA
Professor Emeritus of Accounting
Rochester Institute of Technology
Rochester, New York

SUSAN EASON, EdD.
Chairperson of Accounting
and General Business
San Jacinto College
Pasadena, Texas

Published by

A49 **SOUTH-WESTERN PUBLISHING CO.**

CINCINNATI WEST CHICAGO, IL DALLAS LIVERMORE, CA

ISBN: 0-538-01490-3

Library of Congress Catalog Card Number: 86-62512

2 3 4 5 K 1 0 9 8 7

Printed in the United States of America

PREFACE

As the world of business and the professions continually grows larger and more complicated, a knowledge of accounting becomes more and more essential. More opportunities are thus created for those persons who have an understanding of the accounting process. *Essentials of Accounting* presents a system of accounting that can be used in any business office that is not involved with inventories of goods for resale or for use in manufacturing products for resale. In addition, special attention is paid to accounting problems and situations encountered by attorneys and physicians and dentists.

The accounting cycle and the income statement and balance sheet are presented early in the course. The remaining chapters in the book are an elaboration of the basic material presented earlier. The student is thus continually building upon and reinforcing his or her knowledge of the underlying structure of accounting. Chapter 3 is devoted to accounting for cash and includes a discussion of banking procedures. Chapter 4 covers payroll accounting. The latter chapters of the book that follow those on accounting for attorneys and physicians and dentists take up the end-of-the-period activities.

The appendix to Chapter 5 discusses and illustrates accounting for the professional corporation. The principles illustrated in this appendix can be applied to accounting for any professional corporation.

A new feature in this sixth edition is the appendix to Chapter 6. This appendix discusses other accounting systems and illustrates the one-write accounting system and computer-based accounting systems. Both of these systems can be used by any business.

The features that were new in the fifth edition are continued in this edition. Among them are "Chapter Objectives" at the beginning of each chapter, "Building Your Accounting Knowledge" review questions at the end of each chapter section (there are one or more sections per chapter), and "Expanding Your Business Vocabulary" terms at the end of each chapter. The vocabulary terms are referenced to the textbook pages on which they appear.

Exercises (called Applying Accounting Concepts), Mastery Problems and a Challenge Problem have been included at the end of each chapter. The forms needed for solving these activities are included in the study assignments workbook. Also included in the study assignments is a Report that will review additional chapter concepts.

Two practice sets are available for use with the text. One of the sets covers one month's transactions in the office of an attorney (Sarah E. Burke, Attorney at Law). This set can be effectively started upon the completion of Chapter 5. A second set (Pratt and Walz Physicians and Surgeons) provides practice in recording a month's transactions in a physician's office. This set is designed to be started upon the completion of Chapter 6. For those instructors who wish to emphasize the record keeping of a general business, a third set (Vance Zarmer, Computer Consultant) designed to correlate with *College Accounting* is available for use after Chapter 5 or 6. All three sets are designed to give the student a review of the complete accounting cycle.

Tests are available for use following completion of Chapters 2, 4, 6, and 8.

The authors acknowledge with gratitude the assistance received from the members of the business and professional community whose suggestions contributed to the preparation of this textbook.

M. E. Burnet
S. Eason

CONTENTS

1
THE NATURE OF BUSINESS ACCOUNTING

CHAPTER OBJECTIVES

Careful study of this chapter should enable you to:

- Describe business accounting as it applies to profit-seeking enterprises.
- Define certain business accounting terms.
- Explain how selected business transactions affect the business entity, using the accounting equation.
- Explain the nature of the income statement and the balance sheet, and how they relate to one another.
- Explain the double-entry framework.
- Explain the function of the trial balance.

The purpose of business accounting is to provide information about the current operating results and financial condition of an enterprise to individuals, agencies, and organizations who have the need and the right to be so informed. These user groups normally include:

1. The **owners** of the business—both present and prospective.
2. The **managers** of the business—managers may or may not own the business. (Often, but not always, the owners and the managers are the same persons.)
3. The **creditors** or **suppliers** of the business—both present and prospective. Creditors or suppliers are those who supply goods and services on credit—meaning that payment need not be made on the date of purchase. The creditor category also includes banks and individuals who lend money to the business.
4. **Government agencies**—local, state, and national. For purposes of regulation and taxation, various governmental agencies must be given certain financial information.

In connection with many businesses, some or all of the following also make use of accounting information: customers or clients, labor unions, competitors, trade associations, stock exchanges, commodity exchanges, financial analysts, and financial writers.

Although the information needed by all types of users is not identical, most want data regarding (1) the results of operations — net income or loss — for the most recent period and (2) the financial status of the business as of the most current date available. The demand for the greatest quantity and variety of information usually comes from the managers of the business. They constantly need up-to-the-minute information about the financial activities of every department in their organization. Because accounting relates to so many phases of business, it is not surprising that there are several fields of accounting specialization such as tax work, cost accounting, computer-based accounting systems design and installation, management consulting, and budget preparation.

Many accountants have but one employer whereas others become qualified as public accountants and offer their services as independent contractors or advisors. Public accountants perform various functions. One of their major activities is **auditing**. This involves the application of standard review and testing procedures to the records of an enterprise to be certain that acceptable accounting policies and practices have been consistently followed. The purpose of the audit is to provide an independent opinion that the financial information about a business is fairly presented. Public accountants frequently extend their activities into the area of "management consulting" — a term that covers a variety of specialized management service assignments. Some states license individuals as **Public Accountants** or **Registered Accountants,** although this practice is disappearing. All states grant the designation of **Certified Public Accountant** (CPA) to those who meet various prescribed requirements, including the passing of a uniform examination prepared by the American Institute of Certified Public Accountants.

A uniform examination is also offered in numerous cities throughout the country by the Institute of Management Accounting of the National Association of Accountants, leading to the designation of **Certified Management Accountant** (CMA). This certificate is designed to give professional status to one-employer accountants. Still another uniform examination is offered under similar conditions by the Institute of Internal Auditors, leading to the designation of **Certified Internal Auditor** (CIA). This certificate affords professional status to accountants who review the operating and accounting control procedures adopted by their full-time employers.

All of the foregoing comments have related to accounting and accountants in connection with profit-seeking organizations. There are thousands of not-for-profit organizations such as governments, educational institutions, churches, and hospitals that also need to accumulate and dispense information. These organizations also engage a large number of accountants. While the "rules of the game" are somewhat different in not-for-profit organizations, much of the record keeping is identical with that found in profit-seeking organizations.

The accountant is responsible for accumulating and dispensing the financial information needed by users. Since such activities touch upon nearly every aspect of business operation and since financial information is communicated in accounting terms, accounting is said to be the "language of business." Anyone intending to engage in any type of business activity should learn this language.

THE ACCOUNTING PROCESS

Business accounting may be defined as the art of (1) analyzing and (2) entering financial transactions and certain business-related economic events in a manner that (3) classifies and (4) summarizes the information and (5) reports and (6) interprets the results. The accounting process itself provides the basis for this definition.

Analyzing is the first step in the accounting process. The accountant must look at a transaction or event that has occurred and determine its fundamental significance to the business so that the relevant information may be properly processed.

Entering traditionally meant writing by hand. Much of the record keeping in accounting still is done manually, however, technological advances have introduced a variety of accounting machines that typically combine the major attributes of typewriters, calculators, cathode ray tubes, and electromechanical printing. Today the initial processing sometimes takes the form of terminal keyboard input directly into a computer with the input appearing on a screen or paper roll; of diskettes prepared by keyboard input not directly connected to a computer; or of special characters that can be magnetically or electronically "read" from source documents and thus used to feed information directly into a computer. Because of the multiple ways information may be processed, the term "data entry" may be substituted for the term "recording" in the accounting process.

Classifying relates to the process of sorting or grouping like things together rather than merely keeping a simple, diary-like narrative record of numerous and varied transactions and events.

Summarizing is the process of bringing together various items of information to determine or explain a result.

Final processing or **reporting** refers to the process of communicating the results. In accounting, it is common to use tabular arrangements rather than narrative-type reports. Sometimes, a combination of the two is used.

Interpreting refers to the steps taken to direct attention to the significance of various matters and relationships. Percentage analyses and ratios often are used to help explain the meaning of certain related bits of information. Footnotes to financial reports and special captions may also be valuable in the interpreting phase of accounting.

Accounting and Bookkeeping

A person involved with or responsible for such functions as accounting information systems design, accounting policy making, data analysis, report preparation, and report interpretation may be referred to as an accountant. A person who records or enters information in accounting records may be referred to as a bookkeeper. Bookkeeping is the processing phase of the accounting information processing system. That term goes back to the time when formal accounting records were in the form of books—pages bound together. While this still is sometimes the case, modern practice favors the use of loose-leaf or computer-generated records and cards. When the language catches up with practice, the designation information processor or "record keeper" may replace "bookkeeper."

Accounting Elements

A business entity is a particular individual, association, or other organization for which formal records are kept and periodic reports are made. Properties of value that are owned by a business entity are called assets.

Assets. Properties such as money, accounts receivable, merchandise, furniture, fixtures, machinery, buildings, and land are common examples of business assets. An account receivable is an unwritten promise by a customer to pay at a later date for goods sold or for services rendered.

It is possible to conduct a business or a professional practice with very few assets. A medical doctor, for example, may have relatively few assets, such as money, accounts receivable, instruments, laboratory equipment, and office equipment. In many cases, however, numerous assets are necessary. A merchant must have a large selection of merchandise to sell and store equipment with which to display the merchandise. A manufacturer must have an inventory of parts and materials, tools and various sorts of machinery with which to make or assemble one or more products.

Liabilities. A legal obligation of a business to pay a debt is a business liability. Debts can be paid with money, goods, or services, but usually are paid in cash. Liabilities represent one type of ownership interest in a business—an outside interest.

The most common liabilities are accounts payable and notes payable. An **account payable** is an unwritten promise to pay a supplier for property purchased on credit or for a service rendered. Formal written promises to pay suppliers or lenders specified sums of money at definite future times are known as **notes payable**. A business also may have one or more types of taxes payable classified as liabilities.

Owner's Equity. The amount by which the business assets exceed the business liabilities is termed the **owner's equity** in the business. The word "equity" used in this sense represents a second type of ownership interest in a business—an inside interest. The terms **proprietorship, net worth**, or **capital** are sometimes used as synonyms for owner's equity. If there are no business liabilities, the owner's equity in the business is equal to the total amount of the assets of the business.

A business that is owned by one person traditionally is called a **proprietorship**. The person owning the interest in a business is known as the proprietor. A distinction must be made between the business assets and liabilities and nonbusiness assets and liabilities that a proprietor may have. For example, the proprietor probably owns a home, clothing, and a car, and perhaps owes the dentist for dental service. These are personal, nonbusiness assets and liabilities. The formal accounting records for the enterprise will relate to the business entity only; any nonbusiness assets and liabilities of the proprietor should be excluded. While the term "owner's equity" can be used in a very broad sense, its use in accounting is nearly always limited to the meaning: business assets minus business liabilities.

Frequent reference will be made to the owner's acts of investing money or other property in the business and to the withdrawal of money or other property from the business. In either case, property is changed from the category of a nonbusiness asset to a business asset or vice versa. These distinctions are important if the owner is going to make decisions based on the financial condition and results of the business apart from nonbusiness affairs.

The Accounting Equation

The relationship between the three basic accounting elements can be expressed in the form of a simple equation known as the **accounting equation**.

ASSETS = LIABILITIES + OWNER'S EQUITY

This equation reflects the fact that outsiders and insiders have an interest in all of the assets of a business. When the amounts of any two of these elements are known, the third can always be calculated.

LIABILITIES = ASSETS − OWNER'S EQUITY

OWNER'S EQUITY = ASSETS − LIABILITIES

For example, Harriet Matthews has business assets on December 31 in the sum of $67,100. The business liabilities on that date consist of $2,900 owed for a microcomputer purchased on account and $2,300 owed to a bank on a note. The owner's equity element of the business may be calculated by subtracting the total liabilities from the total assets, $67,100 − $5,200 = $61,900.

ASSETS =	**LIABILITIES** +	**OWNER'S EQUITY**
$67,100	$5,200	$61,900

A closer examination of the owner's equity will show how the equation maintains equality. One way to increase the owner's equity in the business is to increase the assets. To increase the assets and owner's equity, Matthews may (1) invest more money or other property in the business or (2) operate the business profitably.

For example, if one year later the assets are $102,600 and the liabilities are $4,400, the status of the business would be as follows:

ASSETS =	**LIABILITIES** +	**OWNER'S EQUITY**
$102,600	$4,400	$98,200

The fact that Matthews equity in the business increased by $36,300 (from $61,900 to $98,200) does not prove that she had made a profit (often called net income) equal to the increase. Increases and decreases in owner's equity must be analyzed. If the records indicated that she invested additional money during the year in the amount of $7,000 and did not withdraw any funds for personal use, the remainder of the increase in her equity ($29,300) would have been due to profit (net income).

If the records indicated she invested no additional funds, withdrew assets in an amount of $28,700 cash for personal use, and increased her equity by $65,000 as a result of a profitable operation, the net effect would also account for the $36,300 ($65,000 − $28,700) increase. It is essential that the business records show the changes in owner's equity due to events that are part of regular business operations and the changes in owner's equity due to investments and withdrawals of assets by the owner.

Transactions

Any activity of an enterprise which involves the exchange of values is referred to as a **transaction**. These values are typically expressed in terms of money. Buying and selling property and performing services are common transactions. The following typical transactions are analyzed to show that each represents an exchange of values.

Typical Transactions	Analysis of Transactions
1. Purchased equipment for cash, $2,500.	Money was exchanged for equipment.
2. Received cash in payment of professional fees, $800.	Professional service was rendered in exchange for money.
3. Paid office rent, $1,250.	Money was exchanged for the right to use property.
4. Paid an amount owed to a supplier, $825.	Money was given in settlement of a debt that may have resulted from the purchase of property on account or from services rendered by a supplier.
5. Paid wages, $2,975.	Money was exchanged for services rendered.
6. Borrowed $4,500 at a bank giving a 10 percent interest-bearing note due in 60 days.	A liability known as a note payable was incurred in exchange for money.
7. Purchased office equipment on account, $850.	A liability known as an account payable was incurred in exchange for office equipment.

Effect of Transactions on the Accounting Equation

Each transaction affects one or more of the three basic accounting elements. For example, in transaction (1) the purchase of equipment for cash represents both an increase and a decrease in assets. The assets increased because equipment was acquired; the assets decreased because cash was disbursed. The office equipment in transaction (7) was purchased on account, thereby creating a liability. The transaction results in an increase in assets (equipment) with a corresponding increase in liabilities (accounts payable). Neither of these transactions has any effect upon the owner's equity element of the equation.

The effect of any transaction on the basic elements of the accounting equation may be indicated by increasing or decreasing a specific asset, liability, or owner's equity account. To illustrate: assume that Anthony Gonzalez, an attorney, decided to go into practice for himself. During the first month of this venture (June, 1987), the following transactions relating to the practice took place:

Transaction (a)

An Increase in an Asset Offset by an Increase in Owner's Equity

Gonzalez opened a bank account with a deposit of $25,000. This transaction caused the new business to receive the asset cash; and since Gonzalez contributed the assets, the owner's equity element was increased by the same amount. As a result of this transaction, the equation for the business would appear as follows:

ASSETS		LIABILITIES + OWNER'S EQUITY
Cash	=	Anthony Gonzalez, Capital
(a) $25,000		$25,000

Transaction (b)

An Increase in an Asset Offset by an Increase in a Liability

Gonzalez purchased office equipment (desk, chairs, file cabinet, etc.) for $5,700 on 30 days credit. This transaction caused the asset office equipment to increase by $5,700 and resulted in an equal increase in the liability accounts payable. Updating the foregoing equation by this (b) transaction gives the following result:

	ASSETS			LIABILITIES +	OWNER'S EQUITY
	Cash	+ Office Equipment		Accounts Payable	Anthony Gonzalez, Capital
Bal.	$25,000		=		$25,000
(b)		$5,700		$5,700	
Bal.	$25,000	$5,700		$5,700	$25,000

Transaction (c)

An Increase in One Asset Offset by a Decrease in Another Asset

Gonzalez purchased office supplies (stationery, legal pads, pencils, etc.) for cash, $760. This transaction caused a $760 increase in the asset office supplies that exactly offset the $760 decrease in the asset cash. The effect on the equation is as follows:

	ASSETS				LIABILITIES +	OWNER'S EQUITY
Bal.	Cash	+ Office Equipment	+ Office Supplies		Accounts Payable	Anthony Gonzalez, Capital
Bal.	$25,000	$5,700		=	$5,700	$25,000
(c)	− 760		$760			
Bal.	$24,240	$5,700	$760		$5,700	$25,000

Transaction (d)

A Decrease in an Asset Offset by a Decrease in a Liability

Gonzalez paid $2,700 on account to the company from which the office equipment was purchased. (See Transaction (b).) This payment caused the asset cash and the liability accounts payable both to decrease $2,700. The effect on the equation is as follows:

	ASSETS				LIABILITIES +	OWNER'S EQUITY
	Cash	+ Office Equipment	+ Office Supplies	=	Accounts Payable	Anthony Gonzalez, Capital
Bal.	$24,240	$5,700	$760		$5,700	$25,000
(d)	− 2,700				−2,700	
Bal.	$21,540	$5,700	$760		$3,000	$25,000

Transaction (e)

An Increase in an Asset Offset by an Increase in Owner's Equity Resulting from Revenue

Gonzalez received $2,000 cash from a client for professional services. This transaction caused the asset cash to increase $2,000, and since the cash was received for services performed by the business, the owner's equity increased by the same amount. The effect on the equation is as follows:

	ASSETS				LIABILITIES +	OWNER'S EQUITY
	Cash	+ Office Equipment	+ Office Supplies	=	Accounts Payable	Anthony Gonzalez, Capital
Bal.	$21,540	$5,700	$760		$3,000	$25,000
(e)	2,000					2,000
Bal.	$23,540	$5,700	$760		$3,000	$27,000

Transaction (f)

A Decrease in an Asset Offset by a Decrease in Owner's Equity Resulting from Expense

(1) Gonzalez paid $800 for office rent for June. This transaction caused the asset cash to be reduced by $800 with an equal reduction in owner's equity. The effect on the equation is as follows:

	ASSETS				LIABILITIES +	OWNER'S EQUITY
	Cash	+ Office Equipment	+ Office Supplies	=	Accounts Payable	Anthony Gonzalez, Capital
Bal.	$23,540	$5,700	$760		$3,000	$27,000
(f1)	− 800					− 800
Bal.	$22,740	$5,700	$760		$3,000	$26,200

(2) Gonzalez paid a bill for telephone service, $67. This transaction, like the previous one, caused a decrease in the asset cash with an equal decrease in the owner's equity. The effect on the equation is as follows:

	ASSETS				LIABILITIES +	OWNER'S EQUITY
	Cash	+ Office Equipment	+ Office Supplies		Accounts Payable	Anthony Gonzalez, Capital
Bal.	$22,740	$5,700	$760	=	$3,000	$26,200
(f2)	− 67					− 67
Bal.	$22,673	$5,700	$760		$3,000	$26,133

The Financial Statements

A set of records that make up an accounting information system is maintained to fill a variety of needs. Foremost is to provide source data for use in preparing various reports, including those referred to as financial statements. The two most important of these are the income statement and the balance sheet.

The Income Statement. The income statement, sometimes called the profit and loss statement or operating statement, shows the net income (net profit) or net loss for a specified period of time and how it was calculated. A very simple income statement has been prepared relating to the business of Anthony Gonzalez for the first month's operation, June, 1987. This statement contains information that was obtained by analysis of the changes in the owner's equity element of the business for the month. This element went from zero to $26,133. Part of this increase, $25,000, was due to the initial investment made by Gonzalez. Since an owner's investment is not classified as income or expense of the business, it is not considered in the income statement. The remainder of the increase, $1,133, was due to Gonzalez earning income and incurring expense. Transaction (e) involved revenue of $2,000; transactions (f1) and (f2) involved expenses of $800 and $67, respectively. Taken together, these transactions explain the net income of $1,133, as it appears in the statement below:

ANTHONY GONZALEZ, ATTORNEY
Income Statement
For the Month of June, 1987

Professional fees		$2,000
Expenses:		
Rent expense	$800	
Telephone expense	67	867
Net income for month		$1,133

The Balance Sheet. The balance sheet, sometimes called a statement of financial position or statement of financial condition, shows the assets, liabilities, and owner's equity of a business at a specified date. A balance sheet in account form for Gonzalez' business as of June 30, 1987, is shown as follows.

ANTHONY GONZALEZ, ATTORNEY
Balance Sheet
June 30, 1987

Assets		**Liabilities**	
Cash	$22,673	Accounts payable	$ 3,000
Office supplies	760		
Office equipment	5,700	**Owner's Equity**	
		Anthony Gonzalez, Capital	26,133
Total assets	$29,133	Total liabilities and owner's equity	$29,133

The accounting process described above can be illustrated with the following diagram.

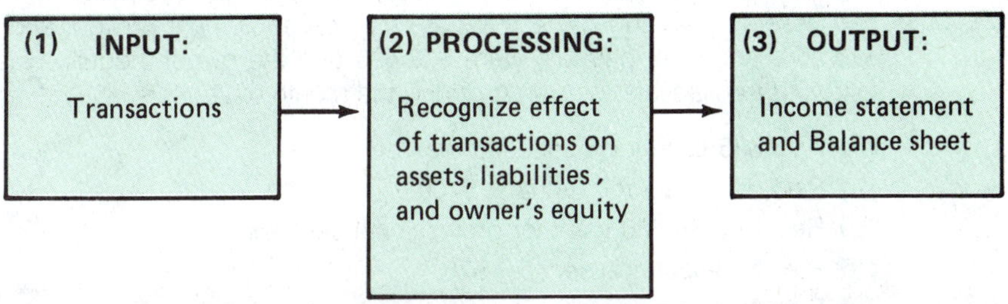

1. Transactions in which property or services are bought or sold by an enterprise provide the necessary **input** for the accounting information system.
2. Recognizing the effect of these transactions on the assets, liabilities and owner's equity of an enterprise is the **processing** function of the accounting information system.
3. The accounting data base generated in the processing function provides the source data for the **output** of the accounting information system—the income statement and the balance sheet.

BUILDING YOUR ACCOUNTING KNOWLEDGE

1. Identify four user groups normally interested in financial information about a business enterprise.
2. Which group of information users usually demands the greatest quantity and variety of information?
3. Why is accounting called the "language of business?"

4. What is the major difference between a public accountant and a management accountant?
5. Identify the six major phases of the accounting process, and indicate what is done in each phase.
6. Why is it necessary to distinguish between the business assets and liabilities and the nonbusiness assets and liabilities of the single proprietor?
7. In what other way than by making a profit can the owner's equity in a proprietorship be increased?
8. In what other way than by suffering a loss can the owner's equity in a proprietorship be decreased?

APPLYING ACCOUNTING CONCEPTS

Exercise 1-1. **(1)** If the amount of the assets is $59,500 and the owner's equity amounts to $37,200, what is the amount of the liabilities? **(2)** If Robert McAfee, a financial planner, has cash in the business bank account in the amount of $29,850, owns office equipment amounting to $11,400, an automobile which is used for business purposes only amounting to $13,200, and other property used in the business amounting to $1,100, and owes business creditors a total of $9,375; what is the owner's equity in the business?

Exercise 1-2. On January 1, 1987, Esther Jacob, a certified public accountant, had assets consisting of cash $21,300, office equipment $6,400, and an automobile $15,200. Accounts payable were $12,600 and the owner's equity was $30,300. The following transactions occurred during the month of January.

(a) Paid $85 cash for a cassette recorder.
(b) Paid office rent for January, $750.
(c) Received $5,200 cash for professional services.
(d) Paid for telephone service, $78.
(e) Paid $2,500 on account.

Indicate the effect of each transaction on the accounting equation: Assets = Liabilities + Owner's Equity. Each amount should be preceded by a plus sign if it represents an increase and by a minus sign if it represents a decrease.

Exercise 1-3. Using the information contained in Exercise 1-2, prepare an income statement for Esther Jacob's business for the month ended January 31, 1987 and a balance sheet as of January 31, 1987.

REPORT NO. 1-1

The work involved in completing Report No. 1-1 requires a knowledge of the principles developed in the preceding textbook discussion. Before proceeding with the following discussion, complete Report No. 1-1 in accordance with the instructions given in the study assignments.

THE DOUBLE-ENTRY FRAMEWORK

The meanings of the terms asset, liability, and owner's equity were explained in the preceding pages. Examples were given to show how each business transaction causes a change in one or more of the three basic accounting elements. Transaction (a) shown on page 7 involved an increase in an asset with a corresponding increase in owner's equity. Transaction (b) involved an increase in an asset which caused an equal increase in a liability. Transaction (c) involved an increase in one asset which was offset by a decrease in another. Each of the transactions illustrated a dual effect. This is always true. A change, increase or decrease, in any asset, any liability, or in owner's equity is always accompanied by an offsetting change within the basic accounting elements.

The fact that each transaction has two aspects—a dual effect upon the accounting elements—provides the basis for what is called double-entry bookkeeping. This term describes a processing system that involves entering the two aspects that are involved in every transaction. Double entry does not mean that a transaction is entered twice; instead it means that both of the two aspects of each transaction are entered.

Double entry is known to have been practiced for at least 500 years. The method has endured largely because it has several virtues; it is orderly, fairly simple, and very flexible. There is no transaction that cannot be entered in a double-entry manner. Double entry promotes accuracy. Its use makes it impossible for certain types of error to remain undetected for very long. For example, if one aspect of a transaction is properly entered but the other aspect is overlooked, it will soon be found that the records as a whole are "out of balance." The accountant then knows that something is wrong, reviews the transaction to discover the trouble and then makes the needed correction.

The Account

It has been explained previously that the assets of a business may consist of a number of items, such as cash, accounts receivable, merchandise, equipment, buildings, and land. The liabilities may consist of one or more items, such as accounts payable and notes payable. A separate record should be kept of each asset and of each liability. Later it will be shown that a separate record should also be kept of the increases and decreases in owner's equity.

A form or record used to keep track of the increases and decreases in each item that result from business transactions is known as an account. There are many types of account forms in general use. They may be ruled on sheets of paper and bound in a book form or kept in a loose-leaf binder;

they may be ruled on cards and kept in a file of some sort; or they may be developed as computer print-outs. An illustration of a standard account form is shown below:

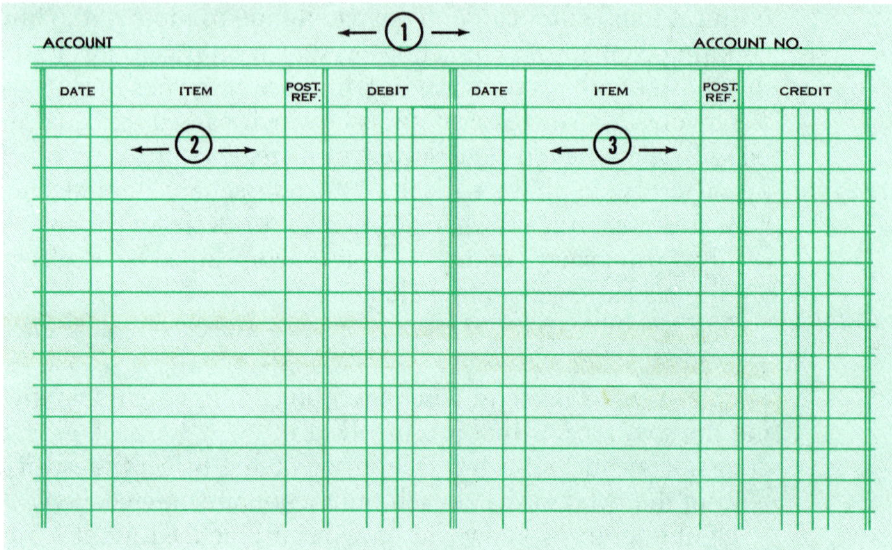

Standard Form of Account

The three major parts of the standard account form are (1) the title and the account number, (2) the debit or left side, and (3) the credit or right side. This account form is designed to facilitate the entering of the essential information regarding each transaction that affects the account. Each account should be given an appropriate title that will indicate whether it is an asset, a liability, or an owner's equity account. Before any entries are made in an account, the title and number of the account should be entered on the horizontal line at the top of the form. The standard account form is divided into two equal parts or sections which are ruled identically to facilitate entering increases and decreases. The left side is called the debit side, while the right side is called the credit side. The Date columns are used for entering the dates of transactions. The Item columns may be used for entering a brief description of a transaction when deemed necessary. The Posting Reference columns will be discussed later. The amount column on the left is headed "Debit" while that on the right is headed "Credit." The Debit and Credit columns are used for entering the amounts of transactions.

To determine the balance of an account at any time, it is necessary only to total the amounts in the Debit and Credit columns, and calculate the difference between the two totals. To save time, a **T account** is commonly used for instructional purposes. It consists of a two-line drawing resembling the capital letter T and is sometimes referred to as a skeleton form of account.

Title	
Debit side	Credit side

T account

Debits and Credits

To **debit** an account means to enter an amount on the left or debit side of the account. To **credit** an account means to enter an amount on the right or credit side of the account. The abbreviation for debit is Dr. and for credit Cr. (based on the Latin terms "debere" and "credere"). Sometimes the word **charge** is used as a substitute for debit. Increases in assets are entered on the left side of the accounts; increases in liabilities and in owner's equity are entered on the right side of the accounts. Decreases in assets are entered on the right side of the accounts; decreases in liabilities and in owner's equity are entered on the left side of the accounts. Entering increases and decreases in the accounts in this manner will reflect the basic equality of assets to liabilities plus owner's equity (Assets = Liabilities + Owner's Equity); at the same time it will maintain equality between the total amounts debited to all accounts and the total amounts credited to all accounts (Debits = Credits). These basic relationships may be illustrated in the following manner:

ASSETS = LIABILITIES + OWNER'S EQUITY

All Asset Accounts	
Debit **to enter increases** (+)	Credit **to enter decreases** (−)

All Liability Accounts	
Debit **to enter decreases** (−)	Credit **to enter increases** (+)

All Owner's Equity Accounts	
Debit **to enter decreases** (−)	Credit **to enter increases** (+)

TOTAL DEBITS = TOTAL CREDITS

Use of Asset, Liability, and Owner's Equity Accounts

To illustrate the application of the double-entry process in handling transactions that affect asset, liability, and owner's equity accounts, the transactions discussed on pages 7-10 will be analyzed and their effect on the accounting elements will be indicated by showing the proper entries in T accounts. As before, the transactions are identified by letters; dates are omitted intentionally.

Transaction (a)

An Increase in an Asset Offset by an Increase in Owner's Equity

Anthony Gonzalez, an attorney, started a business by investing $25,000 in cash.

Cash			
(a)	25,000		

Anthony Gonzalez, Capital			
		(a)	25,000

Analysis: As a result of this transaction the business acquired an asset, cash. The amount of money invested represents Gonzalez' equity in the business; thus the amount of the asset cash is equal to the owner's equity in the business. Separate accounts are kept for the asset cash and for the owner's equity. To enter the transaction as an increase in an asset and an increase in owner's equity, the cash account was debited and Gonzalez' capital account was credited for $25,000.

Transaction (b)

An Increase in an Asset Offset by an Increase in a Liability

Purchased office equipment (desk, chairs, file cabinet, etc.) for $5,700 on 30 days credit.

Office Equipment			
(b)	5,700		

Accounts Payable			
		(b)	5,700

Analysis: As a result of this transaction the business acquired a new asset, office equipment. The debt incurred as a result of purchasing the equipment on 30 days' credit is a liability, accounts payable. Thus, the outside interest in the business has increased by $5,700. Separate accounts are kept for office equipment and for accounts payable. The purchase of office equipment caused an increase in the assets of the business. Therefore, the asset account, Office Equipment, was debited for $5,700. The purchase also caused an increase in a liability. Therefore the liability account, Accounts Payable was credited for $5,700.

Transaction (c)

An Increase in One Asset Offset by a Decrease in Another Asset

Purchased office supplies (stationery, legal pads, pencils, etc.) for cash, $760.

Cash

(a)	25,000	**(c)**	**760**

Office Supplies

(c)	**760**		

Analysis: As a result of this transaction the business acquired a new asset, office supplies. The addition of this asset was offset by a decrease in the asset cash. Notice there is no change in total assets. To enter the transaction properly, Office Supplies was debited and Cash was credited for $760. This is the second entry in the cash account; the account was previously debited for $25,000 when Transaction (a) was recorded.

It is proper to enter office supplies as an asset at the time of purchase even though they will become an expense when used. The procedure used in accounting for supplies will be discussed later.

Transaction (d)

A Decrease in an Asset Offset by a Decrease in a Liability

Paid $2,700 on account to the company from which the office equipment was purchased. (See Transaction (b).)

Cash

(a)	25,000	(c)	760
		(d)	**2,700**

Accounts Payable

(d)	**2,700**	(b)	5,700

Analysis: This transaction resulted in a decrease in the liability accounts payable with a corresponding decrease in the asset cash; hence, it was entered by debiting Accounts Payable and by crediting Cash for $2,700. Note that this is the second entry in the accounts payable account and the third entry in the cash account. At this point in time, the outside interest in the business has decreased by $2,700.

Revenue and Expense

The owner's equity element of a business entity or professional enterprise may be increased in two ways as follows:

1. The owner may invest additional money or other property in the enterprise. Such investments result in an increase both in the assets of the enterprise and in the owner's equity, but they do not further enrich the owner. More property merely is invested in the enterprise and less property outside of the enterprise.
2. Revenue may be derived from sales of goods or services, or from other sources.

As used in accounting, the term revenue in nearly all cases refers to an increase in the owner's equity in a business resulting from transactions involving asset inflows other than the investment of assets in the business by its owner. In most cases, an increase in owner's equity due to revenue results from an addition to the assets without any change in the liabilities. Often it is cash that is increased. However, an increase in cash and other assets can occur in connection with several types of transactions that do not involve revenue. For this reason, revenue is often defined in terms of a change in owner's equity rather than a change in assets. Any transaction that causes owner's equity to increase, except for investments in the business by its owner, involves revenue.

The owner's equity element of a business entity or professional enterprise may be decreased in two ways as follows:

1. The owner may withdraw assets (cash or other property) from the business enterprise.
2. Expenses may be incurred in operating the enterprise.

As used in accounting, the term expense in nearly all cases means a decrease in the owner's equity in a business caused by transactions involving asset outflows other than a withdrawal by the owner. When an expense is incurred, either the assets are reduced or the liabilities are increased. In either event, owner's equity is reduced. If a transaction causing a reduction is not a withdrawal of assets by the owner, an expense is incurred. Common examples of expense are rent of office or store, salaries of employees, telephone service, supplies consumed, and many types of taxes.

If during a specified period of time, the total increases in owner's equity resulting from revenue exceed the total decreases resulting from expenses, it may be said that the excess represents the net income or net profit for the period.

Revenue > Expenses = Net Profit

On the other hand, if the expenses of the period exceed the revenue, such excess represents a net loss for the period.

Expenses > Revenue = Net Loss

The time interval used in the measurement of net income or net loss can be determined by the owner. It may be a month, a quarter (three months), a year, but because of federal, state, and other taxing authority laws, the time interval cannot be longer than a year. Any accounting period of twelve months' duration is usually referred to as a fiscal year. The fiscal year frequently coincides with the calendar year.

Transactions involving revenue and expense always cause a change in the owner's equity element of an enterprise. Such changes could be entered by debiting an account called Owner's Equity for expense and crediting it for revenue. If this practice were followed, however, the credit side of the owner's equity account would contain a mixture of increases due to revenue and to the investment of assets in the business by the owner, while the debit side would contain a mixture of decreases due to expenses and to the withdrawal of assets from the business by the owner. In order to determine the net income or the net loss for each accounting period, a careful analysis of the owner's equity account would be required. It is, therefore, better practice to enter revenue and expenses in separate accounts.

When a transaction produces revenue, the amount of the revenue should be credited to an appropriate revenue account. When a transaction involves expense, the amount of the expense should be debited to an appropriate expense account. The relationship of these accounts to the owner's equity account and the application of the debit and credit theory to the accounts are indicated in the following diagram:

All Owner's Equity Accounts

Debit	Credit
to enter decreases (−)	**to enter increases** (+)

All Expense Accounts

Debit	Credit
to enter increases (+)	**to enter decreases** (−)

All Revenue Accounts

Debit	Credit
to enter decreases (−)	**to enter increases** (+)

The revenue and expense accounts are called temporary owner's equity accounts because it is customary to close them into the owner's equity account (which sets their balances back to zero) at the end of each accounting period. It is important to recognize that the credit side of each revenue account is serving temporarily as a part of the credit side of the owner's equity account. Increases in owner's equity are entered as credits. Thus increases in owner's equity resulting from revenue should be credited to revenue accounts. The debit side of each expense account is serving temporarily as a part of the debit side of the owner's equity account. Decreases in owner's equity are entered as debits. Thus decreases in owner's equity resulting from expense should be debited to expense accounts.

Use of Revenue and Expense Accounts

To illustrate the application of the double-entry process in handling transactions that affect revenue and expense accounts, the transactions discussed on pages 9 and 10 will be analyzed and their effect on the accounting elements will be indicated by showing the proper entries in T accounts. These transactions represent a continuation of the transactions completed by Anthony Gonzalez, an attorney, in the conduct of his practice. (See pages 16-17 for Transactions (a) to (d)).

Transaction (e)

An Increase in an Asset Offset by an Increase in Owner's Equity Resulting from Revenue

Received $2,000 in cash from a client for professional services rendered.

Cash

(a)	25,000	(c)	760
(e)	**2,000**	(d)	2,700

Professional Fees

		(e)	**2,000**

Analysis: This transaction results in an increase in the asset cash with a corresponding increase in owner's equity because of revenue from professional fees. To enter the transaction properly, Cash was debited and an appropriate account for the revenue was credited for $2,000. Accounts should always be given a descriptive title that will aid in classifying them in relation to the accounting elements. In this case the revenue account was given the title, Professional Fees. Note that this is the fourth entry in the cash account and the first entry in the account, Professional Fees.

Transaction (f)

A Decrease in an Asset Offset by a Decrease in Owner's Equity Resulting from Expense

(1) Paid $800 for office rent for one month.

Cash

(a)	25,000	(c)	760
(e)	2,000	(d)	2,700
		(f1)	**800**

Rent Expense

(f1)	**800**		

Analysis: This transaction resulted in a decrease in the asset cash with a corresponding decrease in owner's equity because of expense. To enter the transaction properly, Rent Expense was debited and Cash was credited for $800. This is the first entry in the rent expense account and the fifth entry in the cash account.

(2) Paid bill for telephone service, $67.

Cash			
(a)	25,000	(c)	760
(e)	2,000	(d)	2,700
		(f1)	800
		(f2)	**67**

Telephone Expense			
(f2)	**67**		

Analysis: This transaction is identical with the previous one except that telephone expense rather than rent expense was the reason for the decrease in owner's equity. To enter the transaction properly, Telephone Expense was debited and Cash was credited for $67. This is the first entry in the telephone expense account and the sixth entry in the cash account.

The Trial Balance

It is a fundamental principle of the double-entry framework that the sum of the assets is always equal to the sum of the liabilities and owner's equity. In order to maintain this equality in entering transactions, the sum of the debit entries must always be equal to the sum of the credit entries. To determine whether this equality has been maintained, it is customary to take a trial balance periodically. A **trial balance** is a list of all of the accounts showing the title and balance of each account. The **balance** of any account is the amount of difference between the total debits and the total credits to that account. To determine the balance of each account, first the debit and credit amount columns should be totaled. This procedure is called **footing** the amount columns as illustrated below:

Cash				
(a)		25,000	(c)	760
(e)		2,000	(d)	2,700
	22,673	*27,000*	(f1)	800
			(f2)	67
				4,327

If there is only one item entered in a column, no footing is necessary. To find the balance of an account, it is necessary only to determine the difference between the footings by subtraction.

Since asset and expense accounts are debited for increases, these accounts normally have **debit balances**. Since liability, owner's equity, and revenue accounts are credited to enter increases, these accounts normally have **credit balances**. The balance of an account should be entered on the side of the account that has the larger total. The footings and balances of accounts should be entered in small figures just below the last entry preferably in pencil. If the two footings of an account are equal in amount, the account is said to be **in balance**.

The accounts of Anthony Gonzalez are reproduced below. To show their relationship to the fundamental accounting equation, the accounts are arranged in three columns under the headings of Assets, Liabilities, and Owner's Equity. The footings and the balance are printed in italics. Note the position of the footings directly under the debit and credit amount columns of the cash account, and the position of the balance on the left side of the cash account. The balance of the accounts payable account is shown on the right side in italics. It is not necessary to enter the balances of the other accounts because there are entries on only one side of these accounts.

ASSETS = LIABILITIES + OWNER'S EQUITY

ASSETS

Cash			
(a)	25,000	(c)	760
(e)	2,000	(d)	2,700
22,673	*27,000*	(f1)	800
		(f2)	67
			4,327

Office Supplies			
(c)	760		

Office Equipment			
(b)	5,700		

LIABILITIES

Accounts Payable			
(d)	2,700	(b)	5,700
		3,000	

OWNER'S EQUITY

Anthony Gonzalez, Capital			
		(a)	25,000

Professional Fees			
		(e)	2,000

Rent Expense			
(f1)	800		

Telephone Expense			
(f2)	67		

A trial balance of Anthony Gonzalez' accounts is on page 23. The trial balance was taken on June 30, 1987; therefore, this date is shown on the third line of the heading. The trial balance shows that the debit and credit totals are equal in amount. This is proof that in entering Transactions (a) to (f) inclusive the total of the debits was equal to the total of the credits.

Anthony Gonzalez, Attorney
Trial Balance
June 30, 1987

Account	Dr. Balance	Cr. Balance
Cash	22673 00	
Office Supplies	760 00	
Office Equipment	5700 00	
Accounts Payable		3000 00
Anthony Gonzalez, Capital		25000 00
Professional Fees		2000 00
Rent Expense	800 00	
Telephone Expense	67 00	
	30000 00	30000 00

Anthony Gonzalez' Trial Balance

A trial balance is not a formal statement or report. Normally, it is never seen by anyone except the accountant or bookkeeper. It is used as an aid in preparing the income statement and the balance sheet. If the trial balance is studied in conjunction with the income statement and the balance sheet shown on pages 10 and 11, it will be seen that those statements could have been prepared quite easily from the information that this trial balance provides.

BUILDING YOUR ACCOUNTING KNOWLEDGE

1. Identify at least three ways in which account forms may be developed and kept.
2. What are the three major parts of the standard account form?
3. What is the standard form of account designed to facilitate?
4. Explain the basis of the abbreviations "Dr." for debit and "Cr." for credit.
5. What word is sometimes used as a substitute for debit?
6. In most cases an increase in owner's equity due to revenue results from what event?
7. When an expense is incurred, what may be the effect on the assets? What may be the effect on the liabilities?
8. What is the purpose of the trial balance?

APPLYING ACCOUNTING CONCEPTS

Exercise 1-4. The following transactions were completed by Anna Gilligan who owns a court reporting service. Analyze each transaction carefully and enter the amounts in the proper debit and credit positions in the T accounts.

1. Paid one month's rent, $850.
2. Bought office equipment from Nathan Goldstein on account, $3,200.
3. Received $2,750 in cash for court reporting services rendered.
4. Paid secretary's semimonthly salary, $450.
5. Paid Nathan Goldstein $500.

Exercise 1-5. John Grossman owns and operates a medical laboratory under the name Madison Medical Lab. The balances in his accounts as of November 30, 1987 are as follows:

Cash, $17,980
Office Supplies, $435
Office Equipment, $4,980
Laboratory Equipment, $20,075
Accounts Payable, $1,225
John Grossman, Capital, $20,310
Laboratory Revenue, $25,770
Rent Expense, $1,500
Salary Expense, $2,200
Telephone Expense, $135

Required: Using the two column paper prepare a trial balance for the Madison Medical Lab as of November 30, 1987.

REPORT NO. 1-2

Refer to the study assignments and complete Report No. 1-2 in accordance with the instructions given therein. The work involved in completing the assignment requires a knowledge of the principles developed in the preceding discussion. Any difficulty experienced in completing the report will indicate a lack of understanding of these principles. In such event further study, using the vocabulary words on page 26, should be helpful.

MASTERY PROBLEMS

Problem 1-A Accounting elements—equation form

Jane McDonald is a licensed real estate agent. As of August 31, McDonald owned the following property that related to her business: Cash, $15,961; office equipment, $4,950; and an automobile, $16,075. At the same time McDonald owed business creditors $1,230.

Required: **(1)** On the basis of the above information, compute the amounts of the accounting elements and show them in equation form. **(2)** Assume that during the following year there is an increase in McDonald's business assets of $2,145 and a decrease in business liabilities of $752. Indicate the changes in the accounting elements by showing them in equation form after the changes have occurred.

Problem 1-B T accounts; trial balance

Timothy Ryan has decided to establish an advertising agency to be known as The Ryan Advertising Agency. Ryan's business transactions for the first month's operations ending July 31, 1987, were as follows:

(a) Ryan invested $45,000 cash in the business.
(b) Paid office rent for one month, $850.
(c) Purchased office equipment from the Cucinotta Office Equipment Company, $3,872 on account.
(d) Paid cash for office supplies from the Gallegher Office Supply Co., $675.
(e) Paid telephone bill, $136.
(f) Received $700 for services rendered to The Young-Il Kim Company.
(g) Paid $900 to the Cucinotta Office Equipment Company on account.
(h) Received $475 for services rendered to the Branch Hill Church.
(i) Paid $1,200 salary to office secretary.

Required: **(1)** Using the T accounts, enter the foregoing transactions directly in the accounts. **(2)** Foot the accounts and enter the balances where necessary. **(3)** Prepare a trial balance of the accounts using the ruled paper provided.

CHALLENGE PROBLEM 1

Emily Milstein is the owner of a public relations firm known as the Milstein Public Relations Agency. A trial balance of Milstein's accounts on April 30, 19-- follows:

The Milstein Public Relations Agency
Trial Balance
April 30, 19--

Cash	5,428	
Office Supplies	647	
Office Equipment	10,943	
Accounts Payable		1,287
Emily Milstein, Capital		16,664
Public Relations Fees		2,032
Rent Expense	1,000	
Salary Expense	1,200	
Telephone Expense	219	
Travel and Entertainment Expense	546	
	19,983	19,983

Required: **(1)** Using the paper provided, prepare an income statement for the Milstein Public Relations Agency showing the results for the month of April. **(2)** Using the paper provided, prepare a balance sheet in account form showing the financial condition of the agency as of April 30, 19--.

EXPANDING YOUR BUSINESS VOCABULARY

What is the meaning of each of the following terms?

account **(p. 13)**
accountant **(p. 4)**
accounting equation **(p. 5)**
account payable **(p. 5)**
account receivable **(p. 4)**
analyzing **(p. 3)**
assets **(p. 4)**
auditing **(p. 2)**
balance **(p. 21)**
balance sheet **(p. 11)**
bookkeeper **(p. 4)**
business accounting **(p. 3)**
business entity **(p. 4)**
capital **(p. 5)**
charge **(p. 15)**
classifying **(p. 3)**
credit **(p. 15)**
creditors **(p. 1)**
credit balances **(p. 22)**
debit **(p. 15)**
debit balances **(p. 22)**
double entry bookkeeping **(p. 13)**
entering **(p. 3)**
expense **(p. 18)**
final processing **(p. 3)**
fiscal year **(p. 19)**
footing **(p. 21)**
in balance **(p. 22)**
income statement **(p. 10)**
information processor **(p. 4)**
input **(p. 11)**
interpreting **(p. 4)**
liability **(p. 4)**
net income **(p. 18)**
net loss **(p. 18)**
net worth **(p. 5)**
notes payable **(p. 5)**
operating statement **(p. 10)**
output **(p. 11)**
owner's equity **(p. 5)**
processing **(p. 11)**
profit and loss statement **(p. 10)**
proprietorship **(p. 5)**
reporting **(p. 3)**
revenue **(p. 18)**
statement of financial condition **(p. 11)**
statement of financial position **(p. 11)**
summarizing **(p. 3)**
suppliers **(p. 1)**
T account **(p. 14)**
temporary owner's equity accounts **(p. 19)**
transaction **(p. 6)**
trial balance **(p. 21)**

2
ACCOUNTING PROCEDURE

CHAPTER OBJECTIVES

Careful study of this chapter should enable you to:

- Recognize the flow of the financial data in an accounting information system—the basic accounting cycle.
- Explain the purpose of a book of original entry.
- Describe the chart of accounts as a means of classifying financial information, using an account numbering system.
- Perform the journalizing and posting process.
- Prepare the income statement and the balance sheet.

The double-entry framework of accounting was explained and illustrated in the preceding chapter. To avoid complicating these principles, the mechanics of collecting and classifying information about business transactions were ignored. In actual practice, the first record of a transaction, sometimes called the source document, is in the form of a business paper, such as a check stub, receipt, cash register tape, sales ticket, or purchase invoice. The information supplied by source documents is an aid in analyzing transactions to determine their effect upon the accounts.

This chapter traces the flow of relevant financial data through the accounting information system. The functions of a book of original entry and a set of accounts are described, and their uses in the journalizing and posting process are explained and illustrated. The role of the chart of accounts in classifying financial information also is described and illustrated. Finally, the procedures for preparing the trial balance are again explained and illustrated and the procedures for preparing the income statement and the balance sheet from trial balance information are explained and illustrated.

JOURNALIZING TRANSACTIONS

A collection of the double-entry records of the transactions of a business is called a **journal**. The act of entering transactions in a journal is called **journalizing**. It is necessary to analyze each transaction before it can be journalized properly. The purpose of a series of journal entries is to provide a chronological record of all transactions completed by the business showing the date of each transaction, titles of the accounts to be debited and credited, and the amounts of the debits and credits. The journal then provides all the information needed to transfer the debits and credits to the proper accounts. When the accounts are grouped together, they collectively comprise a ledger. The flow of data concerning transactions can be illustrated in the following manner:

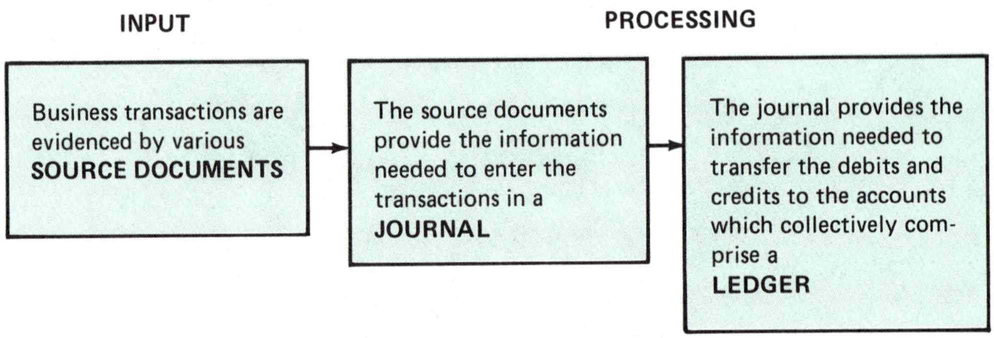

Source Documents

The term **source document** covers a wide variety of forms and papers. Almost any document that provides information about a business transaction can be called a source document.

SOURCE DOCUMENTS

	Examples:	*Provide information about:*
1.	Check stubs or carbon copies of checks	Cash payments
2.	Receipt stubs, carbon copies of receipts, cash register tapes, or memos of cash register totals.	Cash receipts
3.	Copies of sales tickets or sales invoices issued to customers or clients.	Sales of goods or services
4.	Purchase invoices received from suppliers	Purchases of goods or services

The Journal

A journal is commonly referred to as a book of original entry because the first formal accounting record of a transaction is made in a journal from source document information. The format of the pages of a journal varies with the type and size of an enterprise and the nature of its operations. Although a wide variety of journals are used in business, the simplest form of journal is a two-column journal. The following is a standard form of such a journal.

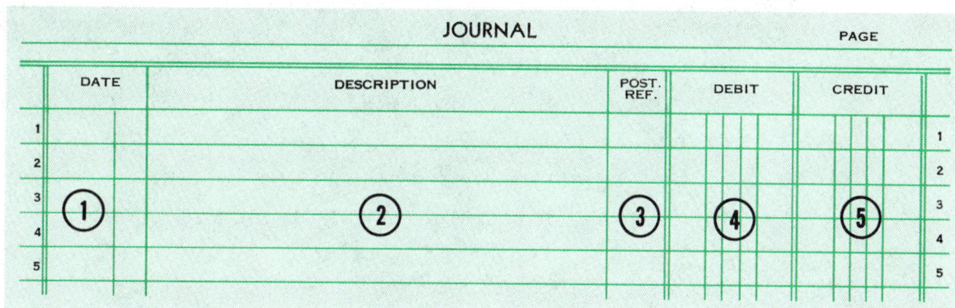

Standard Two-Column Journal

Journal pages usually are numbered in sequence, and the appropriate number is entered after the word "page" in the upper right-hand corner of each page of the journal. A two-column journal has only two amount columns, one for debit amounts and one for credit amounts. In the illustration, the columns have been numbered to facilitate the following discussion.

Column 1 is the Date column. The year is entered in small figures at the top of the column immediately below the column heading and needs to be repeated only at the top of each new page unless an entry for a new year is made further down on the page. The Date column is a double column, the perpendicular single rule being used to separate the month from the day. Thus in entering the date, the name of the month should be entered in full or abbreviated to the left of the single line. The number designating the day of the month should be entered to the right of this line. The name of the month needs to be shown only for the first entry on a page unless an entry for a new month is made farther down on the page.

Column 2 is generally referred to as the Description or explanation column. The Description column is used to enter the titles of the accounts affected by each transaction, together with a description of the transaction. Two or more accounts are affected by each transaction, and the titles of all accounts must be entered. The titles of the accounts debited are entered first, followed by the titles of the accounts credited. A separate line should be used for each account title. The titles of the accounts to be debited are entered at the extreme left of the column, while the titles of the accounts to be credited are usually indented one-half inch (about 1.3 centimeters). The description should be entered immediately following the credit entry and indented an additional one-half inch.

Column 3 is the **Posting Reference column**, sometimes referred to as a folio column. No entries are made in this column at the time of journalizing the transactions; such entries are made only at the time of posting, which is the process of entering the debit and credit elements in the proper accounts in the ledger. This procedure will be explained in detail later in this chapter.

Column 4, the **Debit amount column**, is a column in which the amount that is to be debited to an account should be entered on the same line on which the title of that account appears in the description column.

Column 5, the **Credit amount column**, is a column in which the amount that is to be credited to an account should be entered on the same line on which the title of that account appears in the description column.

Journalizing

Journalizing involves entering the significant information concerning each transaction either (1) at the time the transaction occurs or (2) subsequently, but in the chronological order in which it and the other transactions occurred. For every transaction, the entry should include the date, the title of each account affected, the amounts, and a brief description. Before a transaction can be entered properly, it must be analyzed in order to determine:

1. Which accounts are affected by the transaction.
2. What effect the transaction has upon each of the accounts involved, that is, whether the balance of each affected account is increased or decreased.

To illustrate the journalizing process, assume that a business purchased an electronic calculator on June 25 for $125 in cash. The asset accounts affected are Office Equipment and Cash. Office Equipment was increased and Cash was decreased upon purchase of the calculator. The following information would be entered in a two-column journal.

JOURNAL PAGE

	DATE		DESCRIPTION	POST. REF.	DEBIT	CREDIT	
	1987						
1	June	25	Office Equipment		125 00		1
2			Cash			125 00	2
3			Purchased an electronic calculator				3
4							4
5							5

The Chart of Accounts

In analyzing a transaction prior to journalizing it, the accountant or bookkeeper must know which accounts are being kept. When an accounting information system is established for a new business, the first step is to decide which accounts are required. The accounts used will depend upon the information needed or desired. Ordinarily, it is desirable to keep a separate account for each type of asset and each type of liability, since it is certain that information will be desired in regard to what is owned and what is owed. A permanent **owner's equity** or **capital account** should be kept in order that information may be available as to the owner's interest in the business. Furthermore, it is advisable to keep separate accounts for each type of revenue and each kind of expense. The revenue and expense accounts are temporary accounts that are used in entering increases and decreases in owner's equity from day-to-day business transactions apart from changes caused by the owner's investments and withdrawals. The specific accounts to be kept for increases and decreases in owner's equity depend upon the nature and sources of the revenue and the nature of the expenses incurred in earning the revenue.

A professional person or an individual engaged in operating a small enterprise may need to keep relatively few accounts. On the other hand, a large business may need to keep a great many accounts because of the complexity of the operation. Regardless of the number, accounts can be segregated into the three major classes, assets, liabilities, and owner's equity, and should be grouped according to these classes in the ledger. Asset accounts are placed first, liability accounts second, and owner's equity accounts, including revenue and expense accounts, last. A list of all the accounts used by a business is called a **chart of accounts**. It has become a general practice to give each account a number and to keep the accounts in numerical order. The numbering usually follows a consistent pattern and becomes a code. For example, asset accounts may be assigned numbers that always start with "1" or "2," liability accounts with "3" or "4," owner's equity accounts with "5," revenue accounts with "6," and expense accounts with "7" or "8."

To illustrate, assume that on December 1, 1987, Margaret Schultz, a certified public accountant (CPA) opens an office for the practice of public accounting under the name of Margaret Schultz, CPA. Since the accounts are kept on the calendar year basis, the first accounting period will be for one month only, that is, for the month of December. A two-column journal and a ledger will be used. Schultz realizes that there will not be a need for many accounts at present because the business is new but that additional accounts may be added as the need arises. A chart of accounts for the practice is shown as follows:

MARGARET SCHULTZ, CPA

CHART OF ACCOUNTS

Assets*
111 Cash
151 Office Supplies
211 Office Equipment

Liabilities
311 Accounts Payable

Owner's Equity
511 Margaret Schultz, Capital
521 Margaret Schultz, Drawing

Revenue
611 Professional Fees

Expenses
811 Advertising Expense
825 Miscellaneous Expense
828 Office Supplies Expense
831 Rent Expense
835 Salary Expense
839 Telephone Expense
841 Travel and Entertainment Expense

*Words in heavy type represent headings and not account titles.

Journalizing Procedure Illustrated

To illustrate journalizing procedures, the transactions completed by Margaret Schultz through December 31, 1987, will be journalized. A narrative of the transactions follows which provides all of the information needed in journalizing the transactions. Some of the transactions are analyzed to explain their effect upon the accounts. The analysis will immediately follow the journal entry.

MARGARET SCHULTZ, CPA

Narrative of Transactions

Tuesday, December 1, 1987

Schultz invested $20,000 cash in a professional enterprise to be known as Margaret Schultz, CPA.

JOURNAL PAGE 1

	DATE		DESCRIPTION	POST. REF.	DEBIT	CREDIT	
1	1987 Dec.	1	Cash		20000 00		1
2			Margaret Schultz, Capital			20000 00	2
3			Original investment in				3
4			accounting practice.				4

Analysis: As a result of this transaction, the practice acquired the asset cash in the amount of $20,000. Since Schultz contributed this asset, the transaction caused an increase of $20,000 in owner's equity. Accordingly, the entry for the transaction is a debit to Cash and a credit to Margaret Schultz, Capital, for $20,000.

Note that the following steps are involved:

1. Since this was the first entry on the journal page, the year is entered at the top of the Date column.
2. The month (abbreviated) and day are entered on the first line in the Date column.
3. The title of the account to be debited, Cash, is entered on the first line at the extreme left of the Description column. The amount of the debit, $20,000, is entered on the same line in the Debit column.
4. The title of the account to be credited, Margaret Schultz, Capital, is entered on the second line indented one-half inch from the left side of the Description column. The amount of the credit, $20,000, is entered on the same line in the Credit column.
5. The explanation of the entry is entered on the next line indented an additional one-half inch. The second line of the explanation is also indented the same distance as the first.

Wednesday, December 2

Paid office rent for December, $800.

4						4
5	2	Rent Expense		800 00		5
6		Cash			800 00	6
7		Paid December rent.				7

Analysis: This transaction resulted in an increase in an expense, with a corresponding decrease in the asset cash. The increase in the expense represents a decrease in owner's equity. The transaction is entered by debiting Rent Expense and by crediting Cash for $800.

Schultz ordered several pieces of office equipment. Since the dealer did not have in stock what Schultz wanted, the articles were ordered from the factory. Delivery is not expected until the latter part of the month. Pending arrival of the equipment, the dealer loaned Schultz some used office equipment. No entry is required until the new equipment is received.

Friday, December 4

Purchased office supplies from the Thomas J. Moss Co. on account, $368.

7						7
8	4	Office Supplies		368 00		8
9		Accounts Payable			368 00	9
10		Thomas J. Moss, Co.				10

Analysis: In this transaction, the business acquired a new asset which represented an increase in the total assets. A liability was also incurred because of the purchase on account. The transaction is entered by debiting Office Supplies and crediting Accounts Payable for $368. As these supplies are consumed, the amount will become an expense of the business.

Monday, December 7

Paid the Citizens Telephone Co. $73 covering the cost of installing a telephone in the office, together with the first month's service charges payable in advance.

Date	Description	Post. Ref.	Debit	Credit
7	Telephone Expense		73 00	
	Cash			73 00
	Paid telephone bill.			

Analysis: This transaction caused an increase in an expense and a corresponding decrease in the asset cash. The transaction is entered by debiting Telephone Expense and by crediting Cash for $73.

Tuesday, December 8

Paid $20 for a subscription to an accounting journal.

Date	Description	Post. Ref.	Debit	Credit
8	Miscellaneous Expense		20 00	
	Cash			20 00
	Accounting journal subscription.			

Analysis: This transaction resulted in an increase in an expense and a corresponding decrease in the asset cash. The transaction is entered by debiting Miscellaneous Expense and by crediting Cash for $20.

Wednesday, December 9

Received $550 from R. J. Terrell, Florist, for accounting services.

Date	Description	Post. Ref.	Debit	Credit
9	Cash		550 00	
	Professional Fees			550 00
	Accounting services; R. J.			
	Terrell, Florist.			

Analysis: This transaction resulted in an increase in the asset cash with a corresponding increase in revenue from accounting services. The transaction is entered by debiting Cash and by crediting Professional Fees for $550. In keeping the accounts, Schultz follows the practice of not entering revenue until it is received in cash. This practice is common to professional and personal service enterprises.

Thursday, December 10

Paid the "Daily Gazette" $75 for an advertisement about Schultz' accounting practice.

Date	Description	Debit	Credit
10	Advertising Expense	75 00	
	Cash		75 00
	Accounting practice announcement.		

Analysis: This transaction resulted in an increase in an expense and a corresponding decrease in the asset cash. The transaction is entered by debiting Advertising Expense and by crediting Cash for $75.

Friday, December 11

Paid the Garner Travel Service $195 for an airplane ticket to be used the next week for attendance at an accounting meeting.

Date	Description	Debit	Credit
11	Travel and Entertainment Expense	195 00	
	Cash		195 00
	Airplane fare—accounting meeting		

Analysis: This transaction resulted in an increase in an expense and a corresponding decrease in the asset cash. The transaction is entered by debiting Travel and Entertainment Expense and by crediting Cash for $195.

Tuesday, December 15

Paid Laura Reed $500 covering her salary for the first half of the month. Reed is employed by Schultz as a secretary and bookkeeper at a salary of $1,000 a month.

Date	Description	Debit	Credit
15	Salary Expense	500 00	
	Cash		500 00
	Paid secretary's salary.		

Analysis: This transaction resulted in an increase in salary expense with a corresponding decrease in the asset cash. The transaction is entered by debiting Salary Expense and by crediting Cash for $500. (The matter of payroll taxes is purposely ignored at this point. These taxes will be discussed in detail in Chapter 4.)

Note that the Posting Reference column has been left blank in the nine preceeding journal entry illustrations. This is because the column is not used until the amounts are posted to the accounts in the ledger, a process to be described starting on page 40. Account numbers are shown in the Posting Reference column of the journal illustrated on pages 37–38, since the illustration shows how the journal appears after the posting has been completed.

The journal entries for the following transactions (as well as for those to this point) are illustrated on pages 37–38.

Thursday, December 17

Received $750 from the Valley Drug Store for accounting services.

Friday, December 18

Schultz withdrew $1,000 for personal use.

Analysis: Amounts of cash withdrawn for personal use by the owner of a business enterprise represent a decrease in owner's equity. Although the amounts withdrawn might be entered as debits to the owner's capital account, it is better practice to enter withdrawals in a separate account, Margaret Schultz, Drawing, since this makes it easier to summarize the owner's withdrawals. This transaction is entered in the journal by debiting Margaret Schultz, Drawing and by crediting Cash for $1,000.

Wednesday, December 23

Received $1,500 from the Depenbrock and Patterson Company for accounting services.

Monday, December 28

Received the office equipment ordered December 2. These items were purchased on account from the Tri-City Office Equipment Co. for $3,750. The dealer removed the used equipment that had been loaned to Schultz.

Analysis: Now that the new equipment has been received, it is necessary to enter the transaction by debiting Office Equipment and by crediting Accounts Payable for $3,750.

Tuesday, December 29

Paid the Thomas J. Moss Co. $368 for the office supplies purchased on December 4.

Analysis: This transaction caused a decrease in the liability accounts payable with a corresponding decrease in the asset cash. The transaction is entered by debiting Accounts Payable and by crediting Cash for $368.

Received from Joseph Reilly $600 for participation in an estate planning conference.

JOURNAL PAGE 1

DATE		DESCRIPTION	POST. REF.	DEBIT	CREDIT
1987					
Dec.	1	Cash	111	20000 00	
		Margaret Schultz, Capital	511		20000 00
		Original investment in			
		accounting practice.			
	2	Rent Expense	831	800 00	
		Cash	111		800 00
		Paid December rent.			
	4	Office Supplies	151	368 00	
		Accounts Payable	311		368 00
		Thomas J. Moss Co.			
	7	Telephone Expense	839	73 00	
		Cash	111		73 00
		Paid telephone bill.			
	8	Miscellaneous Expense	825	20 00	
		Cash	111		20 00
		Accounting journal subscription.			
	9	Cash	111	550 00	
		Professional Fees	611		550 00
		Accounting services, R. J.			
		Terrell, Florist.			
	10	Advertising Expense	811	75 00	
		Cash	111		75 00
		Accounting practice announcement.			
	11	Travel and Entertainment Expense	841	195 00	
		Cash	111		195 00
		Airplane fare-accounting meeting.			
	15	Salary Expense	835	500 00	
		Cash	111		500 00
		Paid secretary's salary.			
	17	Cash	111	750 00	
		Professional Fees	611		750 00
		Accounting services, Valley			
		Drug Store.			
	18	Margaret Schultz, Drawing	521	1000 00	
		Cash	111		1000 00
		Withdrawn for personal use.			
	23	Cash	111	1500 00	
		Professional Fees	611		1500 00
				25831 00	25831 00
		Accounting services, Depenbrock			
		& Patterson Co.			

Margaret Schultz, CPA, Journal

(continued on next page)

JOURNAL PAGE 2

DATE		DESCRIPTION	POST. REF.	DEBIT	CREDIT
1987 Dec.	28	Office Equipment	211	3750 00	
		Accounts Payable	311		3750 00
		Tri-City Office Equipment Co.			
	29	Accounts Payable	311	368 00	
		Cash	111		368 00
		Thomas J. Moss Co.			
	29	Cash	111	600 00	
		Professional Fees	611		600 00
		Estate planning conference,			
		Joseph Reilly			
	31	Salary Expense	835	500 00	
		Cash	111		500 00
		Paid secretary's salary			
	31	Office Supplies Expense	828	62 00	
		Office Supplies	151		62 00
		Cost of supplies used		5280 00	5280 00
		during December.			

Margaret Schultz, CPA, Journal
(concluded)

Thursday, December 31

Paid Reed $500 covering her salary for the second half of the month.

Office supplies used during the month, $62.

Analysis: Refer to the transaction of December 4, and note that office supplies amounting to $368 were purchased and were entered as an asset. By taking an inventory, counting the supplies in stock at the end of the month, Schultz was able to determine that $306 of supplies were on hand. This meant that the expense of supplies used during the month amounted to $62 ($368 − $306). The total expenses for the month of December would not be reflected properly if the supplies used during the month were not taken into consideration. Therefore, the expense of supplies used is entered by debiting the expense account, Office Supplies Expense, and by crediting the asset account, Office Supplies, for $62.

Proving The Journal

Because a double entry is made for each transaction, the equality of debit and credit entries on each page of the journal may be proved merely by totaling the amount columns. The total of each column is entered as a footing immediately under the last entry. When a page of the journal is filled, the footings may be entered just under the last single horizontal ruled line at the bottom of the page as shown in the illustration on page 37. When it is desirable to prove the equality of debits and credits on a page that is not filled, the footings should be entered immediately under the last entry as shown in the foregoing illustration.

BUILDING YOUR ACCOUNTING KNOWLEDGE

1. Where are the first formal double-entry records of business transactions usually made?
2. Name a source document that provides information about each of the following types of business transactions:
   (a) cash payment
   (b) cash receipt
   (c) sale of goods or services
   (d) purchase of goods or services
3. What information usually is entered in each of the following columns of the journal?
   (a) Date column
   (b) Description column
   (c) Debit amount column
   (d) Credit amount column
4. What is the first step in establishing an accounting information system for a new business?
5. Name the five types of financial statement items for which it is ordinarily found desirable to keep separate accounts.
6. Which two types of accounts are temporarily used to enter increases and decreases in owner's equity from most day-to-day business transactions?
7. In what order are the accounts customarily placed in the ledger?

APPLYING ACCOUNTING CONCEPTS

Exercise 2-1. Herbert Marquette operates a computer consulting service. Journalize the following transactions which occurred during the first month of operations (March, 19--). Use the two-column journal paper provided.

March	2	Marquette invested $35,000 cash in the business.
	3	Paid office rent, $750.
	5	Purchased office equipment from Johnston Office Supply Co. on account.
	10	Received $800 from Garcia Manufacturing Company for services rendered.
	27	Paid Johnston Office Supply Co. $1,500 on account.

Exercise 2-2. Maynardo Serena operates a detective agency. Journalize the following transactions which occurred during the first month of operations (July, 19--). Use the two-column journal paper provided.

July	1	Serena invested $25,000 cash in the business.
	2	Paid office rent, $800.
	6	Paid Centerville Telephone Co. $78 for telephone installation and first month's service charges.
	9	Paid $80 for an advertisement in the "Centerville News."
	10	Purchased office supplies from Bryant Office Supply Co. on account, $289.

(continued)

July 13	Received $2,500 from the R. S. Williams Co. for services rendered.
31	Paid office secretary $1,100 covering her salary for the month.

Report No. 2-1

Refer to the study assignments and complete Report No. 2-1. To complete this assignment correctly, the principles developed in the preceding discussion must be understood. Review the text assignment if necessary.

POSTING TO THE LEDGER; THE TRIAL BALANCE

The purpose of a journal is to provide a chronological record of financial transactions expressed as debits and credits to accounts. Accounts are kept to supply management with desired information in summary form. Collectively, the accounts are known as the **general ledger**, or often simply as "the ledger." The account forms may be on sheets of paper or on cards. When on sheets of paper, the sheets may be bound in book form or kept in a loose-leaf binder. Usually a separate page or card is used for each account. The accounts should be classified properly in the ledger; that is, the asset accounts should be grouped together, the liability accounts together, and the owner's equity accounts together. Proper grouping of the accounts in the ledger is an aid in preparing the various reports desired by the owner. Schultz decided to keep all of the accounts for the practice in a loose-leaf ledger. The numbers shown in the practice's chart of accounts on page 32 were used as a guide in arranging the accounts in the ledger. The ledger is reproduced on pages 42–48. Note that the accounts are in numerical order.

Since Schultz makes few purchases on account, a separate account is not kept for each supplier. When invoices are received for items purchased on account, the invoices are checked and entered in the journal by debiting the proper accounts and by crediting Accounts Payable. The credit balance of Accounts Payable indicates the total amount owed to suppliers. After each invoice is entered, it is filed in an unpaid invoice file, where it remains until it is paid in full. When an invoice is paid in full, it is removed from the unpaid invoice file and then filed under the name of the supplier for future reference. The balance of the accounts payable may be proved at any time by determining the total of the unpaid amounts of the invoices.

Posting

The process of transferring information from the journal to the ledger is known as **posting**. All amounts entered in the journal should be posted to the accounts kept in the ledger in order to summarize the results. Such posting may be done daily or at frequent intervals. The ledger is not a reliable source of information until all of the transactions entered in the journal have been posted. Since the accounts provide the information needed in preparing financial statements, an accurate posting procedure must be maintained.

Posting from the journal to the ledger involves entering the following information in the accounts:

1. The date of each transaction.
2. The amount of each transaction.
3. The page of the journal from which each transaction is posted.

The posting procedure also requires that after the page of the journal has been posted to the ledger account, the number of that account should be entered in the Posting Reference column in the journal so as to provide a **cross-reference** between the journal and the ledger.

The first entry of the accounting practice to be posted from the journal occurred on December 1, 1987, and required a debit to cash of $20,000. The posting is, as shown in the following illustration, accomplished by (1) entering the year, "1987," the month, abbreviated "Dec.," and the day, "1," in the Date column of the cash account, (2) entering the amount, $20,000, in the Debit column, (3) entering the number "1" in the Posting Reference column since the posting came from Page 1 of the journal, and (4) entering the cash account number 111 in the Posting Reference column of the journal on the same line as the debit to Cash for $20,000. The same pattern is followed in posting the credit part of the entry, $20,000 to Margaret Schultz, Capital, Account No. 511.

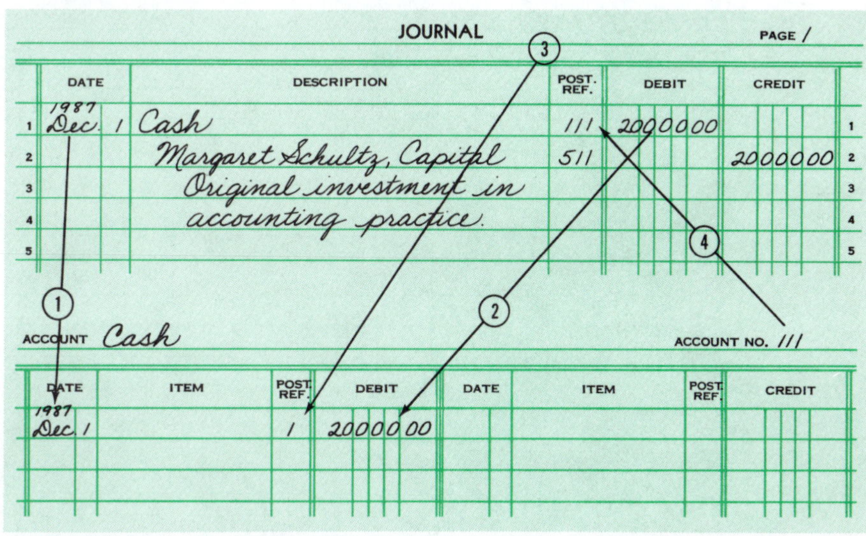

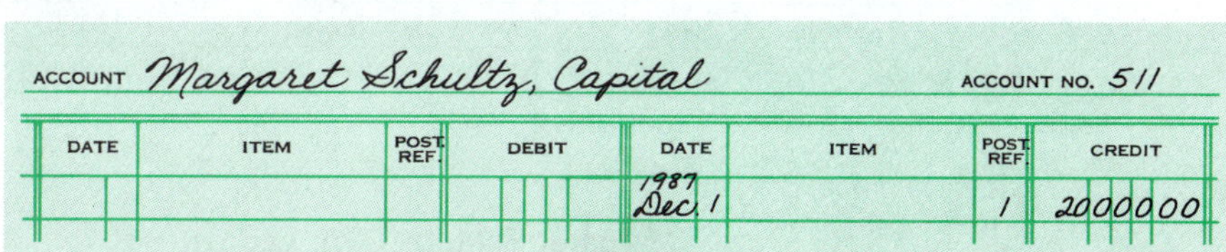

As shown in the journal of Margaret Schultz, CPA, (reproduced on pages 37–38) and its ledger (reproduced on pages 42–44), a similar procedure is followed in posting every amount from the journal. Note also that in the ledger, the year "1987" is entered only at the top of each Date column, and that the month "Dec." is entered only with the first posting to an account.

ACCOUNT *Cash* ACCOUNT NO. 111

DATE		ITEM	POST. REF.	DEBIT	DATE		ITEM	POST. REF.	CREDIT
1987					1987				
Dec.	1		1	20000 00	Dec.	2		1	800 00
	9		1	550 00		7		1	73 00
	17		1	750 00		8		1	20 00
	23		1	1500 00		10		1	75 00
	29		2	600 00		11		1	195 00
		19,869.00		23400 00		15		1	500 00
						18		1	1000 00
						29		2	368 00
						31		2	500 00
									3531 00

ACCOUNT *Office Supplies* ACCOUNT NO. 151

DATE		ITEM	POST. REF.	DEBIT	DATE		ITEM	POST. REF.	CREDIT
1987					1987				
Dec.	4	306.00	1	368 00	Dec.	31		2	62 00

ACCOUNT *Office Equipment* ACCOUNT NO. 211

DATE		ITEM	POST. REF.	DEBIT	DATE		ITEM	POST. REF.	CREDIT
1987									
Dec.	28		2	3750 00					

ACCOUNT *Accounts Payable* ACCOUNT NO. 311

DATE		ITEM	POST. REF.	DEBIT	DATE		ITEM	POST. REF.	CREDIT
1987					1987				
Dec	29		2	368 00	Dec.	4		1	368 00
						28	3,750.00	2	3750 00
									4118 00

Margaret Schultz, CPA, Ledger

(continued on next page)

ACCOUNT *Margaret Schultz, Capital* ACCOUNT NO. 511

DATE	ITEM	POST. REF.	DEBIT	DATE	ITEM	POST. REF.	CREDIT
				1987 Dec. 1		1	2000000

ACCOUNT *Margaret Schultz, Drawing* ACCOUNT NO. 521

DATE	ITEM	POST. REF.	DEBIT	DATE	ITEM	POST. REF.	CREDIT
1987 Dec. 18		1	100000				

ACCOUNT *Professional Fees* ACCOUNT NO. 611

DATE	ITEM	POST. REF.	DEBIT	DATE	ITEM	POST. REF.	CREDIT
				1987 Dec. 9		1	55000
				17		1	75000
				23		1	150000
				29		2	60000
							340000

ACCOUNT *Advertising Expense* ACCOUNT NO. 811

DATE	ITEM	POST. REF.	DEBIT	DATE	ITEM	POST. REF.	CREDIT
1987 Dec. 10		1	7500				

ACCOUNT *Miscellaneous Expense* ACCOUNT NO. 825

DATE	ITEM	POST. REF.	DEBIT	DATE	ITEM	POST. REF.	CREDIT
1987 Dec. 8		1	2000				

ACCOUNT *Office Supplies Expense* ACCOUNT NO. 828

DATE	ITEM	POST. REF.	DEBIT	DATE	ITEM	POST. REF.	CREDIT
1987 Dec. 31		2	6200				

Margaret Schultz, CPA, Ledger
(continued)

ACCOUNT *Rent Expense* ACCOUNT NO. 831

DATE		ITEM	POST. REF.	DEBIT	DATE	ITEM	POST. REF.	CREDIT
1987								
Dec.	2		1	800 00				

ACCOUNT *Salary Expense* ACCOUNT NO. 835

DATE		ITEM	POST. REF.	DEBIT	DATE	ITEM	POST. REF.	CREDIT
1987								
Dec.	15		1	500 00				
	31		2	500 00				
				1000 00				

ACCOUNT *Telephone Expense* ACCOUNT NO. 839

DATE		ITEM	POST. REF.	DEBIT	DATE	ITEM	POST. REF.	CREDIT
1987								
Dec.	7		1	73 00				

ACCOUNT *Travel and Entertainment Expense* ACCOUNT NO. 841

DATE		ITEM	POST. REF.	DEBIT	DATE	ITEM	POST. REF.	CREDIT
1987								
Dec.	11		1	195 00				

Margaret Schultz, Ledger
(concluded)

As shown in the preceding discussion, when the posting is completed, the same information is provided in both the journal and the ledger as to the date, the amount, and the effect of each transaction. A cross-reference from each book to the other book is provided by the Posting Reference column. Each entry in the journal may be traced to the ledger by referring to the account numbers indicated in the Posting Reference column of the journal. The cross reference also makes it possible to trace the entry in the ledger to the journal by referring to the page indicated in the Posting Reference column. Note that the account numbers were inserted in the Posting Reference column of the journal on pages 37–38. This was done as each part of the posting was completed.

The Trial Balance

As indicated in Chapter 1, the purpose of a trial balance is to prove that the totals of the debit and credit balances in the ledger accounts are equal. In a double-entry framework, equality of debit and credit balances in the ledger must be maintained. A trial balance may be taken daily, weekly, monthly, or whenever desired. Before taking a trial balance, all transactions should be journalized and the posting should be completed in order that the effect of all transactions to date will be reflected in the ledger accounts.

Footing Accounts. Prior to taking a trial balance it is necessary to (1) foot—add the amounts entered on the debit and credit side of each account and (2) determine the balance of each account. The footing process is illustrated in the following manner. The footings are entered immediately below the last item in both the debit and credit amount columns of the account. The footings should be entered in small figures close to the preceding line so that they will not interfere with the placing of an item on the next ruled line. At the same time, the balance (the difference between the footings) is computed and entered in small figures in the Item column of the account on the side with the larger footing. In other words, if an account has a debit balance, the balance should be entered in the Item column on the debit or left side of the account just below the line on which the last regular entry appears and in line with the footing. If the account has a credit balance, the balance should be entered in the Item column on the credit or right side of the account just below the line in which the last regular entry appears.

ACCOUNT *Cash* ACCOUNT NO. *111*

DATE		ITEM	POST. REF.	DEBIT	DATE		ITEM	POST. REF.	CREDIT
1987					1987				
Dec.	1		1	20000 00	Dec.	2		1	800 00
	9		1	550 00		7		1	73 00
	17		1	750 00		8		1	20 00
	23		1	1500 00		10		1	75 00
	29		2	600 00		11		1	195 00
		19,869.00		23400 00		15		1	500 00
						18		1	1000 00
						29		2	368 00
						31		2	500 00
									3531 00

In the ledger shown on pages 42–44, the accounts have been footed and the footings and the balances are entered. When only one item has been posted to an account, regardless of whether it is a debit or a credit amount, no footing is necessary.

Care should be used in computing the balances of the accounts. If an error is made in adding the amount columns or in determining the difference between the footings, the error will be carried to the trial balance and considerable time may be required to locate the mistake. Most accounting errors result from carelessness. For example, a bookkeeper may enter an account balance on the wrong side of an account by mistake or may enter figures so carelessly that they may be misread later. Care in entering the amounts is just as important as accuracy in determining the footings and the balances.

Preparing the Trial Balance. It is important that the following procedure be followed in preparing a **trial balance**:

1. Head the trial balance showing (a) the name of the individual, firm, or organization, (b) the title of the report, "Trial Balance," and (c) the date. The date shown is the day of the last transaction that is included in the accounts, which is usually the last day of a month. A December 31 trial balance might be prepared by the bookkeeper on January 3, however, the accounts should reflect only transactions through December 31.
2. List the account titles in order, showing each account number.
3. Enter the account balances, placing debit balances in the left amount column and credit balances in the right amount column.
4. Add the columns and enter the totals, placing a single line across the amount columns above the totals and a double line below the totals in the manner shown in the following illustration.

Margaret Schultz, CPA
Trial Balance
December 31, 1987

Account	Acct. No.	Debit Balance	Credit Balance
Cash	111	19869 00	
Office Supplies	151	306 00	
Office Equipment	211	3750 00	
Accounts Payable	311		3750 00
Margaret Schultz, Capital	511		20000 00
Margaret Schultz, Drawing	521	1000 00	
Professional Fees	611		3400 00
Advertising Expense	811	75 00	
Miscellaneous Expense	825	20 00	
Office Supplies Expense	828	62 00	
Rent Expense	831	800 00	
Salary Expense	835	1000 00	
Telephone Expense	839	73 00	
Travel and Entertainment Expense	841	195 00	
		27150 00	27150 00

Model Trial Balance

A trial balance is usually prepared on ruled paper though it can be prepared on plain paper if desired. The illustration on page 46 shows the trial balance as of December 31, 1987, of the ledger of Margaret Schultz, CPA.

Even though the trial balance indicates that the ledger is in balance, there still may be errors in the ledger. For example, if a journal entry has been made in which the wrong accounts were debited or credited, or if an item has been posted to the wrong account, the ledger will still be in balance. It is important, therefore, that extreme care be used in preparing the journal entries and in posting them to the ledger accounts.

BUILDING YOUR ACCOUNTING KNOWLEDGE

1. What useful purpose is served by proper grouping of the accounts in the ledger?
2. When does the ledger become a reliable source of information?
3. Name the three elements of information normally entered in each ledger account involved in the posting process.
4. What information is entered in the Posting Reference column of the journal as each amount is posted to the proper account in the ledger?
5. Where should the footings of an account be entered?
6. Where should the balance of an account be entered?
7. Explain why there still may be errors in the ledger even though the trial balance indicates that the ledger is in balance. Give examples of two such types of errors.

APPLYING ACCOUNTING CONCEPTS

Exercise 2-3. Using the ledger accounts provided **(a)** post the journal entries from Exercise 2-1 to the appropriate accounts, **(b)** Foot the accounts, enter the balances and prepare a trial balance on the paper provided.

Exercise 2-4. Using the ledger accounts provided **(a)** post the journal entries from Exercise 2-2 to the appropriate accounts, **(b)** Foot the accounts, enter the balances and prepare a trial balance on the paper provided.

Report No. 2-2

Refer to the study assignments and complete Report No. 2-2. To complete this assignment correctly, the principles developed in the preceding discussion must be understood. Review the text assignment if necessary.

THE FINANCIAL STATEMENTS

The transactions completed by Margaret Schultz, CPA, during the month of December were entered in a two-column journal (see pages 37 and 38). The debits and credits were subsequently posted to the proper accounts in a ledger (see pages 42–44). At the end of the month, a trial balance was taken as a means of proving that the equality of debits and credits had been maintained throughout the journalizing and posting process (see page 46).

Although the trial balance of Margaret Schultz, CPA, taken as of December 31 lists all of the accounts and shows the amounts of their debit and credit balances, it does not clearly present all of the information that Schultz may need regarding the results of operations during the month or the status of the business at the end of the month. To meet these needs, it is usual practice for a small personal service enterprise to prepare two financial statements—the income statement and the balance sheet. Preparation of the financial statements is the last step in the flow of the financial data through the accounting information system. This flow can be illustrated as follows:

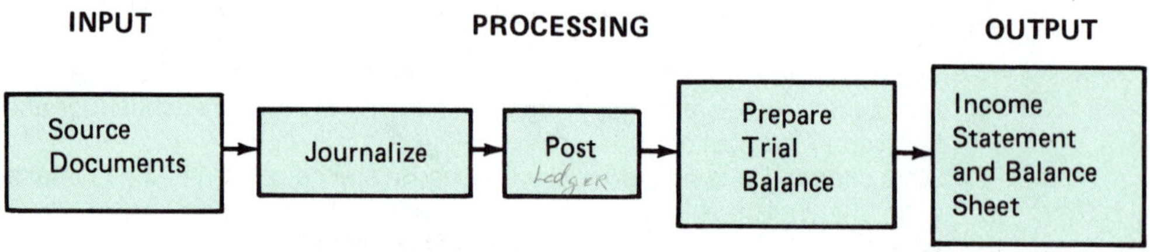

The Income Statement

An income statement is an itemized statement for the purpose of providing information regarding the results of operations during a specified period of time. It is a statement of the changes in owner's equity resulting from the revenue and expenses of a specific period (month, quarter, or year). Such changes are entered originally in temporary owner's equity accounts known as revenue and expense accounts. Changes in owner's equity resulting from investments or withdrawals of assets by the owner are not included in the income statement because they involve neither revenue nor expense.

The **heading** of an income statement consists of the following:

1. The name of the business.
2. The title of the statement.
3. The period of time covered by the statement.

The **body** of an income statement consists of (1) an itemized list of the sources and amounts of revenue received during the period, and (2) an itemized list of the various expenses incurred during the period. The income statement reflects the matching concept (matching the revenues and expenses of a business on a periodic basis). It is said that this matching process is the "heart" of income measurement.

The following income statement prepared from the Margaret Schultz, CPA, trial balance shows the results of operations for the month ended December 31, 1987.

Margaret Schultz, CPA
Income Statement
For the Month Ended December 31, 1987

Revenue:		
Professional fees		$3400 00
Expenses:		
Advertising expense	$ 75 00	
Miscellaneous expense	20 00	
Office supplies expense	62 00	
Rent expense	800 00	
Salary expense	1000 00	
Telephone expense	73 00	
Travel and entertainment expense	195 00	
Total expenses		2225 00
Net income		$1175 00

Income Statement

The financial statements usually are prepared first on ruled paper. Such copies may then be typed or word processed on a microcomputer so that a number of copies will be available for those who are interested in examining the statements. Since the processed copies are not on lined paper, dollar signs are included in the preliminary draft so that the typist or word processor will understand just where they are to be inserted. Note that a dollar sign is placed beside the first amount in each column and the first amount below a ruling in each column. The income statement illustrated is shown on two-column paper; however, the columns do not have any debit-credit significance. The only source of revenue was professional fees that amounted to $3,400. The total expenses for the month amounted to $2,225. The revenue exceeded the expenses by $1,175. This represents the amount of the net income for the month. If the total expenses had exceeded the total revenue, the excess would have represented a net loss for the month. The information provided by the income statement of Margaret Schultz, CPA, may be summarized in equation form as follows:

REVENUE	−	**EXPENSES**	=	**NET INCOME**
$3,400	−	$2,225	=	$1,175

It is apparent that the income statement is more informative than the trial balance as to the results of operations for December. The trial balance contains the necessary data for preparing the income statement, but the income statement presents the data in a more meaningful way.

The Balance Sheet

The **balance sheet** is an itemized statement of the assets, liabilities, and owner's equity of a business enterprise as of a specified date. Its purpose is to provide information regarding the status of these basic accounting elements as of the close of business on the date indicated in the heading.

The **heading** of a balance sheet contains the following:

1. The name of the business.
2. The title of the statement.
3. The date of the statement as of the close of business on that day.

The **body** of a balance sheet consists of an itemized list of the assets, the liabilities, and the owner's equity, the latter being the difference between the total amount of the assets and the total amount of the liabilities. A balance sheet for Margaret Schultz, CPA, showing the status of the business when it closed on December 31, 1987, is reproduced on pages 50 and 51. The balance sheet illustrated is arranged like a standard account with the assets listed on the left side and the liabilities and owner's equity listed on the right side. The information provided by the balance sheet of Margaret Schultz, CPA, may be summarized in equation form as follows:

ASSETS	=	**LIABILITIES**	+	**OWNER'S EQUITY**
$23,925	=	$3,750	+	$20,175

The trial balance was the source of the information needed in listing the assets and liabilities in the balance sheet. The amount of the owner's equity may be determined by subtracting the total liabilities from the total assets. Thus, Schultz' equity as of December 31, 1987, is as follows:

Margaret
Balance
December

Assets		
Cash	$19,869 00	
Office supplies	306 00	
Office equipment	3,750 00	
Total assets		$23,925 00

Balance Sheet—Account Form
(Left Page)

Total assets	$23,925
Less total liabilities	3,750
Owner's equity	$20,175

The owner's equity may also be determined by taking into consideration the following factors:

1. The **amount invested** in the enterprise by Schultz on December 1, as shown by the capital account.
2. The amount of the **net income** of Margaret Schultz, CPA, for December, as shown by the income statement.
3. The total **amount withdrawn** for personal use during December, as shown by Schultz' drawing account.

The trial balance on page 46 shows that Schultz' equity in Margaret Schultz, CPA, on December 1 amounted to $20,000. This is supported by the credit balance of the capital account. The income statement on page 49 shows that the net income of the practice for December amounted to $1,175. The trial balance also shows that the amount withdrawn by Schultz for personal use during the month amounted to $1,000. This is supported by the debit balance of the drawing account. On the basis of this information, Schultz' equity in Margaret Schultz, CPA, as of December 31, 1987, is as follows:

Amount of capital, December 1		$20,000
Net income for December	$1,175	
Less amount withdrawn for personal use during the month	1,000	175
Capital as of close of business, December 31		$20,175

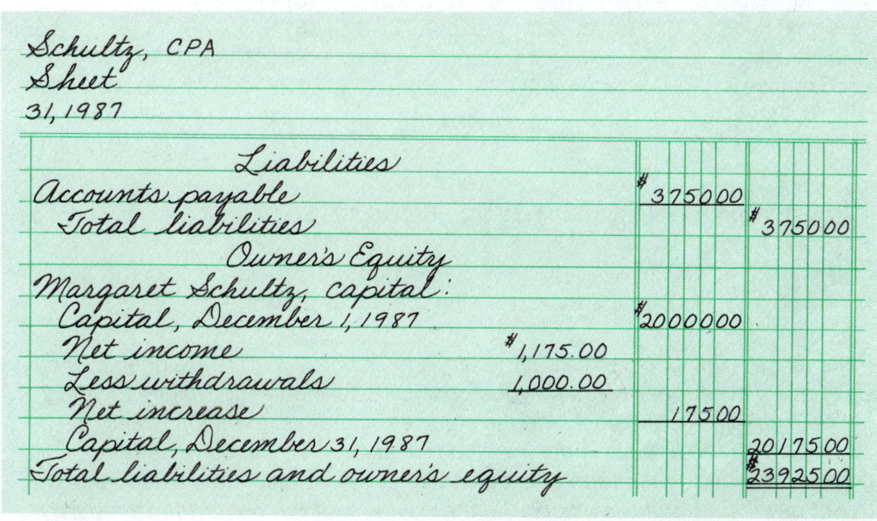

Schultz, CPA
Sheet
31, 1987

Liabilities			
Accounts payable		$3750.00	
Total liabilities			$3750.00
Owner's Equity			
Margaret Schultz, capital:			
Capital, December 1, 1987		$20000.00	
Net income	$1,175.00		
Less withdrawals	1,000.00		
Net increase		175.00	
Capital, December 31, 1987			20175.00
Total liabilities and owner's equity			$23925.00

Balance Sheet—Account Form
(Right Page)

BUILDING YOUR ACCOUNTING KNOWLEDGE

1. What is the purpose of an income statement?
2. Why are changes in owner's equity resulting from investments or withdrawals of assets by the owner not included in the income statement?
3. What are the three parts of the heading of an income statement?
4. What is the purpose of a balance sheet?
5. What are the three parts of the heading of a balance sheet?
6. What is the source of information for preparing both the income statement and the balance sheet?
7. Owner's equity can be calculated by subtracting total liabilities shown by the balance sheet from total assets shown by the balance sheet. What three factors may be used to prove the amount of owner's equity calculated in this manner?

APPLYING ACCOUNTING CONCEPTS

Exercise 2-5. George Rehkamp is a consultant who specializes in a service for mediating partnership disputes. Rehkamp employs a secretary-bookkeeper at a salary of $1,000 a month. The following is the trial balance for Rehkamp's business as of May 31, 19--, the first month of operations.

George Rehkamp, Consultant
Trial Balance
May 31, 19--

Account	No.	Debit	Credit
Cash	111	14,874	
Office Supplies	151	497	
Office Equipment	211	6,438	
Accounts Payable	311		1,586
George Rehkamp, Capital	511		20,000
George Rehkamp, Drawing	521	1,500	
Professional Fees	611		3,560
Rent Expense	711	750	
Salary Expense	721	1,000	
Telephone Expense	731	87	
		25,146	25,146

Prepare an income statement for George Rehkamp, Consultant, using the paper provided.

Exercise 2-6. Refer to Exercise 2-5 and prepare a balance sheet in account form for George Rehkamp, Consultant, using the paper provided.

REPORT NO. 2-3

Refer to the study assignments and complete Report 2-3. This assignment provides a test of your ability to apply the principles developed in Chapters 1 and 2 of this textbook. The textbook and the study assignments go hand in hand, each serving a definite purpose in the learning process. Inability to solve correctly any problem included in the report indicates that you have failed to master the principles developed in the textbook. Further study, with the aid of the vocabulary list on page 56, should be helpful in this regard.

MASTERY PROBLEMS

Problem 2-A Journal entries

Following is a narrative of the transactions completed by A. P. Spencer, the owner of the Spencer Insurance Agency, during the first month of the agency's business operations:

April	1	Spencer invested $25,000 cash in the business.
	1	Paid office rent, $950.
	3	Purchased office furniture for $4,932.20 cash.
	3	Paid $92.18 for installation of telephone and for one month's service.
	6	Purchased stationery and supplies on account from Lopez Stationery Co., $239.70.
	8	Received commission on policy sold to Charlotte Reinecke, $285.
	10	Paid $20 for subscription to a professional magazine. (Debit Miscellaneous Expense.)
	14	Paid personal bill from the Harwood Department Store, $50.11. (Note: This is equivalent to a withdrawal of $50.11 by Spencer for personal use. Debit Spencer's drawing account.)
	15	Received commission on policy sold to the Pieters Manufacturing Co., $730.
	17	Paid $185 for an airplane ticket for a business trip.
	21	Paid other traveling expenses, $309.60.
	23	Paid account of Lopez Stationery Co. in full, $239.70.
	27	Received commission on policy sold to Dr. Harold Guenther, $315.
	30	Paid $1,100 monthly salary to secretary.

Required: Journalize the foregoing transactions using the paper provided. Select the account titles from the chart of accounts shown below.

CHART OF ACCOUNTS

Assets
- 101 Cash
- 121 Stationery and Supplies
- 201 Office Furniture

Liabilities
- 301 Accounts Payable

Owner's Equity
- 501 A. P. Spencer, Capital
- 521 A. P. Spencer, Drawing

Revenue
- 701 Commissions Earned

Expenses
- 801 Miscellaneous Expense
- 803 Rent Expense
- 805 Salary Expense
- 808 Telephone Expense
- 811 Traveling Expense

After journalizing the transactions, prove the equality of the debits and credits by footing the amount columns. Enter the footings in pencil immediately under the line on which the last entry appears.

Problem 2-B Journalizing, Posting, Taking a Trial Balance

Jane Kordenbrock is a certified public accountant (CPA). Following is a trial balance of Kordenbrock's practice taken as of February 28, 19--

Jane Kordenbrock, CPA
Trial Balance
February 28, 19--

Account	No.	Debit	Credit
Cash	100	20,023.96	
Automobile	200	11,548.60	
Office Equipment	210	5,037.88	
Accounts Payable	300		1,178.05
Jane Kordenbrock, Capital	500		26,472.85
Jane Kordenbrock, Drawing	510	5,000.00	
Professional Fees	600		21,052.00
Automobile Expense	700	428.36	
Charitable Contributions Expense	705	125.00	
Miscellaneous Expense	710	21.80	
Rent Expense	715	1,800.00	
Salary Expense	720	4,560.00	
Telephone Expense	725	157.30	
		48,702.90	48,702.90

A narrative of transactions completed by Kordenbrock during the month of March follows below. Kordenbrock has two employees.

March 2 Paid one month's rent, $900.
3 Paid telephone bill, $125.80.
4 Gave the Salvation Army $25.
5 Received $2,250 from Johnson Electric Co. for services rendered.
6 Purchased two new tires for the automobile, $114.66.
10 Received $750 from Midvale Awning Co. for services rendered.
12 Paid the Barstow Department Store $87.21. (Debit Kordenbrock's drawing account.)
16 Kordenbrock withdrew $1,250 for personal use.
18 Paid Chen Office Supply Co. $600 on account.
19 Received $500 from T. R. Lorenz for services rendered.
23 Gave the Shriners Burn Institute, $50.
24 Paid $250 for professional dues.
26 Received $1,850 from Century Cadillac Co. for services rendered.
31 Kordenbrock withdrew $1,300 for personal use.
31 Paid March salaries, $2,260.

Required: **(1)** Journalize the March transactions, using the paper provided. Foot the amount columns. **(2)** Use the ledger accounts provided to open the accounts. Enter the March 1 balances as shown in the February 28 trial balance and post the journal entries for March. **(3)** Foot the ledger accounts and enter the balances. Prove the balances by taking a trial balance as of March 31.

Problem 2-C Financial Statements

The following is the trial balance of the Juan Provedo Advertising Agency.

The Juan Provedo Advertising Agency
Trial Balance
January 31, 19--

Account	No.	Debit	Credit
Cash	101	19,999.71	
Stationery and Supplies	111	406.83	
Automobile	201	10,536.00	
Office Furniture	211	6,107.34	
Accounts Payable	301		241.15
Notes Payable	311		1,200.00
Juan Provedo, Capital	501		32,547.10
Juan Provedo, Drawing	511	2,750.00	
Agency Fees	601		9,820.00
Automobile Expense	701	140.28	
Miscellaneous Expense	706	35.60	
Rent Expense	711	1,000.00	
Salary Expense	716	2,200.00	
Stationery and Supplies Expense	721	60.19	
Telephone Expense	726	93.24	
Traveling Expense	731	479.06	
		43,808.25	43,808.25

Required: **(1)** Prepare an income statement for the Juan Provedo Advertising Agency for the month ended January 31, 19--. Use the paper provided. **(2)** Prepare a balance sheet in account form showing the financial condition of the agency as of January 31. Use the paper provided.

CHALLENGE PROBLEM 2

Louis Schmidt is a manufacturers' agent selling machinery on commission for several machinery manufacturers. Schmidt began the business on January 2, 19--. A trial balance of the accounts as of March 31, 19-- follows:

Louis Schmidt, Manufacturers' Agent
Trial Balance
March 31, 19--

Account	No.	Debit	Credit
Cash	100	5,196.92	
Office Supplies	105	333.92	
Automobile	200	11,778.00	
Office Equipment	205	4,570.31	
Accounts Payable	300		530.40
Louis Schmidt, Capital	500		30,000.00
Louis Schmidt, Drawing	505	6,000.00	
Commissions Earned	600		4,746.00
Automobile Expense	700	389.27	
Office Supplies Expense	705	342.18	
Rent Expense	710	3,000.00	
Salary Expense	715	3,300.00	
Telephone Expense	720	365.80	
		35,276.40	35,276.40

Required: **(1)** Using the paper provided, prepare an income statement for Louis Schmidt, Manufacturers' Agent showing the results of operations for the three months ended March 31, 19--. **(2)** Using the paper provided, prepare a balance sheet in account form showing the financial condition of Louis Schmidt as of March 31, 19--.

EXPANDING YOUR BUSINESS VOCABULARY

What is the meaning of each of the following terms:

balance **(p. 45)**
balance sheet **(p. 50)**
book of original entry **(p. 29)**
capital account **(p. 31)**
chart of accounts **(p. 31)**
Credit amount column **(p. 30)**
cross-reference **(p. 41)**
Date column **(p. 29)**
Debit amount column **(p. 30)**
Description column **(p. 29)**
foot **(p. 45)**
general ledger **(p. 40)**
income statement **(p. 48)**
journal **(p. 28)**
journalizing **(p. 28)**
matching concept **(p. 48)**
net income **(p. 49)**
net loss **(p. 49)**
owner's equity **(p. 31)**
posting **(p. 40)**
Posting Reference column **(p. 30)**
proving the journal **(p. 38)**
source document **(p. 28)**
trial balance **(p. 46)**
two-column journal **(p. 29)**

3
ACCOUNTING FOR CASH

CHAPTER OBJECTIVES

Careful study of this chapter should enable you to:

- Explain the meanings of the term "cash" as it is used in accounting.
- Describe **internal control** as it relates to the handling of cash.
- Explain the operation of a petty cash fund and prepare a special multicolumn record of cash payments.
- Describe banking procedures relating to the use of commercial bank checking accounts, and prepare a bank statement reconciliation.

In the preceding chapters, the purpose and nature of business accounting, transaction analysis, and the double entry framework were introduced. Explanations and illustrations were given of (1) **journalizing** (entering transactions in a journal—a book of original entry), (2) **posting** (transferring the entries to the accounts that, taken together, comprise the general ledger), (3) taking a trial balance, and (4) using the latter to prepare an income statement and a balance sheet (two basic and important financial statements).

This chapter is devoted to a discussion of the handling of and accounting for cash receipts and cash payments. Included in the discussion are the nature of the cash account, cash proof, and the operation of and accounting for a petty cash fund. Also included in the discussion are the operation of both bank checking and savings accounts, the functions performed by commonly used bank forms, and the process of reconciling the bank statement.

CASH RECEIPTS AND CASH PAYMENTS

The term "cash" has several different, though not completely distinctive, meanings. In a very narrow sense, cash means currency and coins. In a broader sense, cash includes checks, drafts, and money orders. All of these, including currency and coins, are sometimes called cash items. Usually, any reference to the cash receipts of a business relates to the receipt of checks, drafts, and money orders payable to the business, as well as to the receipt of currency and coins. The cash account balance, as well as the amount shown for cash in a balance sheet, normally includes cash and cash items on hand plus the amount on deposit in one or more bank checking accounts. On the balance sheet, it is rather rare to make a distinction between "cash on hand" and "cash in bank," but sometimes this is done.

A good policy for a business enterprise to adopt is a system of internal control which requires that all cash and cash items it receives be deposited daily in a bank. When this is done, its total cash receipts will equal its total deposits in the bank. It is also a good policy to make arrangements with the bank so that all checks and other cash items received by the business from customers or others in the usual course of business will be accepted by the bank for deposit only. This will cause the records of cash receipts of the business to agree item by item with the bank's record of deposits.

The Cash Account

The cash account is debited when cash is increased and credited when cash is decreased. This account normally has a debit balance.

Cash Receipts. Cash and cash items received by a business are known as cash receipts. It is vital that an accurate and timely record be kept of cash receipts. When the volume of the receipts is large both in number and in amount, procedures designed to reduce the danger of mistake and embezzlement (the unauthorized taking of business cash by an employee) should be followed. When numerous receipts of currency and coins are accepted from customers who have purchased goods or services, it is customary to use a cash register. Such a machine classifies items sold and amounts. A cash register may also have the capability of accumulating subtotals by departments and calculating sales taxes.

Many business transactions are credit transactions; that is, the goods are sold or the service is rendered and the supplier expects to be paid at a later date. Credit transactions may be billed at various times, usually on a monthly basis. Part of the bill or statement may be a form showing the remitter's name and address and a place for entering the amount of the payment. The form and a check or money order are mailed or given to the supplier. A good example of such a form is the top part of a monthly statement that the patient has received as shown in the following illustration:

Dr. Neville Grant
114 N. Taylor Ave.
St. Louis, MO 63108-1011

PHONE NUMBER	DATE
534-8600	09-01-87

MAKE CHECKS PAYABLE TO THE ABOVE.
TO INSURE PROPER CREDIT
PLEASE RETURN THIS PORTION IN THE ENCLOSED ENVELOPE.

ACCOUNT NO.	PATIENT	PLEASE PAY THIS AMOUNT
342616	Scott Mayfield	300.00

TEAR HERE — RETAIN BOTTOM PORTION FOR INCOME TAX PURPOSES. IT WILL BE THE ONLY RECORD WHICH YOU WILL RECEIVE. (SEE REVERSE SIDE FOR INSTRUCTIONS) — TEAR HERE

ACCOUNT NUMBER	PATIENT NAME & RESPONSIBLE PARTY	PHONE NUMBER	DATE
342616	Scott Mayfield Burton W. Mayfield	872-7818	09-01-87

DATE MO DAY YR	DESCRIPTION	AMOUNT
07:15:87	INITIAL OFFICE VISIT, EXAM	800.00
07:19:87	Appendectomy	
07:23:87	Post-op office visit	
07:24:87	Medical insurance filed, $800	
08:17:87	Received on account	500.00 CR

Grant Medical Clinic, Inc.

BALANCE DUE 300.00

DISREGARD THIS STATEMENT IF IT HAS BEEN PAID WITHIN THE LAST 10 DAYS.

Sometimes a written receipt must be prepared by the business. A copy of the receipt or the returned portion of the monthly statement provides the source document for the cash received. In any case, the initial record of each amount received should be prepared by someone other than the accountant to provide good internal control. The money received, including checks and money orders, is placed in the custody of whoever is authorized to handle bank deposits and cash on hand. The accountant uses the initial records in preparing proper journal entries for cash receipts. Under such a plan, the accountant does not actually handle any cash; instead cash receipts are entered from documents prepared by other persons. The procedure of having transactions involving cash handled by two or more persons reduces the danger of embezzlement and is one of the important features of a system of internal accounting control.

Cash Payments. Cash and cash items paid by a business are known as **cash payments**. Payments may be made in cash or by bank check. When a payment is made in cash, a receipt should be obtained as evidence of the payment. When a payment is made by bank check, it is not necessary to obtain a receipt since the canceled check that is returned by the bank serves as a receipt.

Proving Cash. The process of determining whether the amount of cash, both on hand and in the bank, is the same amount that exists in the accounting records is called **proving cash**. Cash should be proved at least once a week and, more often if the volume of cash transactions is large. The first step is to determine from the ledger the amount of the cash account balance. The most recent cash account balance is determined by adding the total of the receipts to the opening balance and subtracting the total of the payments. The result should be equal to the amount of cash on deposit in the bank as reflected in the checkbook stubs plus the total of currency, coins, checks, and money orders on hand. An up-to-date record of cash in bank is maintained—usually by using check stubs to show deposits as well as checks drawn, and the resulting balance after each deposit made or check drawn. (See check stubs illustrated on page 75.) The amount of cash on hand must be determined by actual count.

Cash Short and Over. If the effort to prove cash is not successful, it means that either (1) the records of receipts, payments, and cash on deposit contain one or more data entry errors, (2) the physical count of cash not deposited is incorrect, or (3) a shortage or an overage exists. If verifications of the records and the cash count do not uncover any error, it is evident that some mistake must have been made in handling cash.

Finding that cash is slightly short or over is not unusual. If there are numerous cash transactions, it is difficult to avoid occasional errors in making change. There is always the danger of shortages due to dishonesty, but most discrepancies are the result of mistakes. Many businesses have a special ledger account entitled **Cash Short and Over** which is used to keep track of day-to-day shortages and overages of cash. If, in the effort to prove cash, it is found that a shortage exists, the amount is treated as a cash payment transaction involving a debit to Cash Short and Over and a credit to cash. Any overage discovered is regarded as a cash receipt transaction involving a credit to Cash Short and Over and a debit to cash.

To illustrate, if Cash was $2 short at the end of the day, the entry would be as follows:

Cash Short and Over	2.00	
Cash		2.00

Conversely, if Cash was $3 over, the entry would be as follows:

Cash	3.00	
Cash Short and Over		3.00

By the end of the fiscal year, it is likely that the cash short and over account will have both debits and credits. If the total of the debits exceeds the total of the credits, the balance represents an expense or loss; if the reverse is the case, the balance represents revenue.

The Petty Cash Fund

When all cash receipts are deposited in a bank, an office fund known as a **petty cash fund** may be established for paying small items. ("Petty" means small or little.) Such a fund eliminates the necessity of writing checks for relatively small amounts.

Operating a Petty Cash Fund. To establish a petty cash fund, a check is written for the amount that is to be set aside in the fund. The amount may be $50, $100, $200, or any amount considered necessary. The check is made payable to the person who will have custody of the fund. That person's name, followed by a comma and the words, "Petty Cashier" appears on the check as the payee. When the check is cashed by the bank, the money is placed in a cash drawer, a cash register, or a safe at the depositor's place of business; and a designated individual in the office is authorized to make payments from the fund. The person responsible for the fund should be able to account for the full amount of the fund at any time.

Payments from the fund should not be made without obtaining some sort of receipt in return. A special form of receipt, showing the name of the payee, the purpose of the payment, and the account to be charged for each petty cash payment, is known as a **petty cash voucher**. A form of petty cash voucher is shown on page 62. Such a voucher should be used for each expenditure.

The check written to establish the petty cash fund may be entered in the journal by debiting Petty Cash Fund and by crediting Cash. When it is necessary to replenish the fund, the petty cashier usually prepares a statement of the payments, properly classified. A check is then written for the exact amount of the total payments. This check is entered in the journal by debiting the proper accounts indicated in the statement and by crediting Cash.

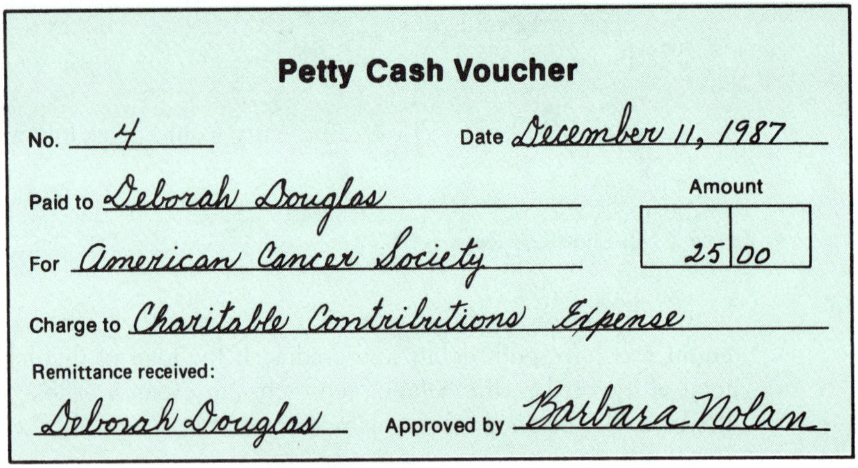

Petty Cash Voucher

No. 4 Date December 11, 1987

Paid to Deborah Douglas

For American Cancer Society

Amount: 25.00

Charge to Charitable Contributions Expense

Remittance received: Deborah Douglas

Approved by Barbara Nolan

Petty Cash Voucher

To illustrate, assume that on June 1, Suzanne's Fashions established a petty cash fund for $100, and that on June 30 the fund was replenished for $85.25 after classifying and totaling the petty cash vouchers. The journal entries for these transactions are:

			Debit	Credit
June	1	Petty Cash Fund	100.00	
		Cash		100.00
		To establish petty cash fund.		
	30	Automobile Expense	22.00	
		Supplies Expense	32.00	
		Postage Expense	26.00	
		Miscellaneous Expense	5.25	
		Cash		85.25
		Replenishment of petty cash fund.		

The petty cash fund is thus a revolving fund. The petty cash account balance does not change in amount unless the fund is increased or decreased. The actual amount of cash in the fund plus the total of the petty cash vouchers should be equal to the amount originally deposited in the petty cash fund. This commonly used method for handling petty cash is referred to as the **imprest method**.

Petty Cash Payments Record. When a petty cash fund is maintained, it is good practice to keep a formal record of all payments from the fund. The **petty cash payments record** is a special multicolumn record that supplements the regular accounting records. No posting is done from this special record. Various types of records also called **auxiliary records** have been designed for this purpose. One of the standard forms is illustrated on pages 64 and 65. The headings of the Distribution columns may vary with each enterprise, depending upon the desired classification of the expenditures. The headings represent accounts that eventually are to be charged for the expenditures. The desired headings may either be printed on the form or they may be typed or written in. Often account numbers instead of account titles are used in the headings to indicate the accounts to be charged.

The petty cashier should have a document for each payment made from the petty cash fund. Whether or not a receipt or receipted invoice is obtained, the petty cashier should prepare a voucher. The vouchers should be numbered consecutively.

A typical petty cash payment record is reproduced on pages 64 and 65. It is a part of the records of Barbara Nolan, a business consultant. Since Nolan is out of the office much of the time, a petty cash fund is provided from which her secretary is authorized to make petty cash payments not to exceed $35 each. A narrative of the petty cash transactions completed by Robert Mardis, Nolan's secretary, during the month of December follows:

BARBARA NOLAN

NARRATIVE OF PETTY CASH TRANSACTIONS

Dec. 1 Issued check for $200 payable to Robert Mardis, Petty Cash Fund Cashier. The check is cashed and the proceeds placed in a petty cash fund.

This transaction is entered in the journal by debiting Petty Cash Fund and by crediting Cash. A memorandum entry is also made in the Description column of the petty cash payments record reproduced on pages 64 and 65.

JOURNAL PAGE

	DATE		DESCRIPTION	POST. REF.	DEBIT	CREDIT	
1	19-- Dec.	1	Petty Cash Fund		20000		1
2			Cash			20000	2
3			To establish petty cash				3
4			fund				4
5							5

During the month of December, the following payments were made from the petty cash fund:

7 Paid $22.80 to Bill Glasgow of Glasgow's Auto for having the company automobile serviced. Petty Cash Voucher No. 1.

PAGE 1 — PETTY CASH PAYMENTS

	DAY	DESCRIPTION		VOU. NO.	TOTAL AMOUNT	Tel. Exp.	Auto Exp.	
1		AMOUNTS FORWARDED						1
2	1	Received in fund	200.00					2
3	7	Automobile repairs		1	22 80		22 80	3
4	8	Client luncheon		2	12 75			4
5	9	Barbara Nolan, personal use		3	30 00			5
6	11	American Cancer Society		4	25 00			6
7	15	Typewriter repairs		5	13 25			7
8	17	Traveling expense		6	14 50			8
9	21	Washing automobile		7	6 00		6 00	9
10	22	Postage expense		8	9 50			10
11	23	Care and Counseling, Inc.		9	15 00			11
12	29	Postage stamps		10	40 00			12
13	30	Long distance call		11	4 80	4 80		13
					193 60	4 80	28 80	
14					193 60	4 80	28 80	14
15	31	Balance	6.40					15
16	31	Received in fund	193.60					16
17		Total	200.00					17

Barbara Nolan's Petty Cash Payments Record (Left Page)

Dec. 8 Reimbursed Nolan $12.75 for the amount spent in entertaining a client at lunch. Petty Cash Voucher No. 2.

9 Gave Nolan $30 for personal use. Petty Cash Voucher No. 3.

This item is entered in the Amount column provided at the extreme right of the petty cash payments record since no special distribution column has been provided for entering amounts withdrawn by the owner for personal use.

11 Gave the American Cancer Society a $25 donation. Petty Cash Voucher No. 4.

15 Paid $13.25 for typewriter repairs. Petty Cash Voucher No. 5.

17 Reimbursed Nolan $14.50 for traveling expenses. Petty Cash Voucher No. 6.

21 Paid $6.00 to Gary Bronson of Gary's Car Care for having the company automobile washed. Petty Cash Voucher No. 7.

22 Paid $9.50 for mailing a package. Petty Cash Voucher No. 8.

23 Donated $15 to Care and Counseling, Inc. Petty Cash Voucher No. 9.

29 Paid $40 for postage stamps. Petty Cash Voucher No. 10.

30 Reimbursed Nolan $4.80 for a long distance telephone call made from a public telephone. Petty Cash Voucher No. 11.

FOR MONTH OF *December* 19*87* PAGE *1*

	DISTRIBUTION OF DEBITS							
	Post. Exp.	*Char. Cont. Exp.*	*Travel + Ent. Exp.*	*Misc. Exp.*		ACCOUNT	AMOUNT	
1								1
2								2
3								3
4			*12 75*					4
5						*Barbara Nolan, Drawing*	*30 00*	5
6		*25 00*						6
7				*13 25*				7
8			*14 50*					8
9								9
10	*9 50*							10
11		*15 00*						11
12	*40 00*							12
13	*49 50*	*40 00*	*27 25*	*13 25*			*30 00*	13
14	*49 50*	*40 00*	*27 25*	*13 25*			*30 00*	14
15								15
16								16
17								17

Barbara Nolan's Petty Cash Payments Record (Right Page)

Proving the Petty Cash Payments Record. To prove the petty cash payments record, it is first necessary to foot all of the amount columns. The sum of the footings of the Distribution columns should equal the footing of the Total Amount column. After proving the footings, the totals are entered and the record is ruled as shown in the illustration. The illustration shows that a total of $193.60 was paid out during December. Since this is an appropriate time to replenish the petty cash fund, the following statement of the payments for December is prepared.

Statement of Petty Cash Payments for December

Telephone Expense	$ 4.80
Automobile Expense	28.80
Postage Expense	49.50
Charitable Contributions Expense	40.00
Travel and Entertainment Expense	27.25
Miscellaneous Expense	13.25
Barbara Nolan, Drawing	30.00
Total payments	$193.60

The statement of petty cash payments provides the information for the issuance of a check for $193.60 to replenish the petty cash fund. On

December 31, Nolan issued a check for $193.60 payable to Robert Mardis, Petty Cashier, to replenish the petty cash fund. This transaction was treated as a compound entry in the journal by debiting the proper accounts and by crediting Cash for the total amount of the expenses. A **compound entry** is one that affects more than two accounts, with the sum of the debits equal to the sum of the credits. Such an entry is usually required for petty cash fund replenishment. The entry is posted from the journal to the affected ledger accounts.

JOURNAL PAGE 15

	DATE		DESCRIPTION	POST. REF.	DEBIT	CREDIT	
1	19-- Dec.	31	Telephone Expense		4 80		1
2			Automobile Expense		28 80		2
3			Postage Expense		49 50		3
4			Charitable Contributions Expense		40 00		4
5			Travel + Entertainment Expense		27 25		5
6			Miscellaneous Expense		13 25		6
7			Barbara Nolan, Drawing		30 00		7
8			Cash			193 60	8
9			Replenishment of petty				9
10			cash fund.				10
11							11

After the petty cash payments record is footed and ruled, the balance in the fund and the amount received to replenish the fund may be entered in the Description column below the ruling as shown in the illustration. It is customary to carry the total forward to the top of a new page as a memorandum entry before entering any of the transactions for the following month.

BUILDING YOUR ACCOUNTING KNOWLEDGE

1. What is the usual source documentation of cash receipts when they are numerous and presented in person? What form of source documentation usually accompanies money that comes in by mail?
2. Why should transactions involving cash be handled by two or more persons?
3. Why is it not unusual to find that the cash balance at the time of proof is slightly short or over?
4. What does a debit balance in the cash short and over account represent? What does a credit balance in this account represent?
5. What is the purpose of a petty cash fund?
6. What should be obtained from the receiving party each time a petty cash payment is made?
7. From what source is the information obtained for issuing a check to replenish the petty cash fund?

APPLYING ACCOUNTING CONCEPTS

Exercise 3-1. **(a)** In attempting to prove cash, a shortage of $6.75 is found. Prepare the appropriate journal entry to recognize the shortage. **(b)** Assume that cash was found to be over by $3.58. Prepare the appropriate journal entry to recognize the overage. Use journal paper for making these entries.

Exercise 3-2. **(a)** On November 2, Marcia's Tea Room established a petty cash fund in the amount of $100. Prepare the journal entry for this transaction. **(b)** The following payments were made from the fund in November:

Automobile Expense	$25.80
Miscellaneous Expense	19.36
Postage Expense	22.00
Supplies Expense	10.48
Telephone Expense	4.20
	$81.84

Prepare the journal entry to replenish the fund on November 30. Use journal paper for making these entries.

Report No. 3-1

Refer to the study assignments and Complete Report No. 3-1.

BANKING PROCEDURES

A bank is a financial institution that receives deposits, lends money, makes collections, and renders a variety of other services, such as providing vaults for the safekeeping of valuables, handling trust funds, and buying and selling securities and insurance for its customers. Most banks offer facilities for both checking accounts and savings accounts.

Checking Account

The majority of all money payments in the United States are made by checks. A piece of commercial paper drawn on funds in a bank account and payable on demand is called a check. Such a paper involves three original parties: (1) the depositor who orders the bank to pay a certain amount of money—known as the drawer (2) the bank in which the drawer has money on deposit—known as the drawee; and (3) the person or entity directed to receive the money—known as the payee. The drawer and payee may be the same. In such a case the actual name of the payee is used or the word "Cash" can be substituted.

A check is negotiable (meaning that the right to receive the money can be transferred to someone else) if it complies with the following requirements: (1) it is in writing; (2) it is signed by the drawer; (3) it contains an unconditional order to pay a specified amount of money; (4) it is payable on demand; and (5) it is payable to the order of another party or to the bearer. The payee transfers the right to receive the money by indorsing the check. This procedure requires stamping or writing his or her name and sometimes other pertinent information on the back of the check. If the payee simply signs on the back of the check, customarily near the left end, the signature is called a blank indorsement. This makes the check payable to any bearer. If there are added words such as "For deposit," "Pay to any bank or banker," or "Pay to Lois McGregor only," it is called a restrictive indorsement. A business practice widely used when indorsing checks for deposit involves using a rubber stamp similar to that shown in the following illustration:

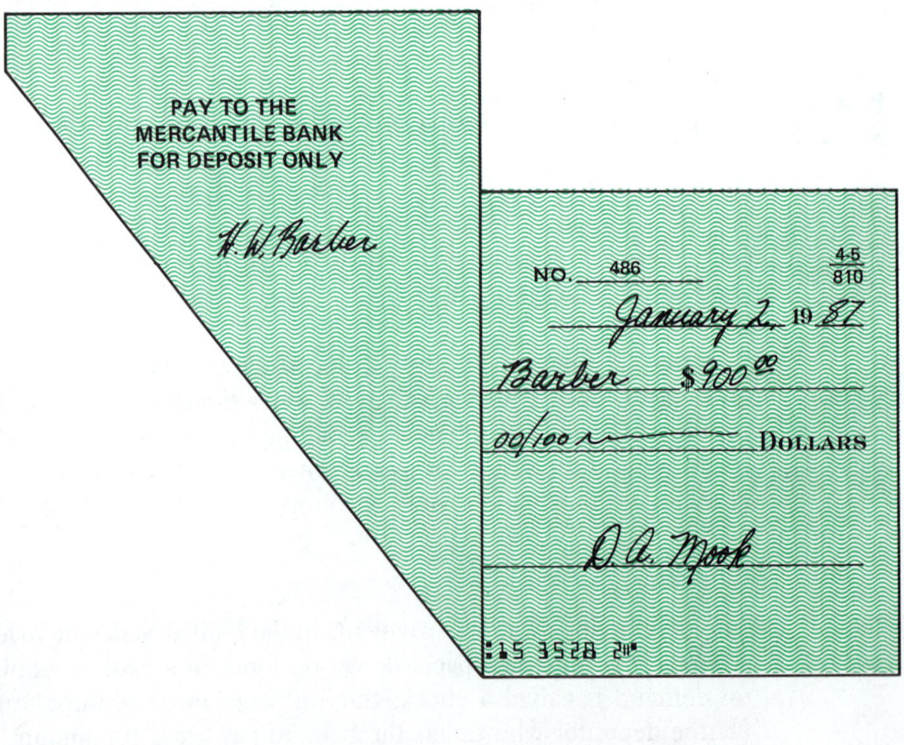

Restrictive Indorsement for Deposit (Rubber Stamp)

Important activities in connection with using a checking account are: (1) opening the account, (2) making deposits, (3) making withdrawals, (4) recording banking transactions, and (5) reconciling the bank statement.

Opening a Checking Account. To open a checking account with a bank, it is necessary to obtain the approval of an official of the bank and to make an initial deposit. Money, checks, bank drafts, money orders, and other cash items usually are accepted for deposit, subject to their verification as to amount and validity.

Banks usually require new depositors to sign their names on a card or form as an aid in verifying the depositor's signature on checks that may be issued, on cash items that may be indorsed for deposit, and on other business papers that may be presented to the bank. The form a depositor signs to give the bank a sample signature is called a **signature card**. If desired, depositors may authorize others to sign checks and other business forms on their behalf. A person who is so authorized is required to sign the depositor's name along with his or her own signature on a signature card and on all documents subsequently executed on behalf of the depositor. To aid in identification, the depositor's social security number is also shown. A signature card is one of the safeguards that a bank uses to protect its own interests as well as the interests of its depositors.

Making Deposits. To make a deposit with a bank, it is necessary to use certain forms prescribed by that bank and to observe the rules of the bank with regard to acceptable and unacceptable deposit items. In preparing the deposit, paper money should be arranged in the order of the denominations, the smaller denominations being placed on top. The bills should be all stacked face up and top up. Coins (pennies, nickels, dimes, quarters, half dollars and dollars) that are to be deposited in considerable quantities should be wrapped in coin wrappers, which the bank provides, unless the bank has a coin-sorting machine. The name and account number of the depositor should be written on the outside of each coin wrapper as a means of identification in the event that a mistake has been made in counting the coins. All checks being deposited must be indorsed. As mentioned earlier, the indorsement on the check illustrated on page 68 was made by means of a rubber stamp.

Deposit Ticket. A printed form with a detailed listing of items being deposited is called a **deposit ticket**. Banks provide these forms for depositors. A filled-in deposit ticket, typical of the type that most banks provide, is reproduced on page 70. Note that the number of the depositor's account is preprinted at the bottom in numbers that can be "read" by electronic equipment used by banks. These numbers are called **MICR numbers**, which stands for magnetic ink character recognition. This series of digits, which is also preprinted at the bottom of all of the depositor's checks, is actually a code used in sorting and routing deposit slips and checks. In the first set of digits, 081000210, the first "8" indicates that the bank is in the Eighth Federal Reserve District. The third digit "1" is the reserve bank or branch serving the district. The fourth digit "0" indicates that the item is for immediate credit. A

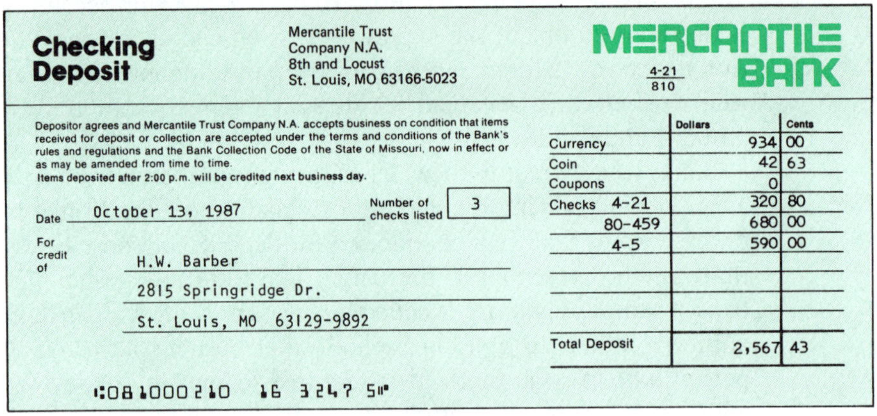
Checking Deposit

Mercantile Trust Company N.A.
8th and Locust
St. Louis, MO 63166-5023

MERCANTILE BANK

4-21 / 810

Depositor agrees and Mercantile Trust Company N.A. accepts business on condition that items received for deposit or collection are accepted under the terms and conditions of the Bank's rules and regulations and the Bank Collection Code of the State of Missouri, now in effect or as may be amended from time to time.
Items deposited after 2:00 p.m. will be credited next business day.

Date October 13, 1987 Number of checks listed 3

For credit of H.W. Barber
2815 Springridge Dr.
St. Louis, MO 63129-9892

	Dollars	Cents
Currency	934	00
Coin	42	63
Coupons	0	
Checks 4-21	320	80
80-459	680	00
4-5	590	00
Total Deposit	2,567	43

⑆081000210 16 3247 5⑈

Deposit Ticket

"1" in the fourth position would indicate that the credit to the bank is delayed by one day. In either case the depositor's account receives immediate credit. The number "21" is a number assigned to the Mercantile Bank. The last number position ("0" in this case) is a check digit position and may be used to verify the accuracy of the eight preceding digits in computer processing. This numbering method was established by the American Bankers Association for use in sorting and routing deposit tickets. The second set of digits, 16-3247-5, is the number assigned by the Mercantile Bank to H. W. Barber's account.

It is not unusual for a depositor to receive a duplicate deposit ticket receipted by a bank teller. However, a more common practice today is to obtain a machine-printed receipt from the bank, which serves as a source document of the deposit. In preparing a deposit ticket, the date, number of checks, and account number should be written in the spaces provided. The amounts of cash represented by currency, coins, matured bond coupons and checks that are deposited should be entered in the amount column of the deposit ticket on the lines provided for these items.

Each check to be deposited should be listed on a separate line of the deposit ticket as shown in the illustration. In listing checks on the deposit ticket, the instructions of the bank should be observed in describing the checks for identification purposes. Banks usually prefer that depositors identify checks being deposited by showing the **ABA number** of the bank on which the check is drawn. This number is frequently located in the upper right hand corner of the check. The ABA number for the first check listed on the deposit ticket is $\frac{4\text{-}21}{810}$. The number "4" is the number assigned to the city in which the bank is located and the number "21" is assigned to the specific bank. The denominator "810" is the check routing number, but only the numerator is used in identifying the deposit.

The total of the cash and other items deposited should be entered on the deposit ticket. The deposit ticket, together with the cash and the other items deposited, should be delivered to the receiving teller of the bank. The teller processes the deposit ticket and gives the depositor a machine-printed receipt.

A depositor may personally obtain cash at the time of making a deposit by indicating on the deposit ticket what portion of the total of items listed is to be returned to him or her, with the remainder to constitute the deposit. Alternatively, a check may be drawn payable to the depositor, or usually, just to "Cash."

Most banks use teller-operated machines in preparing machine-printed receipts for deposits. The use of such machines saves the time required to make manual entries and eliminates the need for making duplicate copies of deposit tickets. Such machines are not only time-saving, but they also promote accuracy in the handling of deposits.

The deposits handled by each teller during the day may be accumulated in the teller-operated machine so that at the end of the day the total amount of the deposits received by the teller is automatically recorded by the machine. This amount may be proved by counting the cash and cash items accepted by a teller for deposit during the day.

Deposits by Mail. Bank deposits may be made by mail since it may not always be convenient to make deposits over the counter. Such deposits may consist of checks and matured bond coupons. When deposits are made by mail, the bank may provide the depositor with a supply of deposit tickets, and a self-addressed, prestamped envelope. A machine-printed receipt for the deposit is subsequently returned by the bank.

Night Deposits. Many banks provide night deposit service. A common practice is for the bank to have a night safe with an opening on the exterior of the bank building. Upon signing a night depository contract, the bank supplies the depositor with a key to the outside door of the safe, together with a bag that has an identifying number and in which valuables may be placed, and two keys to the bag itself. Once the depositor places the bag in the night deposit safe, it cannot be retrieved because it moves to a vault in the bank that is accessible to bank employees only. Since only the depositor is provided with keys to the bag, the depositor or an authorized representative must go to the bank to unlock the bag. The depositor may or may not deposit the funds that had been placed previously in the night deposit safe.

Night deposit banking service is especially valuable to those individuals and concerns that accumulate cash and other cash items which they cannot take to the bank during regular banking hours and that do not have safe facilities in their own places of business.

Dishonored Checks. A check that a bank refuses to pay is described as a dishonored check. A depositor guarantees all items deposited and is liable to the bank for the amount involved if any item is not honored when presented for payment. When a check or other cash item is deposited with a bank and is not honored upon presentation to the bank upon which it is drawn, the depositor's bank may charge the amount of the dishonored item to the depositor's account or may present it to the depositor for reimbursement. It is not uncommon for checks that have been deposited to be returned to the depositor for various reasons accompanied with a debit advice. As indicated on the following debit advice, the most common reason for checks being returned unpaid is that they are NSF checks ("not sufficient funds" remain in the drawer's account to cover them).

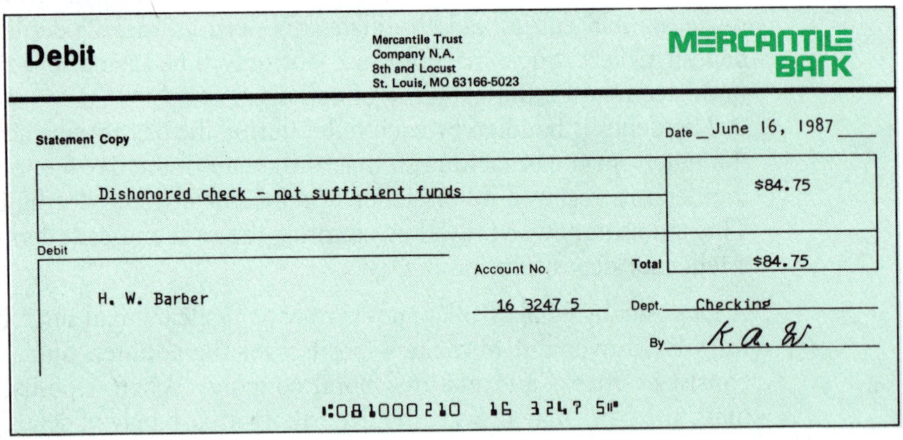
Debit

Mercantile Trust
Company N.A.
8th and Locust
St. Louis, MO 63166-5023

MERCANTILE BANK

Statement Copy

Date June 16, 1987

Dishonored check - not sufficient funds	$84.75
Total	$84.75

Debit
H. W. Barber

Account No. 16 3247 5
Dept. Checking
By K. a. W.

⑆081000210 16 3247 5⑈

Debit Advice

Issuance of a check on a bank without sufficient funds on deposit with that bank to cover the check when it is presented for payment is called an overdraft. Under the laws of most states, issuance of such a check is illegal. When a dishonored check is charged to the depositor's account, the amount should be deducted from the balance shown on the depositor's checkbook stub.

Most overdraft checks are not the result of any dishonest intent on the part of the drawer of such checks. Either the depositor thought that there was money in the account when the check was written, due to an error in keeping the checkbook, or expected to get a deposit to the bank in time to "cover" the check before it reached the bank for payment. It is commonly considered to be something of a disgrace to the drawer of a check if the bank will not honor (pay) it. In recent years, many banks have made available plans that guarantee that all checks, within prescribed limits as to amount, will be honored even if the depositor's balance is too low. This amounts to a prearrangement with the bank to make a loan to the depositor, and in some cases, interest may be automatically computed and charged against the depositor's account. These plans have been given names such as "Ready Reserve Account," "Instant Cash," and others. Arrangements of this sort are parts of larger plans that involve such things as picture checks, no minimum balance requirement, bank statements that list checks paid in numerical order, check guarantee cards, travelers checks without fee, safe-deposit boxes, and bank credit cards. The bank may charge a monthly fee for any or all of these services. Such comprehensive plans are not widely subscribed to by businesses (in contrast to individuals).

Postdated Check. A check dated after the date that the check was written and issued is known as a postdated check. For example, a check written and issued on March 2 is dated March 16. The recipient of the postdated check should not deposit it before the date specified on the check (March 16) because it is not legally acceptable as cash until that date. One reason for issuing a postdated check may be that the drawer does not have sufficient funds in the bank at the time of issuance which in this case is March 2, but expects to have a sufficient amount on deposit by the time the check is presented for payment on or after the date of the check (March 16). When a postdated check is presented to the bank on which it is drawn and payment is not made, it is handled by the bank in the same manner as any other dishonored check. Generally it is not considered good practice for a business to issue postdated checks.

Making Withdrawals. The amount deposited in a bank checking account may be withdrawn either by the depositor or by any other person who is properly authorized to make withdrawals from the depositor's account. Such withdrawals are accomplished by the use of plastic cards inserted in automated teller machines or by the use of checks signed by the depositor or by others having the authority to sign checks drawn on the account.

Automated Teller Machines. Many banks now make automated teller machines available at all times to depositors. Although such machines may be used to make deposits, they are used far more frequently to make withdrawals.

Each depositor electing to use automated teller machines is provided with a plastic card and a secret code number. The depositor inserts the card into the machine, keys in the "password" code number, presses another key to indicate either (1) a withdrawal or (2) a deposit, and then keys in the amount. The machine next asks for a keyed-in verification ("yes" or "no") of the amount and—after a slight pause—instructs the depositor to open a drawer or door on the front of the machine.

If the transaction is a withdrawal, the cash requested can be found and removed. If a deposit, the deposit ticket and deposit items are placed in the drawer or compartment. The machine then asks the depositor whether another transaction will take place, and if the keyed-in answer is "no," the drawer or compartment locks automatically. The depositor then removes the plastic card from the machine, which deactivates it until the next depositor arrives.

Checkbook. Checks used by businesses are usually bound in the form of a book with two or three blank checks to a page and perforated so that they may be removed singly. Checks may be provided by the bank (often for a charge) or purchased directly from firms that specialize in the manufacture of check forms.

To the left of each check is a small form called a **check stub** that contains space to record all relevant information about the check. Sometimes the depositor is provided with a **checkbook** that, instead of containing stubs, is accompanied by a small **check register** book in which the relevant information is noted. The information contained on the stub or on the register includes the check number, date, payee, amount, the purpose of the check and often the account to be charged, along with the bank balance before the check was issued, current deposits if any, and the resulting balance after issuing the check.

The depositor's name and address normally are printed on each check and the MICR numbers are shown along the bottom edge. Often the check number is preprinted in the upper right corner. Sometimes, checks come bound in the form of a pad. There may be a blank page after each check for use in making a carbon copy of the check. The copy is not a check; it is merely a copy of what was typed or written on the original check and provides the essential information for making an entry in the formal records.

Preparing a Check. The first step in preparing a check is to complete the **check stub** or **check register.** This plan insures that the drawer will retain a record of each check issued. The purpose is to keep a detailed record of deposits made and checks issued to indicate the balance in the checking account after each check is drawn. Second, the name of the payee is entered on the check. Third, the amount of the check is entered on the check in both figures and words. If the amount shown on the check in figures does not agree with the amount shown in words, the bank usually contacts the drawer for the correct amount or returns the check unpaid.

Care must be used in entering the amount on the check in order to avoid any possibility that the payee or a subsequent holder may change the amount. If the instructions below are followed in the preparation of a check, it will be difficult to change the amount.

1. The amount shown in figures should be entered so that there is no space between the dollar sign and the first digit of the amount.

2. The amount stated in words should be entered beginning at the extreme left on the line provided for this information. The cents should be entered in the form of a common fraction; if the check is for an even number of dollars, use two zeros or the word "no" as the numerator of the fraction. If a vacant space remains, a line should be drawn from the amount stated in words to the word "Dollars" on the same line with it, as shown in the following illustration.

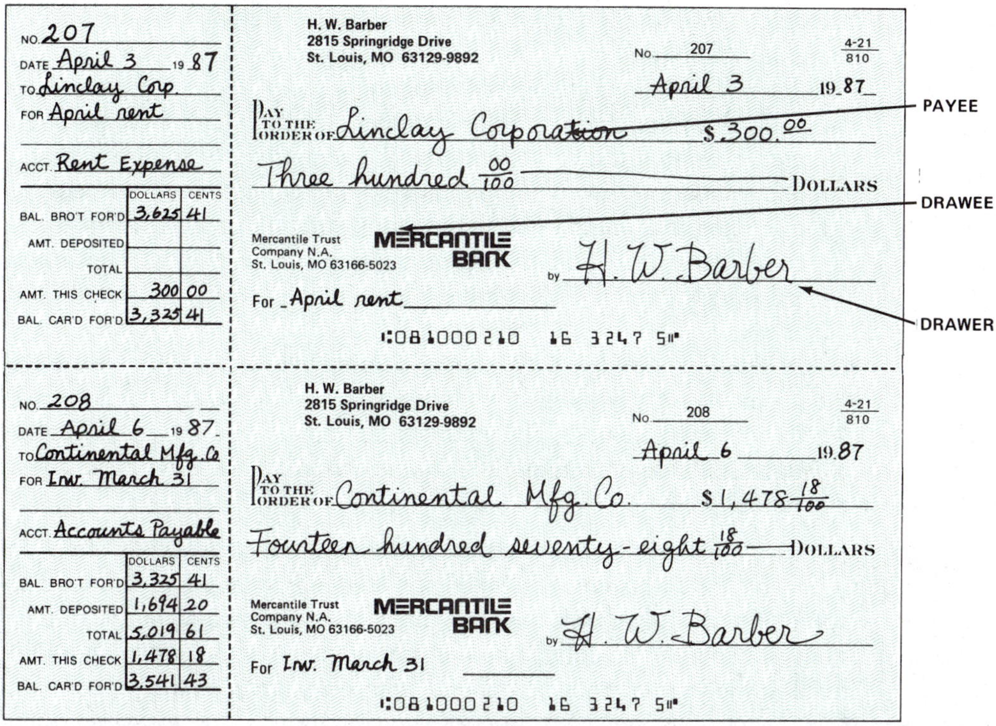

Checks and Stubs

A machine frequently used to print the amount of a check in figures and in words is known as a **checkwriter**. The use of a checkwriter is desirable because it practically eliminates the possibility of changing the amount of a check.

As the fourth step in writing a check, the purpose for which a check is drawn is often noted in the lower left-hand corner of the check itself. Indicating the purpose on the check provides information for the benefit of the payee and provides a specific receipt for the drawer. In the fifth step, the signature of the drawer is written on the lower right hand corner of the check in the same manner as on the signature card.

Each check issued by a depositor will be returned by the bank on which it is drawn after the check has been paid. Canceled checks are returned to the depositor with the bank statement, which is usually sent by mail each month.

Canceled checks will have been indorsed by the payee and any subsequent holders. They constitute receipts that the depositor should retain for future reference. They may be attached to the stubs from which they were removed originally or they should be filed in numerical order.

Electronic Processing of Checks. It is now nearly universal practice to use checks that, like deposit tickets, can be processed by MICR (magnetic ink character recognition) equipment. Imprinted in magnetic ink along the lower margin of the check is a series of magnetic numbers or digits in the form of a code that indicates (1) the identity of the Federal Reserve district in which the bank is located and a routing number, (2) the identity of the bank, and (3) the account number assigned to the depositor. Sometimes that check number is also imprinted. In processing checks with electronic equipment, the first bank that handles the check imprints the amount in magnetic ink characters to further aid in the processing of the check. The amount is printed directly below the signature line in the lower right-hand corner of the check.

Checks imprinted with the bank's number, the depositor's number, and the amount—all in MICR characters—can be posted electronically to the customer's account. The two checks reproduced on page 75 illustrate magnetic ink characters along the lower margins, as well as check stubs properly completed.

Entering Banking Transactions in the Journal. Checkbook stubs contain much of the information needed for keeping a record of the transactions completed with the bank, but they are not a journal and no posting is done from the checkbook stubs. The amount of each check written should be entered in the journal and then posted from the journal to the proper accounts. Checkbook stubs provide a line for showing the purpose for which the check is written, but they do not provide detailed information about the source of the amounts deposited. This information must come, for example, from fees for services rendered, additional investments by the owner, or sales invoices. Depending upon the nature of the deposit, the journal entry will be a debit to Cash and a credit to the proper income account.

As the amount of each check is entered in the journal, a check mark is placed immediately after the account title written on the stub to indicate that the check was entered. When the canceled check is subsequently received from the bank, the amount shown on the stub may be checkmarked to indicate that the canceled check was received.

Records Kept by a Bank. The usual transactions completed by a bank with a depositor are:

1. Accepting deposits made by the depositor.
2. Paying checks issued by the depositor.

3. Lending money to the depositor.
4. Collecting the amounts of various kinds of commercial paper, such as matured notes or bonds and bond interest coupons, for the account of the depositor.
5. Buying and selling securities and insurance for the depositor.

The bank keeps an account for each depositor. Each transaction affecting the depositor's account is entered by either debiting or crediting the depositor's account, depending upon the effect of the transaction.

When a bank accepts a deposit, the account of the depositor is credited (increased) for the amount of the deposit. The deposit increases the bank's liability to the depositor. When the bank pays a check that has been drawn on the bank, it debits (decreases) the account of the depositor for the amount of the check. If the bank makes a collection for the depositor, the net amount of the collection is credited to the account. At the same time, the bank notifies the depositor that the collection has been made using a credit advice form similar to the illustration below.

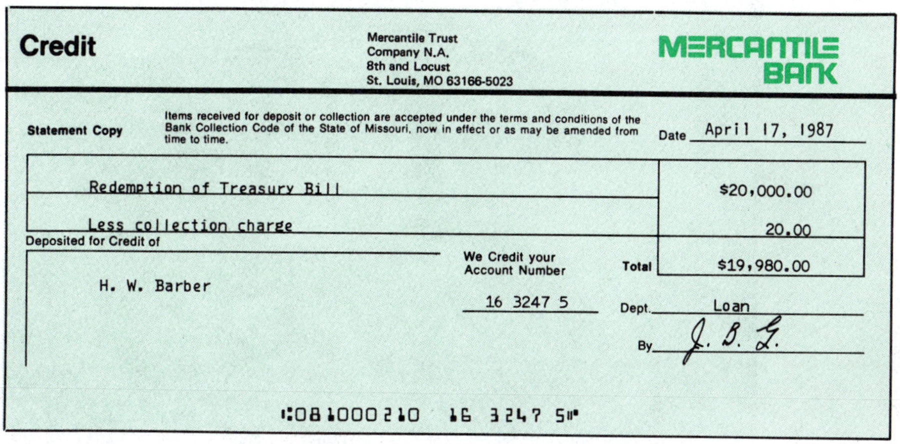
Credit
Mercantile Trust
Company N.A.
8th and Locust
St. Louis, MO 63166-5023
MERCANTILE BANK

Statement Copy
Items received for deposit or collection are accepted under the terms and conditions of the Bank Collection Code of the State of Missouri, now in effect or as may be amended from time to time.
Date April 17, 1987

Redemption of Treasury Bill	$20,000.00
Less collection charge	20.00
Total	$19,980.00

Deposited for Credit of
H. W. Barber
We Credit your Account Number 16 3247 5
Dept. Loan
By J. B. G.

⑆081000210 16 3247 5⑈

Credit Advice

Bank Statement. A statement of account issued to each depositor once a month by a bank is called a bank statement. An illustration of a widely used form of bank statement is shown on page 78. Some banks provide statements that also present information regarding savings accounts and loan accounts, for those depositors who have such accounts. Very commonly, however, a separate statement is furnished for each type of account.

The statement illustrated is for a checking account. It is a report showing (1) the balance on deposit at the beginning of the period, (2) the amount of deposits and credits added during the period (credits), (3) the amounts of withdrawals by check and other charges subtracted during the period (debits), (4) the balance on deposit at the end of the period, (5) the average daily balance during the period, and (6) the minimum balance in the period. With the bank statement, the depositor also receives all checks paid by the bank during the period, together with any forms representing items charged or credited to the account.

Statement MERCANTILE BANK

H. W. Barber
2815 Springridge Dr.
St. Louis, MO 63129-9892

Reference Number: 16 3247 5
Page Number:
Statement Date: Nov. 30, 1987
Statement Instructions:

Beginning Balance	No. of Deposits and Credits	We have added these deposits and credits totaling	No. of Withdrawals and Charges	We have subtracted these withdrawals and charges totaling	Resulting in a statement balance of
$2,721.51	2	$2,599.31	15	$3,572.73	

Document Count	Average daily balance this statement period	Minimum balance this statement period Date	Amount
17	$2,258.18	11/25/87	$ 1,748.09

If your account does not balance, please see reverse side and report any discrepancy to our Customer Service Department.

Date	Deposits and Credits	Withdrawals and Charges				Balance
				Previous Statement		2,721.51
10/27		242.00				2,479.51
10/28		68.93	58.00			2,352.58
10/29	867.00					3,219.58
11/3	1,732.31	19.88	228.11	452.13	94.60	4,157.17
11/17		2,000.00	32.42	64.08	210.87	1,849.80
11/25		18.00	23.31	58.60	1.80 SC	1,748.09

AD - Credit Advance
CM - Credit Memo
CR - Deposit
DM - Debit Memo
EC - Error Correction
FB - Fingertip Banking
IC - Internal Credit (float)
IE - Internal Entry
LS - List of Checks
M - Credit or Debit Memo
OD - Overdrawn
RC - Return Check Charge
RT - Returned Check
SC - Service Charge
SP - Sure Pay
ST - Savings Transfer
TC - Transfer to Checking
TR - Wire Transfer

Depositor agrees and Bank accepts business upon the terms and conditions of Bank's rules and regulations now in effect or as may be hereafter adopted.

Bank Statement

Reconciling the Bank Statement. A depositor ordinarily keeps one or more records of bank-related transactions. A bank also keeps records of tansactions with each depositor. The depositor's records of transactions with the bank should be brought into agreement with the bank's records of transactions with the depositor at periodic intervals—usually once a month.

As soon as possible after a bank statement is received, the depositor should try to make it agree with the bank balance record kept on the check stubs, a procedure known as **reconciling the bank statement**. The balance shown on the bank statement may not be the same as the amount shown on the check stubs for one or more of the following reasons:

1. Checks issued during the period may not have been presented to the bank for payment before the statement was prepared. These are known as **outstanding checks**. Some of the checks may fall into this category.
2. Deposits may not have been entered by the bank on the bank statement. These are known as **deposits in transit**. Such a deposit may have been mailed, or placed in the automated teller or night depository and not entered by the bank until the day following the date of the statement.
3. The bank may have credited the depositor's account for an amount collected, but the depositor may not as yet have noted it on the check stubs since the credit advice has not yet been received.
4. Service charges or other charges may appear on the bank statement that the depositor has not entered on the check stubs.
5. The depositor may have erred in keeping the bank account record.
6. The bank may have erred in keeping its account with the depositor.

Each bank usually provides a form for completing the bank reconciliation on the back of the bank statement. If a depositor is unable to reconcile the bank statement, a report on the matter should be made to the bank immediately.

The following is a suggested procedure in reconciling the bank statement:

1. The amount of each deposit entered on the bank statement is compared with the amount entered on the check stubs. Any deposit entered on the check stub but not entered on the bank statement should be added to the bank statement balance as a deposit in transit.
2. The amount of each canceled check is compared both with the amount entered on the bank statement and with the amount entered on the depositor's check stubs. When making this comparison, it is a good plan to place a check mark by the amount entered on each check stub to indicate that the canceled check has been returned by the bank and its amount verified.
3. The outstanding checks are listed, totaled, and deducted from the bank balance. The information needed for this list may be obtained by examining the check stubs and noting the amounts that have not been checkmarked.
4. The amounts of any items listed on the bank statement that represent credits or charges to a depositor's account which have not been entered on the check stubs are added to or deducted from the balance on the check stubs and are entered in the journal that is being used for cash receipts and payments.
5. Any error discovered on the check stubs or bank statement will require an adjustment to the check stub balance or bank balance depending on the nature of the error. A journal entry will also be necessary to correct for any check stub errors.

After completion of the foregoing procedure, the adjusted balance shown on the check stubs should equal the adjusted bank balance. A reconciliation of the bank balance shown in the statement reproduced on page 78 with the most recent check stub balance as follows:

H. W. BARBER
Reconciliation of Bank Statement
November 30, 1987

1.	Balance, November 30, per bank statement		$1,748.09
2.	Add deposit, November 30		782.91
			$2,531.00
3.	Less checks outstanding, November 30:		
	No. 525	$163.00	
	No. 530	28.47	
	No. 532	247.20	438.67
4.	Adjusted bank balance		$2,092.33
5.	Balance, November 30, per check stub		$2,095.03
6.	Less: Bank service charge	$ 1.80	
7.	Error on stub for Check No. 503	.90	2.70
8.	Adjusted check stub balance		$2,092.33

In making the reconciliation of the H. W. Barber bank statement as of November 30, 1987, the following steps, which correspond with the numbers in the reconciliation, were completed:

1. The November 30 bank balance, $1,748.09 was copied from the bank statement.
2. A deposit of $782.91, placed in the night depository on November 30 and therefore not shown on the bank statement, was added to the November 30 bank balance to agree with the check stub that reflected the deposit on that date.
3. The outstanding Checks Nos. 525, 530, and 532 were listed, totaled, and $438.67 was subtracted from the bank balance. These checks had not been presented to the bank for payment and thus were not returned with the bank statement.
4. The adjusted bank balance as of the close of business November 30 was calculated as $2,092.33.
5. The check stub balance as of November 30 was copied from the last check stub bearing that date, in the amount of $2095.03.
6. A bank service charge of $1.80 shown at the bottom of the bank statement was subtracted from the check stub balance.
7. A checkbook error was discovered. Check No. 503 was written for $19.88 and recorded in the check stub as $18.98. This error required the check stub balance to be decreased by $.90.
8. The adjusted check stub balance as of the close of business, November 30, was calculated as $2,092.33 and was equal to the adjusted November 30 bank balance.

In step number 6, a bank service charge was mentioned. A service charge may be made by a bank for the handling of checks and other items. The basis and the amount of such charges vary with different banks in different localities.

When a bank statement indicates that a service charge has been made, the depositor should enter the amount of the service charge by debiting an expense account, such as Miscellaneous Expense, and by crediting Cash.

Miscellaneous Expense	1.80	
Cash		1.80
Bank service charge for November.		

The error noted in step number 7 was discovered when the canceled checks that were returned with the bank statement were matched against the check stubs. It was found that, although Check No. 503 had been written for $19.88, the amount was shown as $18.98 on its stub. This is called a **transposition error**, because the "9" and the "8" were transposed; i.e., their order was reversed. On Stub No. 503, and the others that followed, the bank balance shown was $.90 overstated. The correct amount, $19.88, should be shown on Stub No. 503, and the bank balance shown on the stub of the last check used should be corrected by reducing the amount by $.90. If Check No. 503 was in payment of a telephone bill, an entry should be made debiting Telephone Expense and crediting Cash.

Telephone Expense	.90	
Cash		.90
Correction of checkbook error.		

Keeping a Ledger Account For Each Bank

As explained previously, the depositor may keep a checkbook for each bank account. The depositor may also keep a ledger account for each bank. The title of such an account usually is the name of the bank. Sometimes, more than one account is kept with a bank, in which case each account should be correctly labeled. Such terms as "commercial," "executive," and "payroll" are used to identify the accounts.

The bank account is debited for the amount of each deposit and should be credited for the amount of each check written. The account should also be debited or credited for any other items that may have been handled directly by the bank, including collections and service charges.

Savings Account

When a **savings account** is opened in a bank, a signature card must be signed by the depositor. By signing the signature card, the depositor agrees to abide by the rules and regulations of the bank. These rules and regulations vary with different banks and may be altered and amended from time to time. At this time, a **passbook** may be given to the depositor. This is a small book in which the bank teller enters the date and amount of each deposit or withdrawal. The passbook is to be presented at the bank or mailed to the bank along with a deposit or withdrawal slip, each time money is deposited or withdrawn from the account. An alternative practice for depositing or withdrawing money from a savings account is to give the depositor a small register for recording deposits and withdrawals and a pad of deposit-withdrawal forms. This procedure eliminates the use of the passbook. Each time a deposit or withdrawal from savings is made, the appropriate part of one of the forms is filled in, signed, entered in the register and presented to or mailed to the bank with deposit items or other documents. The bank gives a machine-printed receipt to the depositor or returns it by mail. There should be a separate savings account in the ledger in which to enter these activities. Sometimes, the name of the bank is in the title of the account, for example, "Cash—Mercantile Bank Savings Account."

At least once each quarter, the bank mails a credit advice to the depositor, indicating the amount of interest credited to the account. This should be entered in the depositor's register upon receipt. If a passbook is used, it should be presented or mailed to the bank, so that the credit advice can be entered by a teller. The depositor should also enter the amount in the business accounts by a debit to the savings account and by a credit to Interest Earned. The interest is revenue earned whether withdrawn or not and is taxable to the depositor.

Cash—Mercantile Bank Savings Account	xxx	
Interest Earned		xxx
Quarterly interest earned.		

Traditionally, the principal differences between a savings account and a checking account are that interest is paid regularly by the bank on a savings account and withdrawals from a savings account may be made at the bank or by mail by the depositor or an authorized agent. Depositors use checking accounts primarily as a convenient means of making payments, while savings accounts are used primarily as a means of accumulating funds with interest.

An increasingly common practice is for the bank to combine savings and checking accounts and get depositor permission to make automatic transfers of funds from the savings portion to the checking portion whenever the latter falls below a specified minimum balance. This amounts to giving the depositor an interest-earning checking account.

Interest-Earning Checking Accounts

Many checking accounts now earn interest on their average daily balances. The amount of such interest usually is determined and reported monthly on the depositor's bank statement. Such accounts commonly specify that a minimum balance must be maintained, and higher rates of interest may be offered if depositors agree to maintain larger minimum balances.

Electronic Funds Transfer

Electronic funds transfer (EFT) uses a computer rather than money or checks to complete transactions with the bank. Increasingly, this approach is being used to meet payrolls, process social security payments, and pay for retail purchases.

If employees agree to sign authorization forms, each pay period their employers will send a magnetic tape containing payroll information directly to the bank. The bank's computer will then debit the employer's account for the total payroll and credit each employee's checking account. The U.S. government will, on authorization, process social security payments in a similar manner. Customers of retail stores can insert special pre-coded plastic cards in store terminals and automatically transfer cash from their checking accounts to the store's checking account at the bank in payment for their purchases.

BUILDING YOUR ACCOUNTING KNOWLEDGE

1. Name the five requirements with which a check must comply in order to be negotiable.
2. Why do banks usually require a new depositor to fill out a signature card? Why may more than one name appear on a signature card?
3. What is the reason for a depositor to obtain a printed receipt from the bank teller?
4. Describe the use of MICR numbers in the electronic processing of checks.
5. Briefly describe how a depositor uses an automated teller machine.
6. Name the six major dollar amounts summarized on a bank statement.
7. If a depositor is unable to reconcile a bank statement, what should be done?
8. What journal entry should a depositor make when a bank statement indicates that there has been a service charge?
9. What is the primary purpose of a checking account? What is the primary purpose of a savings account?
10. Name three applications of electronic funds transfer in current use.

APPLYING ACCOUNTING CONCEPTS

Exercise 3-3. The following information relates to the bank account of Janet Noguchi's financial consulting service on June 30:

Balance, June 30, per check stub		$15,852.37
Balance, June 30, per bank statement		15,197.59
June 30 deposit not shown on bank statement		1,135.00
Bank service charge shown on bank statement		4.75
Checks outstanding, June 30:		
No. 1012	$163.28	
No. 1015	278.13	
No. 1019	43.56	484.97

Prepare a reconciliation of the bank statement with the check stub balance of June 30.

Exercise 3-4. **(a)** A depositor's bank statement shows a service charge of $5.35. Prepare the journal entry for this service charge. **(b)** Comparison of the cancelled checks with the check stubs revealed that Check No. 1214 which had been written for $21.56 was shown as $25.16 on the check stub. Check No. 1214 was used to pay a bill for gasoline and oil for the company car. Prepare the journal entry to correct this error.

REPORT NO. 3-2

Refer to the study assignments and complete Report No. 3-2. This assignment provides a test of your ability to apply the principles developed in the first three chapters of the textbook.

MASTERY PROBLEMS

Problem 3-A Journalizing, posting, taking a trial balance

Frieda Von Lehman is a certified public accountant (CPA). Following is the trial balance of the business taken as of September 30:

FRIEDA VON LEHMAN, CPA
Trial Balance
September 30, 19--

Cash	111	35,712.72	
Automobile	211	13,575.00	
Office Equipment	221	5,390.00	
Accounts Payable	311		530.63
Frieda Von Lehman, Capital	511		39,222.36
Frieda Von Lehman, Drawing	521	18,000.00	
Professional Fees	611		62,860.00
Automobile Expense	711	2,742.50	
Charitable Contributions Expense	713	1,285.00	
Electricity Expense	715	617.42	
Miscellaneous Expense	718	263.01	
Rent Expense	720	10,800.00	
Salary Expense	723	11,700.00	
Telephone Expense	725	954.18	
Travel and Entertainment Expense	727	1,573.16	
		102,612.99	102,612.99

The following transactions were completed in the month of October:

Oct. 1 Paid October office rent, $1,200.
1 Paid electric bill, $61.02.
2 Paid telephone bill, $98.47.
2 Received a check from Harper Chemical Co. for $1,155 for services rendered.
6 Received $1,800 from the Hagedorn Dry Wall Co. for services rendered.
7 Donated $25 to the United Way.
7 Paid garage bill, $102.30.
12 Received a check for $2,250 from the Quality Printing Co. for services rendered.
15 Von Lehman withdrew $1,000 for personal use.
15 Paid secretary's salary for the half month, $650.
16 Purchased a secretarial work center on credit from the Mack Furniture Co., $683.55.
20 Paid $7.50 to send a registered letter.
20 Received $2,500 from the Suburban Lumber Co. for services rendered.
22 Paid traveling expenses to attend an accounting meeting, $279.80.
23 Donated $50 to the Salvation Army.
27 Paid the October 1 balance due in Accounts Payable, $530.63.
28 Von Lehman withdrew $1,000 for personal use.
30 Paid secretary's salary for the second half of the month, $650.

***Required:* (1)** Journalize the October transactions using the two-column journal paper. Number the first page 19. Foot the journal pages to be sure the total of the debit column equals the total of the credit column. **(2)** Using the ledger accounts enter the October 1 balances and post the journal entries. Enter the cross references in the journal and the ledger. Foot the ledger accounts and enter the balances. **(3)** Take a trial balance as of October 31, 19-- using the paper provided.

Problem 3-B Reconciliation of bank statement

Michael Sheridan, an insurance agent, completed the following transactions with the Philipsburg Bank during the month of September:

Sept.	1	Balance in bank per record kept on check stubs	$8,628.30
	1	Deposit	2,000.00
	1	Check No. 739	788.20
	3	Check No. 740	20.00
	3	Check No. 741	1,860.00
	3	Check No. 742	750.00
	3	Check No. 743	18.29
	4	Check No. 744	90.00
	7	Check No. 745	390.26
	7	Check No. 746	75.00
	7	Check No. 747	412.25
	7	Deposit	1,543.85
	8	Check No. 748	336.09
	10	Check No. 749	190.00
	10	Check No. 750	62.85
	11	Check No. 751	189.52

Sept. 14	Check No. 752	41.80
14	Check No. 753	509.18
14	Deposit	3,481.27
16	Check No. 754	150.00
18	Check No. 755	265.01
21	Check No. 756	104.17
21	Deposit	2,791.00
23	Check No. 757	209.16
25	Check No. 758	415.02
28	Check No. 759	382.45
29	Check No. 760	183.00
30	Check No. 761	656.13
30	Deposit	945.24

Required: **(1)** Using the paper provided, prepare a record of the bank account as it would appear on the check book stubs. **(2)** Prepare a reconciliation of the bank statement for September that indicated a balance of $12,845.50 on September 30 with Checks Nos. 748, 759, 760, and 761 outstanding and a service charge of $3.45. Use the paper provided.

Problem 3-C Petty cash payments record

Linda Carr operates a court reporting service. On November 1 she had a balance of $125 in the petty cash fund. During November the following petty cash transactions were completed:

Nov. 2 Paid $15.67 for typewriter ribbons. Petty Cash Voucher No. 111.
4 Paid $22 for postage stamps. Petty Cash Voucher No. 112.
9 Paid $8.30 for gas and oil for the company car. Petty Cash Voucher No. 113.
11 Reimbursed Carr $4.50 for a long distance call made from a booth. Petty Cash Voucher No. 114.
12 Gave $5 to the Salvation Army. Petty Cash Voucher No. 115.
16 Paid for newspapers for the month of October, $13.45. Petty Cash Voucher No. 116.
19 Paid garage for washing car, $5.75. Petty Cash Voucher No. 117.
23 Gave Carr's daughter $5. (Debit Linda Carr, Drawing.) Petty Cash Voucher No. 118.
26 Paid supper money to secretary who worked overtime in the evening, $7.50. Petty Cash Voucher No. 119.
27 Paid for window washing, $15. Petty Cash Voucher No. 120.
30 Paid for car lubrication, $8.50. Petty Cash Voucher No. 121.

Required: **(1)** Record the foregoing transactions in the petty cash payments record. Distribute the expenditures as follows:

Linda Carr, Drawing	Office Supplies Expense
Automobile Expense	Postage Expense
Donations Expense	Telephone Expense
Miscellaneous Expense	

(2) Prove the petty cash payments record by footing the amount columns and proving the totals. Enter the totals and rule the amount columns with single and double lines. **(3)** Using the paper provided, prepare a statement of the petty cash payments for

November. **(4)** Bring down the balance of the petty cash fund below the ruling in the Description column. Enter the amount received to replenish the fund and record the total. **(5)** Prepare a compound journal entry as of November 30, using the journal paper provided.

CHALLENGE PROBLEM 3

Johanna Heidrich is a financial planner. The balance in the petty cash fund on April 1 was $125. During April the following petty cash transactions were completed:

April 1 Paid $8.95 for client luncheon. Petty Cash Voucher No. 27.
6 Paid $4.50 for parking car. Petty Cash Voucher No. 28.
9 Paid $7.10 for office supplies. Petty Cash Voucher No. 29.
13 Paid for newspapers for the month of March, $14.30. Petty Cash Voucher No. 30.
17 Paid $22 for postage stamps. Petty Cash Voucher No. 31.
22 Gave Heidrich's son $5.00 (Debit Johanna Heidrich, Drawing.) Petty Cash Voucher No. 32.
27 Gave $15 to the American Red Cross. Petty Cash Voucher No. 33.
30 Paid $18.95 for typewriter repairs. Petty Cash Voucher No. 34.
30 The cash in the petty cash drawer was counted and was found to be $30.50.
30 Rendered a report of petty cash expenditures for April and received the amount needed to replenish the fund.

Required: **(1)** Record the foregoing transactions in the petty cash payments record. **(2)** As the last item in the petty cash payments record, enter the cash overage on April 30 by placing the amount of the overage in the Total column and drawing a circle around it. Also enter the account title Cash Short and Over in the Account column and the dollar amount of the overage in the amount column with a circle around the figures. The circle around the amount of the overage in the Total column means that it is a debit to Cash. The overage should be subtracted from the other figures in the column. The circle around the figures in the amount column means that the overage is a credit to Cash Short and Over. **(3)** Prove the petty cash payments record by footing the amount columns and proving the totals. Enter the totals and rule the amount columns with single and double lines. **(4)** Prepare a statement of the petty cash payments for April including the overage, using the ruled paper provided. **(5)** Prepare a compound journal entry for the transactions in the petty cash payments record, using the journal paper. **(6)** Assuming that the balance in the fund was found to be $27.45, prepare a statement of the petty cash payments for April including the shortage, using the ruled paper. **(7)** Prepare a compound journal entry for the transactions in the petty cash payments record, using the journal paper.

EXPANDING YOUR BUSINESS VOCABULARY

What is the meaning of each of the following terms?

ABA numbers **(p. 70)**
automated teller machines **(p. 73)**
auxiliary records **(p. 62)**
bank **(p. 67)**

4
PAYROLL ACCOUNTING

CHAPTER OBJECTIVES

Careful study of this chapter should enable you to:

- Explain and perform the three major functions of payroll accounting: **(1)** determination of employee earnings and deductions, **(2)** determination of employer payroll taxes, and **(3)** proper data entry of the expenses, liabilities, and cash payments in connection with (1) and (2).
- Explain those government laws and regulations that primarily affect payroll accounting.
- Describe and prepare selected forms and records that are required or desirable in payroll accounting.
- Explain selected record-keeping methods and procedures used in the payroll area in connection with a computer-based accounting information system.

Employers need to maintain detailed and accurate payroll accounting records for both financial and legal reasons. The financial reason is simply that payroll expenditures represent a major part of the total expenditures of most companies. Payroll accounting records provide data useful in the analysis, classification, and control of these expenditures. In addition, payroll accounting information is invaluable in contract discussions with labor unions, in the settlement of company-union grievances, and in determining employee pension benefits.

The legal reason for maintaining payroll accounting records is that employers are required by federal, state, and local laws to do so. Companies must accumulate payroll data both for the business as a whole and for each employee. Clearly, accurate payroll accounting is essential to the survival of most businesses.

EMPLOYEE EARNINGS AND DEDUCTIONS

The first step in determining the amount to be paid to an employee is to calculate the employee's total or gross earnings for the pay period. The second step is to determine the amounts of deductions that are required either by law or by specific agreement between the employer and the employee. Depending upon a variety of circumstances, either or both of these steps may be relatively simple or quite complicated. An examination of the factors that must be considered in performing these two steps follows.

Employees and Independent Contractors

Not every individual who performs services for a business is considered to be an employee. A public accountant, lawyer, or management consultant who sells services to a business does not necessarily become its employee. Neither does a plumber nor an electrician who is hired to make specific repairs or installations on business property. These people are told what to do, but not how to do it, and the compensation that they receive for their services is called a **fee**. Any person who agrees to perform a service for a fee and is not subject to the control of those for whom the service is performed is called an **independent contractor**

In contrast, an **employee** is one who is under the control and direction of an employer with regard to the performance of services. The difference between an independent contractor and an employee is an important legal distinction. The nature and extent of the responsibilities of the contractor and the client to each other and to third parties are quite different from the mutual obligations of the employer and the employee. Of particular importance for payroll accounting purposes is the fact that the various government laws and regulations regarding employee deductions, employer payroll taxes, records, and reports apply only to employees.

Types of Compensation

Compensation for managerial or administrative services usually is called **salary**. A salary normally is expressed in weekly, biweekly, monthly, or annual terms. Compensation either for skilled or for unskilled labor usually is referred to as **wages**. Wages ordinarily are expressed in terms of hours, weeks, or pieces of accomplishment. The terms salaries and wages often are used interchangeably in practice.

Supplements to basic salaries or wages of employees include bonuses, commissions, cost-of-living adjustments, pension and profit sharing plans, and vacation pay. Compensation also may take the form of goods, lodging, meals, or other property, and as such is measured by the fair market value of the property or service given in payment for the employee's efforts. This chapter demonstrates proper accounting for basic salaries and wages of employees paid in cash.

Determination of Total Earnings

An employee's earnings commonly are based on the time worked during the payroll period. Sometimes earnings are based on units of output or of sales during the period. Compensation based on time requires a record of the time worked by each employee. If there are only a few employees, a record of times worked may be kept in a memorandum book. Where there are many employees, time clocks commonly are used to record time spent on the job each day. With time clocks, a time card is provided for each employee and the clock is used to record arrival and departure times on the card. Alternatively, plastic cards or badges encoded with basic employee data are now being used in computer-based timekeeping systems. Whatever method is used, the total time worked during the payroll period must be computed.

Employees often are entitled to compensation at more than their regular rate of pay for work during certain hours or on certain days. If the employer is engaged in Interstate Commerce, the Federal Fair Labor Standards Acts (commonly known as the Wages and Hours Law) provides that all employees covered by the Act must be paid one and one-half times the regular rate for all hours worked over 40 per week. Labor-management agreements often require extra pay for certain hours or days. In such cases, hours worked in excess of eight per day or work on Sundays and specified holidays may be paid for at higher rates.

To illustrate, assume that the company which employs Donald Kawasaki pays time and a half for all hours worked in excess of 40 per week and double time for work on Sunday. Kawasaki's regular rate is $12 per hour; and during the week ended April 11, Kawasaki worked nine hours each day Monday through Friday, six hours on Saturday and four on Sunday. Kawasaki's total earnings or gross pay for the week ended April 11, is computed as follows:

40 hours @ $12	$480
11 hours @ $18	198*
4 hours (on Sunday) @ $24	96
Total earnings for the week	$774

*Kawasaki worked 9 hours each day Monday through Friday and 6 hours on Saturday—a total of 51 hours. Forty hours would be paid for at the regular rate and 11 hours at time and a half.

An employee who is paid a regular biweekly, monthly or annual salary may also be entitled to premium pay for any overtime. If this is the case, it is necessary to compute the regular hourly rate of pay before computing the overtime rate. To illustrate, assume that Jean Meyer receives a regular salary of $2,000 a month and that Meyer is entitled to overtime pay at the rate of one and one-half times the regular hourly rate for any time worked in excess of 40 hours per week. Meyer's overtime pay is computed as follows:

$2,000 × 12 months	$24,000 annual pay
$24,000 ÷ 52 weeks	$461.54 pay per week
$461.54 ÷ 40 hours	$11.54 pay per regular hour
$11.54 × 1½	$17.31 overtime pay per hour

Deductions from Total Earnings

An employee's take-home or **net pay** typically is significantly less than the total earnings or **gross pay**. The difference between an employee's gross and net pay generally can be explained by three factors: (1) employee FICA (Federal Insurance Contributions Act) tax withheld by the employer, (2) employee federal income taxes (and state and city income taxes where applicable) withheld by the employer, and (3) other deductions based on special agreements between the employer and the employee.

Employees' FICA Tax Withheld. The Federal Insurance Contributions Act (FICA) requires most employers to withhold certain amounts from employees' earnings for contributions to the old-age, survivors, and disability insurance (OASDI) and health insurance for the aged (HIP) programs. These withheld amounts are commonly referred to as **FICA taxes**.

Each employee is required to have a **social security number** for payroll accounting purposes. An illustration of a completed form SS-5, the official form used in applying for an account number is shown on page 93.

The earnings base against which the FICA tax is applied and the tax rate have been changed several times since the law was first enacted and are subject to change by Congress at any time in the future. These base and rate changes, however, do not affect the accounting principles and procedures for payroll. Therefore, for the sake of convenience in this chapter, the rate is assumed to be 6.0% of taxable wages paid during the calendar year for OASDI plus 1.5% for HIP for a total FICA rate of 7.5%. It is also assumed that the first $47,000 of earnings paid to each employee in any calendar year is taxable. Any amount of compensation paid in excess of $47,000 is assumed to be exempt from the tax.

State and Local Taxes. In addition to the foregoing federal requirements, a few states require employers to withhold a percentage of the employees' wages for unemployment compensation benefits or for disability benefits. In some states and cities, employers are also required to withhold a percentage of the employees' wages for other types of payroll taxes.

Employees' Income Tax Withheld. Under federal law, employers are required to withhold certain amounts from the total earnings of each employee to be applied toward the payment of the employee's federal income tax. The

FORM SS-5 — APPLICATION FOR A SOCIAL SECURITY NUMBER CARD (Original, Replacement or Correction)

MICROFILM REF. NO. (SSA USE ONLY)

Unless the requested information is provided, we may not be able to issue a Social Security Number (20 CFR 422-103(b))

INSTRUCTIONS TO APPLICANT ▶ Before completing this form, please read the instructions on the opposite page. You can type or print, using pen with dark blue or black ink. Do not use pencil.

		First	Middle	Last
NAA	NAME TO BE SHOWN ON CARD	John	Herman	Metzger
NAB 1	FULL NAME AT BIRTH (IF OTHER THAN ABOVE)			
ONA	OTHER NAME(S) USED			

STT 2 MAILING ADDRESS 218 Audubon Place (Street/Apt. No., P.O. Box, Rural Route No.)

CTY CITY Fort Mitchell Kentucky | STE STATE Kentucky | ZIP ZIP CODE 41017

CSP 3 CITIZENSHIP (Check one only)
- [X] a. U.S. citizen
- [ ] b. Legal alien allowed to work
- [ ] c. Legal alien not allowed to work
- [ ] d. Other (See instructions on Page 2)

SEX 4 SEX
- [X] MALE
- [ ] FEMALE

ETB 5 RACE/ETHNIC DESCRIPTION (Check one only) (Voluntary)
- [ ] a. Asian, Asian-American or Pacific Islander (Includes persons of Chinese, Filipino, Japanese, Korean, Samoan, etc., ancestry or descent)
- [ ] b. Hispanic (Includes persons of Chicano, Cuban, Mexican or Mexican-American, Puerto Rican, South or Central American, or other Spanish ancestry or descent)
- [ ] c. Negro or Black (not Hispanic)
- [ ] d. Northern American Indian or Alaskan Native
- [ ] e. White (not Hispanic)

DOB 6 DATE OF BIRTH ▶ MONTH 6 DAY 29 YEAR 69 | AGE 7 PRESENT AGE 18 | PLB 8 PLACE OF BIRTH ▶ CITY Claiborne | STATE OR FOREIGN COUNTRY Louisiana | FCI [ ]

		First	Middle	Last
MNA 9	MOTHER'S NAME AT HER BIRTH	Jeanne	Louise	Rouan (Her maiden name)
FNA	FATHER'S NAME	George	Leonard	Metzger

PNO 10 a. Has a Social Security number card ever been requested for the person listed in item 1? [ ] YES(2) [X] NO(1) [ ] Don't know(1) If yes, when: → MONTH YEAR

b. Was a card received for the person listed in item 1? [ ] YES(3) [X] NO(1) [ ] Don't know(1) **If you checked yes to a or b, complete items c through e; otherwise go to item 11.**

SSN c. Enter Social Security number assigned to the person listed in item 1. ☐☐☐–☐☐–☐☐☐☐

NLC d. Enter the name shown on the most recent Social Security card issued for the person listed in item 1.

PDB e. Date of birth correction (See Instruction 10 on page 2) ▶ MONTH DAY YEAR

DON 11 TODAY'S DATE ▶ MONTH 7 DAY 13 YEAR 87 | 12 Telephone number where we can reach you during the day. Please include the area code. ▶ HOME 482-5519 OTHER

ASD **WARNING: Deliberately furnishing (or causing to be furnished) false information on this application is a crime punishable by fine or imprisonment, or both.**

13 YOUR SIGNATURE *John H. Metzger* | 14 YOUR RELATIONSHIP TO PERSON IN ITEM 1 [X] Self [ ] Other (Specify)

Application for Social Security Number (Form SS-5)

amount to be withheld each pay period is based on (1) the total earnings of the employee, (2) the marital status of the employee, (3) the number of withholding allowances claimed by the employee, and (4) the length of the employee's pay period.

Each employee is required to furnish the employer with an Employee's Withholding Allowance Certificate, Form W-4, showing marital status and the number of allowances claimed. The marital status of the taxpayer and the number of allowances claimed determine the dollar amount of earnings subject to withholding tax. According to 1984 federal income tax laws, \$2,300 for single taxpayers and \$3,400 for married taxpayers filing jointly is excluded from withholding tax. These amounts on which no withholding tax is levied are known as zero bracket amounts, that is, they represent income brackets or levels at which the withholding tax is zero. A withholding allowance is an allowance of $1,000 on which no federal income tax is withheld from the employee's pay. Each federal income taxpayer is permitted one personal withholding allowance, one for a spouse, and one for each dependent who qualifies. Thus, the taxpayer is entitled to one or more exemptions of $1,000 each from federal income tax based on family status and dependency relationships. The law specifies the relationship that must exist, the extent of support required, and the amount of support that must be provided in order for a person to qualify as a dependent.

In addition to these withholding allowances for personal, spouse, and dependent exemptions, a taxpayer can qualify for two other types of withholding allowances. First, one special withholding allowance can be claimed by each single taxpayer who has only one job, or each married taxpayer whose spouse is not employed. Second, additional withholding allowances are permitted to taxpayers who anticipate child-care tax credits or large itemized deductions. In order to claim one or more additional withholding allowances, an employee's expected total earnings, credits, and itemized deductions for the coming year have to be estimated. Based on these expected total earnings and itemized deductions, the schedule illustrated below is used to determine the number of additional withholding allowances to which the employee is entitled. An allowance certificate completed by John Herman Metzger is shown below.

Form **W-4** Department of the Treasury Internal Revenue Service | **Employee's Withholding Allowance Certificate** ▶ **For Privacy Act and Paperwork Reduction Act Notice, see instructions.** | OMB No. 1545-0010

1 Type or print your full name: John Herman Metzger | 2 Your social security number: 281-92-4638

Home address (number and street or rural route): 218 Audubon Place

City or town, state, and ZIP code: Fort Mitchell, Kentucky 41017

3 Marital Status: ☐ Single ☒ Married ☐ Married, but withhold at higher Single rate
Note: *If married, but legally separated, or spouse is a nonresident alien, check the Single box.*

4 Total number of allowances you are claiming (from the Worksheet on page 3) 6

5 Additional amount, if any, you want deducted from each pay (see Step 4 on page 2) . . . . . $ -0-

6 I claim exemption from withholding because (see Step 2 above and check boxes below that apply):

a ☐ Last year I did not owe any Federal income tax and had a right to a full refund of **ALL** income tax withheld, **AND**

b ☐ This year I do not expect to owe any Federal income tax and expect to have a right to a full refund of **ALL** income tax withheld. If both a and b apply, enter the year effective and "EXEMPT" here . . . . ▶ Year 19

c If you entered "EXEMPT" on line 6b, are you a full-time student? . . . . . ☐ Yes ☐ No

Under penalties of perjury, I certify that I am entitled to the number of withholding allowances claimed on this certificate or, if claiming exemption from withholding, that I am entitled to claim the exempt status

Employee's signature ▶ John H. Metzger **Date** ▶ January 2, 19 87

7 Employer's name and address **(Employer: Complete 7, 8, and 9 only if sending to IRS)** | 8 Office code | 9 Employer identification number

Withholding Allowance Certificate (Form W-4)

To illustrate the use of the schedule, John Metzger is married, has a spouse who is not employed, and has one dependent child. Metzger expects earnings of $39,000 and itemized deductions of $5,500 in the coming year. As computed in the schedule, Metzger is therefore entitled to 1 additional withholding allowance. On line 1 of the W-4 form, Metzger claims 6 allowances, calculated as follows:

Personal allowances:		
Self	1	
Wife	1	2
Special withholding allowance		1
Allowance for dependent		1
Allowance for estimated deductions		1
Allowance for payments to a Keogh (H.R. 10) retirement plan		1
Total withholding allowances		6

Metzger's Withholding Allowance Schedule

Most employers use the **wage-bracket method** of determining the amount of tax to be withheld from an employee's pay by tracing the employee's gross pay for a specific time period into the appropriate wage-bracket table provided by the Internal Revenue Service. These tables cover monthly, semimonthly, biweekly, weekly, and daily or miscellaneous periods, and there are separate tables for single and married taxpayers. Copies may be obtained from any local Internal Revenue Service office. A portion of a weekly income tax wage-bracket withholding table for married persons is illustrated on page 96. To use this table, assume that John Metzger (who claims 6 allowances) had gross earnings of $750 for the week ending December 18, 1987. On the line showing the tax on wages of "at least $750, but less than $760," in the column headed "6 withholding allowances," $112.00 is given as the amount to be withheld.

Whether the wage-bracket method or some other method is used in computing the amount of tax to be withheld, the sum of the taxes withheld from an employee's wages only approximates the tax on actual income derived solely from wages. An employee may be liable for a tax larger than the amount withheld. This additional tax will be remitted with the employee's federal income tax return. On the other hand, the amount of the taxes withheld by the employer may be greater than the employee's actual tax liability. In such an event, the employee will be entitled to a refund of the excess taxes withheld, or the excess can be applied to the employee's tax liability for the following year.

Several states and cities have adopted state and city income tax procedures. Some of these states and cities supply employers with withholding allowance certificate forms and income tax withholding tables that are similar in concept and appearance to those used by the federal Internal Revenue Service. Other states determine the amount to be withheld merely by applying a fixed percentage to the federal withholding amount.

WEEKLY Payroll Period—Employee MARRIED

And the wages are-		And the number of withholding allowances claimed is—										
At least	But less than	0	1	2	3	4	5	6	7	8	9	10 or more
		The amount of income tax to be withheld shall be—										
$490	$500	$75	$70	$66	$61	$57	$52	$48	$45	$41	$38	$34
500	510	78	73	68	63	59	55	50	47	43	39	36
510	520	80	75	70	66	61	57	52	48	45	41	38
520	530	83	78	73	68	63	59	55	50	47	43	39
530	540	85	80	75	70	66	61	57	52	48	45	41
540	550	88	83	78	73	68	63	59	55	50	47	43
550	560	90	85	80	75	70	66	61	57	52	48	45
560	570	93	88	83	78	73	68	63	59	55	50	47
570	580	95	90	85	80	75	70	66	61	57	52	48
580	590	98	93	88	83	78	73	68	63	59	55	50
590	600	101	95	90	85	80	75	70	66	61	57	52
600	610	103	98	93	88	83	78	73	68	63	59	55
610	620	106	101	95	90	85	80	75	70	66	61	57
620	630	109	103	98	93	88	83	78	73	68	63	59
630	640	112	106	101	95	90	85	80	75	70	66	61
640	650	115	109	103	98	93	88	83	78	73	68	63
650	660	117	112	106	101	95	90	85	80	75	70	66
660	670	120	115	109	103	98	93	88	83	78	73	68
670	680	123	117	112	106	101	95	90	85	80	75	70
680	690	126	120	115	109	103	98	93	88	83	78	73
690	700	129	123	117	112	106	101	95	90	85	80	75
700	710	132	126	120	115	109	103	98	93	88	83	78
710	720	136	129	123	117	112	106	101	95	90	85	80
720	730	139	132	126	120	115	109	103	98	93	88	83
730	740	142	136	129	123	117	112	106	101	95	90	85
740	750	146	139	132	126	120	115	109	103	98	93	88
750	760	149	142	136	129	123	117	112	106	101	95	90
760	770	152	146	139	132	126	120	115	109	103	98	93
770	780	155	149	142	136	129	123	117	112	106	101	95
780	790	159	152	146	139	132	126	120	115	109	103	98
790	800	162	155	149	142	136	129	123	117	112	106	101
800	810	165	159	152	146	139	132	126	120	115	109	103
810	820	169	162	155	149	142	136	129	123	117	112	106
820	830	172	165	159	152	146	139	132	126	120	115	109
830	840	175	169	162	155	149	142	136	129	123	117	112

*As of the date of printing, the above Weekly Federal Income Tax Withholding Table is the most current available.

Portion of Weekly Federal Income Tax Wage-Bracket Withholding Table for Married Persons

Other Deductions. In addition to the compulsory deductions from employee earnings for FICA and income taxes, there are many other possible deductions that generally are voluntary and depend on specific agreements between the employee and employer. Some examples of these deductions are for:

1. United States savings bond purchases.
2. Life, accident or health insurance premiums.
3. Credit union deposits.
4. Pension plan payments.
5. Charitable contributions.

Payroll Records

The needs of management and the requirements of various federal and state laws make it necessary for employers to keep records that will provide the following information for each employee:

1. Name, address, and social security number.
2. The gross amount of earnings, the date of payment, and the period of employment covered by each payroll.
3. The gross amount of earnings accumulated since the first of the year.
4. The amount of any taxes or other items withheld.

Regardless of the number of employees or type of business, three types of payroll records usually need to be prepared by the employer. They are: (1) the **payroll register** or payroll journal; (2) the payroll check with earnings statement attached; and (3) the **earnings record** of the individual employee (on a weekly, monthly, quarterly, or annual basis). While these records can be prepared either by manual or by automated methods, payroll is a major application of computer-based accounting systems.

Record-Keeping Methods. A purely **manual system** is one in which all records, journals and ledgers are prepared by hand. Such systems are rare today. Even very small businesses use cash registers, electronic calculators and other machines in performing accounting tasks. In this sense, virtually all accounting information systems today are at least partially automated, i.e., they use some kind of machines in the accounting process.

In a manual system, all employee data on the payroll records, such as name, address, social security number, pay rate, hours worked, current earnings, and taxes withheld, are determined, calculated, and entered by hand. In such a system, it often is necessary to enter the same data a number of times. For example, identical employee earnings amounts would be entered on the payroll register, paycheck, and earnings record.

Automated systems can be broken down into two types: mechanical and electronic. A **mechanical system** is one in which various types of accounting machines are used for posting accounts, billing customers, entering payroll, and printing paychecks. An **electronic system** is one in which data are processed using electronic computers. On the following pages, a payroll register, payroll check, and individual employee's earnings record that are prepared using a microcomputer are illustrated.

In a mechanical system, much of the payroll information is entered simultaneously on the payroll register, paycheck, and earnings record. This is an example of the **write-it-once principle**. It is often desirable to enter data on a number of documents and records at the same time, because each time the same information is recopied there is another chance for an error. Many accounting machines are available that perform these functions. Most of these machines also are capable of performing the arithmetic operations necessary in preparing the payroll. Each pay period, accounting personnel still need to provide input to the machines indicating information such as employee name, social security number, gross earnings, taxes withheld, and other deductions.

In a system using electronic computers, not only are the payroll register, paycheck, and earnings record generated simultaneously, but a number of inputs need not be repeated each pay period. Computers have the ability to store internally large amounts of information, such as employee names, social security numbers, withholding allowances, pay rates, FICA and income tax withholding rates, and earnings to date. They also can perform the arithmetic and logic functions required in payroll accounting. In a given pay period, based on inputs of employee social security numbers and hours worked, the computer can supply the related employee names and other data and calculate gross earnings, all appropriate deductions, and net pay. The computer can then print the paychecks and the payroll register, and update the employee's earnings records.

Both mechanical and electronic processing systems also are available through companies external to an employer's business. These companies, known as **service bureaus** (or automation companies), perform payroll accounting, among other accounting functions, for businesses on a contract basis. A common approach is for the employer to provide a service bureau with whatever inputs the employer would need if the payroll were being prepared on the employer's own mechanical or electronic payroll system. The service bureau then processes these inputs and provides the employer with the completed payroll register, paychecks, and updated employee earnings records. The use of service bureaus is diminishing as a result of rapid growth in the use of personal computer systems.

Computers are also used with payroll accounting systems on a **time sharing** basis. This refers to the use of a single computer by a number of small- to medium-sized businesses who share time on the computer. Thus it is possible for businesses that cannot afford their own computer to have the use of one by sharing it with other companies. Companies using time sharing have record keeping and processing situations similar to those for companies having their own computers. The main difference is that communication between time sharing users and the computer is normally by means of special telephone lines, remote computer terminals, and other electronic devices at each business location. Time sharing also is diminishing in use as personal computer systems increase in use, largely because the latter are believed to be less costly.

An important point to note in connection with this discussion of payroll record-keeping methods is that the same inputs and outputs are required in all of the different systems. Even given an electronic computer with substantial data stored in its memory, the inputs required for payroll processing have to be provided to the system at some point in time. The outputs in the form of a payroll register, paychecks, and employee earnings records are basically the same under all of the different systems. This means that the illustrations of payroll records under any of these systems are quite similar. For the sake of convenience and in order to avoid duplication, the illustrations in this chapter are based on a computer system only. The forms and procedures illustrated are equally applicable to a manual or a mechanical system.

Payroll Register. A **payroll register** is a multi-column form used to assemble, compute, and summarize the data required at the end of each payroll period. The payroll register used by Central States Diversified, Inc. for the payroll period ended December 4, 19--, is illustrated on pages 100 and 101. The columnar headings are basically self-explanatory. Detailed information on earnings, taxable earnings, deductions, and net pay is summarized for each employee.

Central States Diversified, Inc. has eight employees. George Schuester and James Toerner each claim only one allowance because each has two jobs. Carolyn Hughes claims two allowances because she has only one job. Jane Irwin claims four allowances because she provides the sole support for her two children. Thomas Hartley is single and gets the special withholding allowance and an additional allowance because he expects to have large itemized deductions. He claims three allowances. Albert Napier claims six withholding allowances because his wife does not work and he has three children. Lawrence Kathman is blind. He is married and his wife does not work. He claims four withholding allowances. Michael Armstrong is married and his wife works but does not claim her allowance on a separate W-4 form. Armstrong is making payments to a Keogh plan. He claims three allowances.

In this example, assume the first $47,000 of earnings received in any calendar year is subject to FICA tax. As indicated in the taxable earnings columns, Napier's earnings for the week ending December 4 are exempt from the FICA tax because earnings totaling $47,000 have already been taxed. In addition to their use in determining the employees' FICA tax, the columns for taxable earnings are needed for determining the employer's payroll taxes. These taxes are discussed on pages 106-107.

Regular deductions are made from the earnings of employees for FICA tax, federal income tax, city earnings tax, pension plan, and health insurance. In addition, voluntary deductions are made for the company credit union and for the United Way contribution according to agreement with individual employees. Hughes has authorized Central States Diversified to withhold $3.00 the first week of each month for her United Way contribution and Toerner has authorized the withholding of $2 the first week of each month. After the data for each employee have been entered, the amount columns in the payroll register should be footed and the footings verified as shown on pages 100–101. In a computer-based accounting system the software package for the payroll application will perform this proof without the need for a separate verification.

PAYROLL

NAME	EMPL. NO.	NO. OF ALLOW.	MARITAL STATUS	EARNINGS REGULAR	EARNINGS OVERTIME	EARNINGS TOTAL	CUMULATIVE TOTAL	TAXABLE EARNINGS UNEMPLOYMENT COMP.	TAXABLE EARNINGS FICA
ARMSTRONG, MICHAEL	1	3	M	360.00	54.00	414.00	17,848.00		414.00
HARTLEY, THOMAS	2	3	S	400.00		400.00	19,600.00		400.00
HUGHES, CAROLYN	3	2	S	620.00	46.50	666.50	31,310.00		666.50
IRWIN, JANE	4	4	S	540.00		540.00	26,460.00		540.00
KATHMAN, LAWRENCE	5	4	M	560.00		560.00	27,440.00		560.00
NAPIER, ALBERT	6	6	M	1,000.00		1,000.00	48,000.00		
SCHUSTER, GEORGE	7	1	M	400.00		400.00	19,600.00		400.00
TOERNER, JAMES	8	1	M	520.00	39.00	559.00	6,435.00	559.00	559.00
				4,400.00	139.50	4,539.50	196,693.00	559.00	3,539.50

Payroll Register—Computer Prepared (Left Page)

Regular earnings		$4,400.00
Overtime earnings		139.50
Gross earnings		$4,539.50
Deductions:		
FICA tax	$265.47	
Federal income tax	725.00	
City earnings tax	45.40	
Pension plan	226.98	
Health insurance premiums	78.00	
Credit union	49.00	
United Way	5.00	1,394.85
Net amount of payroll		$3,144.65

An error in the payroll register could cause the payment of an incorrect amount to an employee or remittance of an incorrect amount to the companies or government agencies for whom funds are deducted from the employees' gross pay.

Payroll Check. Employees may be paid in cash or by check. In some cases today, the employee does not even handle the paycheck. Rather, salary is paid via a **direct deposit** of the check or electronic funds transfer by the employer to the employee's bank. The employee receives the deduction stub from the check and a printed deposit receipt. Payment by check or direct deposit is strongly preferred because it provides better internal accounting control. Many businesses prepare a single check for the net amount of the total payroll and deposit it in a special payroll bank account. Individual paychecks are then drawn on the account for the amount due to each employee. Data needed to prepare an individual paycheck for each employee are contained in the payroll register. (In a computer-based system, the paychecks normally are prepared at the same time as the payroll register.) The employer furnishes a

REGISTER

			DEDUCTIONS							
FICA TAX	FEDERAL INCOME TAX	CITY TAX	PENSION PLAN	HEALTH INS.	CREDIT UNION	UNITED WAY	TOTAL	DATE	NET PAY	CHECK NUMBER
31.05	45.00	4.14	20.70	10.00			110.89	DEC 04, 19--	303.11	2511
30.00	55.00	4.00	20.00	8.00	12.00		129.00	DEC 04, 19--	271.00	2512
49.99	138.00	6.67	33.33	8.00	12.00	3.00	250.99	DEC 04, 19--	415.51	2513
40.50	87.00	5.40	27.00	12.00	5.00		176.90	DEC 04, 19--	363.10	2514
42.00	73.00	5.60	28.00	12.00			160.60	DEC 04, 19--	399.40	2515
	192.00	10.00	50.00	12.00	10.00		274.00	DEC 04, 19--	726.00	2516
30.00	50.00	4.00	20.00	8.00	10.00		122.00	DEC 04, 19--	278.00	2517
41.93	85.00	5.59	27.95	8.00		2.00	170.47	DEC 04, 19--	388.53	2518
265.47	725.00	45.40	226.98	78.00	49.00	5.00	1,394.85		3,144.65	

Payroll Register — Computer Prepared (Right Page)

statement of payroll deductions to each employee along with each wage payment. Paychecks with detachable stubs, like the one for Carolyn Hughes illustrated on page 104, are widely used for this purpose. Before such a check is deposited or cashed, the stub should be detached and retained by the employee as a permanent record of earnings and payroll deductions.

Employee's Earnings Record. A separate record of each employee's earnings, called an **employee's earnings record**, is kept in order to provide the information needed in preparing the various federal, state, and local reports required of employers. A computer-prepared employee's earnings record used by Central States Diversified, Inc., for Carolyn Hughes during the last two quarters of the current calendar year is illustrated on pages 102-103.

This record usually is kept on separate sheets or cards, which may be filed alphabetically or by employee number for ready reference. The information printed on this form is obtained from the payroll register in a computer-based system, in which the employee's earnings record can be updated simultaneously with the preparation of the payroll register. This is done with multiple-copy forms and special paper, which can be machine-separated after printing.

Hughes' earnings for the last half of the year up to December 4 are shown on this form. The entry for the pay period ended December 4 is the same as that in the payroll register illustrated above.

The payroll register is a summary of the earnings of all employees for each pay period, while the earnings record is a summary of the annual earnings of each employee. The earnings record illustrated on pages 102-103 is designed so that quarterly and yearly totals can be accumulated. Thus the form provides a complete record of the earnings of an employee for the year—

EMPLOYEE'S

NAME	Carolyn Anne Hughes	SEX	Female
ADDRESS	6926 Vista Court	MARITAL STATUS	Single
CITY	St. Louis, MO 64075-4326	NO. OF ALLOWANCES	2

EARNINGS				TAXABLE EARNINGS	
REGULAR	OVERTIME	TOTAL	CUMULATIVE TOTAL	UNEMPLOY-MENT COMP.	FICA
620.00		620.00	17,670.00		620.00
620.00		620.00	18,290.00		620.00
620.00	46.50	666.50	18,956.50		666.50
620.00		620.00	19,576.50		620.00
620.00	69.75	689.75	20,266.25		689.75
620.00		620.00	20,886.25		620.00
620.00		620.00	21,506.25		620.00
620.00	46.50	666.50	22,172.75		666.50
620.00	93.00	713.00	22,885.75		713.00
620.00		620.00	23,505.75		620.00
620.00		620.00	24,125.75		620.00
620.00	23.25	643.25	24,769.00		643.25
620.00	69.75	689.75	25,458.75		689.75
THIRD QUARTER					
8,060.00	348.75	8,408.75			8,408.75
620.00		620.00	26,078.75		620.00
620.00		620.00	26,698.75		620.00
620.00	38.75	658.75	27,357.50		658.75
620.00		620.00	27,977.50		620.00
620.00	69.75	689.75	28,667.25		689.75
620.00	116.25	736.25	29,403.50		736.25
620.00		620.00	30,023.50		620.00
620.00		620.00	30,643.50		620.00
620.00	46.50	666.50	31,310.00		666.50
FOURTH QUARTER					
YEARLY TOTAL					

Employee's Earnings Record — Computer Prepared (Left Page)

information that is needed in preparing an annual report to the employee and the Internal Revenue Service on a form called a Wage and Tax Statement. This report is explained in the following section. The earnings record also provides information on an employee's quarterly earnings that is needed for filing quarterly reports to government agencies on various forms. These reports will be discussed later in this chapter.

Wage and Tax Statement

Not later than January 31 of each year, the law requires employers to furnish each employee from whom income taxes have been withheld an annual report called a Wage and Tax Statement, Form W-2, showing the total

EARNINGS RECORD

DEPARTMENT	Accounting	SOCIAL SECURITY NUMBER	314-07-2906
OCCUPATION	Accountant	DATE OF BIRTH	March 2, 1952
PAY RATE	$620 Weekly	DATE EMPLOYED	April 3, 1977
EMPLOYEE NO.	3	DATE EMPLOYMENT TERMINATED	

DEDUCTIONS										
FICA TAX	FEDERAL INCOME TAX	CITY TAX	PENSION PLAN	HEALTH INS.	CREDIT UNION	UNITED WAY	TOTAL	DATE	NET PAY	CK. NO.
46.50	124.00	6.20	31.00	8.00	12.00	3.00	230.70	JUL 10,'87	389.30	2345
46.50	124.00	6.20	31.00	8.00	12.00		227.70	JUL 17,'87	392.30	2353
49.99	138.00	6.67	33.33	8.00	12.00		247.99	JUL 24,'87	418.51	2361
46.50	124.00	6.20	31.00	8.00	12.00		227.70	JUL 31,'87	392.30	2369
51.73	144.00	6.90	34.49	8.00	12.00	3.00	260.12	AUG 07,'87	429.63	2377
46.50	124.00	6.20	31.00	8.00	12.00		227.70	AUG 14,'87	392.30	2385
46.50	124.00	6.20	31.00	8.00	12.00		227.70	AUG 21,'87	392.30	2393
49.99	138.00	6.67	33.33	8.00	12.00		247.99	AUG 28,'87	418.51	2401
53.48	155.00	7.13	35.65	8.00	12.00	3.00	274.26	SEP 04,'87	438.74	2409
46.50	124.00	6.20	31.00	8.00	12.00		227.70	SEP 11,'87	392.30	2417
46.50	124.00	6.20	31.00	8.00	12.00		227.70	SEP 18,'87	392.30	2425
48.24	131.00	6.43	32.16	8.00	12.00		237.83	SEP 25,'87	405.42	2433
51.73	144.00	6.90	34.49	8.00	12.00	3.00	260.12	OCT 02,'87	429.63	2441
	THIRD QUARTER									
630.66	1,718.00	84.10	420.45	104.00	156.00	12.00	3,125.21		5,283.54	
46.50	124.00	6.20	31.00	8.00	12.00		227.70	OCT 09,'87	392.30	2449
46.50	124.00	6.20	31.00	8.00	12.00		227.70	OCT 16,'87	392.30	2457
49.41	134.00	6.59	32.94	8.00	12.00		242.94	OCT 23,'87	415.81	2465
46.50	124.00	6.20	31.00	8.00	12.00		227.70	OCT 30,'87	392.30	2473
51.73	144.00	6.90	34.49	8.00	12.00	3.00	260.12	NOV 06,'87	429.63	2481
55.22	162.00	7.36	36.81	8.00	12.00		281.39	NOV 13,'87	454.86	2489
46.50	124.00	6.20	31.00	8.00	12.00		227.70	NOV 20,'87	392.30	2497
46.50	124.00	6.20	31.00	8.00	12.00		227.70	NOV 27,'87	392.30	2505
49.99	138.00	6.67	33.33	8.00	12.00	3.00	250.99	DEC 04,'87	415.51	2513
	FOURTH QUARTER									

Employee's Earnings Record—Computer Prepared (Right Page)

amount of wages paid and the amount of such tax withheld during the preceding calendar year. A completed form W-2 is illustrated on page 105.

If the employee's wages are subject to FICA tax as well as federal, state, or local income tax, the employer must report total wages paid and the amounts deducted both for income tax and for FICA tax. Information for this purpose is contained in the employee's earnings record.

The **employer's identification number** appearing on the Wage and Tax Statement is an identification number assigned to the employer by the Internal Revenue Service. An employer who employs one or more persons must file for an identification number. This number must be shown on all reports required of Central States Diversified, Inc., under the Federal Insurance Contributions Act.

OFFICE PAYROLL

NUMBER
2513

CSD **CENTRAL STATES DIVERSIFIED, INC.**
5221 NATURAL BRIDGE ST. LOUIS, MO. 63115-8230
PLANTS: ST. LOUIS - PALATKA, FLA.

4-97 / 810

PAY TO THE ORDER OF	DATE	NAME	DOLLARS		CENTS
	Dec 4,'87	Carolyn Hughes	$ 415	AND	51

CENTRAL STATES DIVERSIFIED, INC.

MOUND CITY TRUST CO.
ST. LOUIS, MO.

BY Albert Napier

⑆0810009741⑆ 49 053 2⑈

CSD **CENTRAL STATES DIVERSIFIED, INC.**
ST. LOUIS, MO.

STATEMENT OF EARNINGS

EARNINGS				TAXABLE EARNINGS		DEDUCTIONS											
REGULAR	OVERTIME	TOTAL	CUMULATIVE TOTAL	UNEMPLOY-MENT COMP.	FICA	FICA TAX	FEDERAL INC. TAX	CITY TAX	PENSION PLAN	HEALTH INS.	CREDIT UNION	UNITED WAY	TOTAL	DATE	NET PAY	CK. NO.
620.00	46.50	666.50	31,310.00		666.50	49.99	138.00	6.67	33.33	8.00	12.00	3.00	250.99	Dec. 4, '87	415.51	2513
29,760.00	1,550.00	31,310.00	31,310.00		31,310.00	2,348.25	6,226.00	311.30	1,556.50	384.00	576.00	144.00	11,546.05	Yr-to-Date	19,763.95	

NON-NEGOTIABLE

Paycheck and Deduction Stub — Computer Prepared

[Form W-2]

1 Control number	22222
For Paperwork Reduction Act Notice, see back of Copy D. OMB No. 1545-0008	For Official Use Only ►
2 Employer's name, address, and ZIP code	Central States Diversified 5221 Natural Bridge St. Louis, MO 63115-8230
3 Employer's identification number	43 0211630
4 Employer's state I.D. number	21 686001
5 Statutory employee ☐ Deceased ☐ Legal rep. ☐ 942 emp. ☐ Subtotal ☐ Void ☐	
6 Allocated tips	
7 Advance EIC payment	
8 Employee's social security number	314 07 2906
9 Federal income tax withheld	$6,872.00
10 Wages, tips, other compensation	$34,014.00
11 Social security tax withheld	$2,551.05
12 Employee's name (first, middle, last)	Carolyn Ann Hughes
13 Social security wages	$34,014.00
14 Social security tips	
15 Employee's address and ZIP code	6926 Vista Court St. Louis, MO 64075-4326
16 *	
17 State income tax	
18 State wages, tips, etc.	
19 Name of state	MO
20 Local income tax	$340.14
21 Local wages, tips, etc.	$34,014.00
22 Name of locality	St. Louis

Wage and Tax Statement (Form W-2)

Wage and Tax Statements must be prepared in quadruplicate. Copy A goes to the Social Security Administration. Copies B and C are furnished to the employee; Copy B must be sent in with the employee's federal income tax return, and Copy C is for the employee's files. Copy D is kept by the employer as part of the accounting records. In states or cities which have state or city income tax withholding laws, two more copies are furnished. Copy 1 is sent by the employer to the appropriate state or city tax department, and Copy 2 is sent by the employee with the state or city income tax return.

Accounting for Employee Earnings and Earnings Deductions

In accounting for employee earnings and deductions from earnings, it is desirable to keep separate accounts for (1) earnings and (2) earnings deductions. Various account titles are used in entering wages, such as Payroll Expense, Salaries Expense, and Salaries and Commissions Expense. The accounts needed in entering earnings deductions depend upon what deductions are involved. It helps in understanding the accounting for these deductions if we recognize that in withholding amounts from employees' earnings, the employer basically is serving as an agent for various groups such as the federal government, insurance companies, and credit unions. Amounts that are withheld and deducted from an employee's gross earnings must be paid by the employer to these groups. Therefore, a separate account should be kept for the liability incurred under each type of deduction, such as employee income tax, FICA tax, and insurance premiums. Examples of several of the major accounts involved in payroll accounting and of a typical journal entry for payroll are presented in the following sections.

Payroll Expense. This is an expense account which is debited for the total amount of the gross earnings of all employees for each pay period. Sometimes separate payroll accounts are kept for the employees of different departments. Thus separate accounts may be kept for Office Salaries Expense, Sales Salaries Expense, and Factory Payroll Expense.

Payroll Expense

Debit	
to enter gross earnings of employees for each pay period.	

FICA Tax Payable. This is a liability account which is credited for (1) the FICA tax withheld from employees' earnings and (2) the FICA tax imposed on the employer. FICA taxes imposed on the employer are discussed later in the chapter. The account should be debited for amounts paid to the Internal Revenue Service. When all of the FICA taxes have been paid, the account should be in balance.

FICA Tax Payable

Debit	Credit
to enter payment of FICA tax previously withheld or imposed.	to enter FICA taxes (1) withheld from employees' earnings and (2) imposed on the employer.

Employees Income Tax Payable. This is a liability account which should be credited for the total income tax withheld from employees' earnings. The account is debited for amounts paid to a bank depository for the Internal Revenue Service. When all of the income taxes withheld have been paid, the account will be in balance. A city or state earnings tax payable account is used in a similar manner.

Employees Income Tax Payable

Debit	Credit
to enter payment of income tax previously withheld.	to enter income tax withheld from employees' earnings.

Other Deductions. Pension Plan Deductions Payable is a liability account which is credited with amounts withheld from employees' earnings for any pension plan contributions. The account should be debited for the subsequent payment of these amounts to the pension plan trustee. Accounts for health insurance premiums payable, credit union contributions payable, and United Way contributions payable are similarly used.

Journalizing Payroll Transactions. The information needed to properly enter the payment of employee wages and salaries is contained in the payroll register. The totals at the bottom of the columns of the payroll register on pages 100-101 provide the basis for the following two-column journal entry for wages paid on December 4, 1987:

Dec. 4	Payroll Expense	4,539.50	
	FICA Tax Payable		265.47
	Employees Income Tax Payable		725.00
	City Earnings Tax Payable		45.40
	Pension Plan Deductions Payable		226.98
	Health Insurance Premiums Payable		78.00
	Credit Union Contributions Payable		49.00
	United Way Contributions Payable		5.00
	Cash		3,144.65
	Payroll for week ended December 4.		

These amounts are posted to payroll expense and liability accounts such as those illustrated in the preceding paragraphs.

BUILDING YOUR ACCOUNTING KNOWLEDGE

1. Why is it important for payroll accounting purposes to distinguish between an employee and an independent contractor?
2. Name three factors that generally explain the difference between an employee's gross pay and net pay.
3. Identify the four factors that determine the amount of federal income tax that is withheld from an employee's pay each pay period.
4. What factors determine the number of withholding allowances to which a taxpayer is entitled?
5. Identify the three types of payroll records usually needed by an employer.
6. Describe the information contained in the payroll register.
7. Why is it important to foot and verify the footings of the payroll register after the data for each employee have been entered?
8. Distinguish between the payroll register and the employee earnings record.
9. Explain what an employer does with the amounts withheld from an employee's pay.

APPLYING ACCOUNTING CONCEPTS

Exercise 4-1. Hilda Gutfreund's regular hourly rate is $11. She receives time and a half for any time worked over 40 hours a week, and double time for work on Sunday.

During the past week Gutfreund worked 8 hours each day Monday through Friday, 4 hours on Saturday, and 3 hours on Sunday.

Compute Gutfreund's gross pay for the past week.

Exercise 4-2. The payroll register of the Smith and Jones Company for the payroll period ended October 31 showed the following amount column totals for the week:

Regular earnings	$5,406.00
Overtime earnings	374.00
Deductions:	
FICA tax	$ 433.50
Federal income tax	867.00
City earnings tax	57.50
Pension plan	231.20
Health insurance	115.00
Credit union	175.00
United Way	50.00

Based on the foregoing payroll register amounts, prepare the two-column journal entry for the payment of wages on October 31.

Report No. 4-1

Complete Report No. 4-1 in the study assignments and submit your working papers to the instructor for approval.

PAYROLL TAXES IMPOSED ON THE EMPLOYER

The various taxes discussed thus far have had one thing in common—they all were levied on the employee. The employer withholds them from the employees' earnings only for the purpose of subsequently paying them to some agency or organization. They do not represent any additional expense of the employer.

In addition to these employee taxes, however, certain taxes are also imposed directly on the employer for various purposes, such as: old-age, survivors, and disability insurance benefits; hospital insurance benefits for the aged; and unemployment, relief, and welfare. Most employers are subject to payroll taxes imposed under the Federal Insurance Contributions Act (FICA) and the Federal Unemployment Tax Act (FUTA). An employer may also be subject to the payroll tax imposed under the unemployment compensation laws of one or more states. This tax is commonly called a **State Unemployment Tax**. All of these employer taxes do represent additional payroll expenses of the employer, as will be demonstrated in subsequent sections.

Employer's FICA Tax

The taxes imposed under the Federal Insurance Contributions Act are levied on employers for exactly the same amounts as employees. As explained on page 92, the rate and the taxable earnings base of the tax may be changed by Congress at any time. It was assumed in this chapter that the combined rate (OASDI and HIP) is 7.5% and the base is $47,000. Thus the employer would be required to pay the employer's share of the FICA tax at a rate of 7.5% on the first $47,000 of each employee's earnings. Any amount of earnings paid to an employee during a year in excess of $47,000 is exempt from FICA tax. (Note that a total of 15% of each employee's taxable earnings — the employer's share and the employee's share — must be paid periodically to an authorized bank or the Internal Revenue Service.)

Employer's FUTA Tax

Under the Federal Unemployment Tax Act, a payroll tax, called the **FUTA tax**, is levied on employers for the purpose of financing the cost of administering the federal-state unemployment compensation program. This tax is levied only on employers and is not deducted from employees' earnings. Employers who employ one or more persons for at least one day in each of 20 or more calendar weeks in a calendar year, or who pay wages of $1,500 or more in any calendar quarter are subject to this tax. The federal law imposes a specific rate of tax on a specific earnings base but allows a substantial credit against this levy for amounts paid into state unemployment compensation programs. Since all states have such programs, the amounts actually paid to the federal government by most employers are substantially less than the legal maximum. Most of the total amount of tax levied under the FUTA program typically is paid to the state governments.

As in the case of the FICA tax, Congress can and does change both the rate and the taxable base of the FUTA tax from time to time. For the purpose of this discussion, a rate of 6.2% with a credit of 5.4% for payments to state unemployment programs is assumed. The difference, 0.8% (6.2%-5.4%) is the effective federal rate. It is further assumed that the taxable base is the first $7,000 of compensation paid to each employee during the calendar year. Note that both the rate and base are substantially lower than the 7.5% and $47,000 for the FICA tax. It is also important to note that all of the payroll taxes relate to gross wages paid — not to wages earned. Sometimes wages are earned in one quarter or year, but not paid until the following period.

Employer's State Unemployment Tax

All of the states and the District of Columbia have enacted unemployment compensation laws providing for the payment of benefits to qualified unemployed workers. The cost of administering the state unemployment compensation laws is borne by the federal government. Under the federal law an appropriation is made for each year by the Congress from which grants are made to the states to meet the proper administrative costs of their unemployment compensation laws. As a result of this provision, the entire amount paid into the state funds may be used for the payment of benefits to qualified workers. While in general there is considerable uniformity in the provisions of the state laws, there are many variations in coverage, rates of tax imposed, and benefits payable to qualified workers. The date of payment of unemployment taxes also varies from state to state, and a penalty generally is imposed on the employer for late payment. Not all employers covered by the Federal Unemployment Tax Act are covered by the unemployment compensation laws of the states in which they have employees. But most employers of one or more individuals are covered by the federal law.

There are frequent changes in the state laws with respect to coverage, contribution rates required, eligibility to receive benefits, and amounts of benefits payable. In this discussion, it is assumed that the state tax rate is 2.7% of the first $7,000 of wages paid each employee each year. However, under the laws of most states there is a **merit-rating system** which provides a tax-saving incentive to employers to stabilize employment. Under this system, an employer's rate may be considerably less than the maximum rate if steady work is provided for the employees, i.e., if none or very few of the employer's workers have applied for unemployment compensation. If an employer is qualified for a lower state rate, the full credit of 2.7% would still be allowed in computing the federal unemployment tax due.

To illustrate the merit-rating system and the functioning of the federal-state unemployment tax program as a whole, assume that an employer has a favorable merit rating and is required to pay only 1.0% rather than 2.7% to the state government. If an employee earns $5,000, this employer would be required to pay a total of $90 in unemployment taxes; $50 to the state government and $40 to the federal government, calculated as follows:

Taxable earnings		$5,000
State unemployment tax rate		×1.0%
State unemployment tax		$ 50
Taxable earnings		$5,000
Total FUTA rate	6.2%	
Credit for state program	5.4%	
		×0.8%
Federal unemployment tax		$ 40

Accounting for Employer Payroll Taxes

In accounting for employer payroll taxes, it is acceptable either to use separate accounts for FICA Tax Expense, FUTA Tax Expense, and State Unemployment Tax Expense, or to enter all of these taxes in a single account such as Payroll Taxes Expense. Liabilities for FICA, FUTA, and state unemployment taxes normally should be entered in separate accounts. Examples of payroll taxes expense and liability accounts and a typical journal entry for payroll taxes are presented in the following sections.

Payroll Taxes Expense. All of the payroll taxes imposed on an employer under the federal and state social security laws are an expense of the employer. For the purpose of this discussion, it is assumed that a single account entitled Payroll Taxes Expense is used in summarizing such taxes. This is an expense account that is debited for all payroll taxes imposed on the employer.

Payroll Taxes Expense

Debit	
to enter FICA, FUTA, and state unemployment taxes imposed on the employer.	

FICA Tax Payable. This is the same liability account that was illustrated on page 92 and was used to recognize the FICA tax withheld from employees' earnings. As used here, the account is credited to enter the FICA tax imposed on the employer. The account is debited when the tax is paid to the Internal Revenue Service. When all of the FICA taxes have been paid, the account should be in balance.

FICA Tax Payable

Debit	Credit
to enter payment of FICA tax.	to enter FICA taxes (1) withheld from employees' earnings and (2) imposed on the employer.

FUTA Tax Payable. In entering the federal unemployment tax, it is customary to keep a separate liability account entitled FUTA Tax Payable. This is a liability account that is credited for the tax imposed on employers under the Federal Unemployment Tax Act. The account is debited for amounts paid to apply on such taxes. When all of the FUTA taxes have been paid, the account should be in balance.

FUTA Tax Payable

Debit	Credit
to enter payment of FUTA tax.	to enter FUTA tax imposed on the employer.

State Unemployment Tax Payable. In entering the tax imposed under state unemployment compensation laws, it is customary to keep a separate liability account entitled State Unemployment Tax Payable. This is a liability account that is credited for the tax imposed on employers under the state unemployment compensation laws. The account is debited for the amount paid to apply on such taxes. When all of the state taxes have been paid, the account should be in balance. Some employers who are subject to taxes imposed under the laws of several states keep a separate liability account for the tax imposed by each state.

State Unemployment Tax Payable

Debit	Credit
to enter state unemployment tax paid.	to enter state unemployment tax imposed on the employer.

Journalizing Employer's Payroll Taxes. The payroll taxes imposed on employers may be entered periodically, such as monthly or quarterly. It is more common to enter such taxes at the time that wages are paid so that the employer's liability for such taxes and related expenses may be entered in the same period as the wages on which the taxes are based.

The information needed to properly enter employer payroll taxes is contained in the payroll register such as the one illustrated on pages 100-101. The totals at the bottom of the two columns for "Taxable Earnings" headed "Unemployment Comp." and "FICA" indicate the total employee earnings on which employer taxes would be levied. The FICA taxable earnings for the pay period involved amounted to $3,539.50. Assuming that the combined rate of the tax imposed on the employer was 7.5%, which is the same as the rate of the tax imposed on each employee, the tax would amount to $265.47. The only earnings in the payroll register that were subject to unemployment compensation taxes were Toerner's earnings for the week because they had not exceeded the $7,000 taxable base. Toerner began working for Central States Diversified, Inc. on September 14, 1987. Federal and State unemployment taxes in this situation can be computed as follows:

State unemployment tax, 2.7% of $559	$15.09
FUTA tax, 0.8% of $559	4.47
Total unemployment taxes	$19.56

The following two-column journal entry would therefore be made for the employer payroll taxes expense on wages paid on December 4. These amounts would be posted to payroll taxes expense and liability accounts such as those illustrated in the preceding paragraphs.

Dec. 4	Payroll Taxes Expense	285.03	
	FICA Tax Payable		265.47
	FUTA Tax Payable		4.47
	State Unemployment Tax Payable		15.09
	Employer payroll taxes for the week ended December 4.		

An alternative approach employed by some businesses is to enter employer payroll taxes only when they are paid. Under this approach, the above entry would not be made on December 4. Instead, if the employer taxes on Central States Diversified's November 1987 payroll totaled $1,150.18, and were due on December 15, 1987, the following journal entry would be made:

Dec. 15	Payroll Taxes Expense	1,150.18	
	Cash		1,150.18
	Employer payroll taxes for November.		

The business illustrated in the following chapter accounts for employer payroll taxes in this manner.

It is important to note in connection with these illustrations the total cost incurred by an employer in order to employ a person. The employer must of course pay the gross wages of an employee, either in whole or in part to the employee, or in part to various government agencies and other organizations. In addition to these gross wages, however, the employer must pay payroll taxes on wages paid to an employee up to certain dollar limits. To illustrate this point, assume that an employee earns $25,000 for a year. The total cost of this employee to the employer can be calculated as follows:

Gross wages	$25,000
Employer FICA tax, 7.5% of $25,000	1,875
State unemployment tax, 2.7% of $7,000	189
FUTA tax, 0.8% of $7,000	56
	$27,120

Thus, the total cost to an employer of employing a person whose stated compensation is $25,000 is not $25,000, but $27,120. Employer payroll taxes clearly are a significant cost of doing business.

Filing Returns and Making Payroll Tax Payments

Employer responsibilities for filing reports and making payroll tax payments can be broken down into two areas: (1) responsibility with respect to FICA and federal income taxes, and (2) responsibility with respect to state and federal unemployment taxes. These two areas are discussed in the following sections.

Responsibilities for FICA and Federal Income Taxes. Federal reporting and payment regulations deal jointly with requirements for employee FICA taxes withheld, federal income taxes withheld, and employer FICA taxes. When the cumulative amount withheld from employees for FICA and income tax purposes plus the cumulative amount of employer FICA tax exceeds certain specified dollar amounts as of particular dates, an employer is required to deposit the amount in a Federal Reserve bank or branch or to some other authorized commercial bank depository. The dollar amounts and dates have been changed several times in recent years and are subject to change at any time in the future. In general, large employers are required to make deposits about every four days. Medium-size employers generally are required to make deposits by the 15th of the following month.

At the time any one of these tax deposits is made, the employer should submit to the depository bank a completed copy of the Federal Tax Deposit of Withheld Income and FICA Tax, Form 8109. An example of this form is shown below.

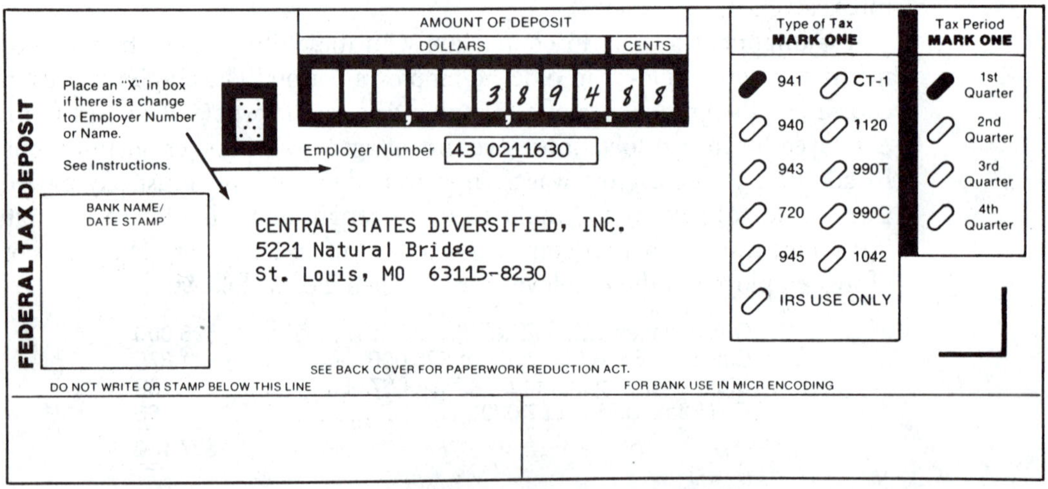

FEDERAL TAX DEPOSIT

AMOUNT OF DEPOSIT

DOLLARS | CENTS

3,894.88

Place an "X" in box if there is a change to Employer Number or Name.

See Instructions.

Employer Number 43 0211630

BANK NAME/ DATE STAMP

CENTRAL STATES DIVERSIFIED, INC.
5221 Natural Bridge
St. Louis, MO 63115-8230

Type of Tax MARK ONE: 941 (marked), CT-1, 940, 1120, 943, 990T, 720, 990C, 945, 1042, IRS USE ONLY

Tax Period MARK ONE: 1st Quarter (marked), 2nd Quarter, 3rd Quarter, 4th Quarter

SEE BACK COVER FOR PAPERWORK REDUCTION ACT.

DO NOT WRITE OR STAMP BELOW THIS LINE

FOR BANK USE IN MICR ENCODING

Federal Tax Deposit Form (Form 8109)

To illustrate the accounting procedure for entering the payment of the employer's and employees' taxes, assume that after the payroll was paid on January 24, the employees' FICA and income taxes withheld and the employer's FICA tax were sufficiently large to require the payment of these taxes by January 28. Central States Diversified, Inc. issued a check in payment of the following taxes imposed with respect to wages paid from the week ending January 10, through the week ending January 24.

Employees' income tax withheld from wages		$2,191.00
FICA tax:		
Withheld from employees' wages	$1,028.78	
Imposed on employer	1,028.78	2,057.56
Amount of check		$4,248.56

The journal entry for this transaction would be as follows:

Jan. 28	Employees' Income Tax Payable	2,191.00	
	FICA Tax Payable	2,057.56	
	Cash		4,248.56
	Remitted $4,248.56 in payment of taxes.		

Another major form that the employer must file in connection with employee FICA and income taxes withheld and cumulative employer FICA taxes is Form 941. This is the Employer's Quarterly Federal Tax Return which must be filed with the Internal Revenue Service by the end of the month following the end of each quarter involved. A completed copy of Form 941 which would be used by Central States Diversified, Inc., on April 30, 1988, to file for the quarter ended March 26, 1988, is shown on page 116. This form summarizes employee FICA and federal income taxes withheld and employer FICA taxes due for the quarter. Portions of the information needed to complete Form 941 are obtained from the payroll register.

Responsibilities for State and Federal Unemployment Taxes. The amount of the tax imposed on employers under the state unemployment compensation laws must be remitted to the proper state office by the end of the month following the close of each calendar quarter involved. Each state provides an official form to be used in making a return of the taxes due. To illustrate the accounting procedure for entering the payment of state unemployment taxes, assume that a check for $1,371.11 was issued on April 30 in payment of state unemployment compensation taxes on wages paid during the preceding quarter ended March 26. This transaction would be entered in a two-column journal as follows:

April 30	State Unemployment Tax Payable	1,371.11	
	Cash		1,371.11
	Paid state unemployment tax.		

Federal unemployment tax must be computed on a quarterly basis. If the amount of the employer's liability under the Federal Unemployment Tax Act during any quarter is more than $100, the total must be paid to a Federal Reserve Bank or some other authorized depository by the last day of the first month following the close of the quarter. If the amount is $100 or less, no

Form **941** (Rev January 1986) Department of the Treasury Internal Revenue Service

Employer's Quarterly Federal Tax Return

▶ For Paperwork Reduction Act Notice, see page 2.

4141 **Please type or print**

OMB No. 1545-0029 Expires: 8-31-88

Your name, address, employer identification number, and calendar quarter of return. (If not correct, please change.)

Name (as distinguished from trade name)

Date quarter ended: March 26, 1988

Trade name, if any: Central States Diversified, Inc.

Employer identification number: 43 0211630

Address and ZIP code: 5221 Natural Bridge, St. Louis, MO 63115-8230

T / FF / FD / FP / I / T

IRS Use: 1 1 1 1 1 1 1 1 1 1 2 2 2 2 2 2 2 2 2 3 3 3 3 3 3
4 5 5 5 6 6 6 7 8 9 9 9 9 9 9 10 10 10 11 11 11 11 11 11 11 11 11 11

If address is different from prior return, check here ▶ ☐

If you are not liable for returns in the future, check here . . . ▶ ☐ Date final wages paid . . . . ▶

	Complete for First Quarter Only			
1a	Number of employees (except household) employed in the pay period that includes March 12th ▶	1a	8	
b	If you are a subsidiary corporation AND your parent corporation files a consolidated Form 1120, enter parent corporation employer identification number (EIN) ▶ 1b —			
2	Total wages and tips subject to withholding, plus other compensation ▶	2	59,187	50
3	Total income tax withheld from wages, tips, pensions, annuities, sick pay, gambling, etc. ▶	3	9,470	00
4	Adjustment of withheld income tax for preceding quarters of calendar year (see instructions) ▶	4	-0-	
5	Adjusted total of income tax withheld	5	9,470	00
6	Taxable social security wages paid $ 59,187 50 X 15% (.15)	6	8,878	13
7a	Taxable tips reported $ -0- X 7.5% (.075)	7a	-0-	
b	Tips deemed to be wages (see instructions) $ -0- X 7.5% (.075)	7b	-0-	
c	Taxable hospital insurance wages paid $ -0- X 2.9% (.029)	7c	-0-	
8	Total social security taxes (add lines 6, 7a, 7b, and 7c)	8	8,878	13
9	Adjustment of social security taxes (see instructions for required explanation) ▶	9	-0-	
10	Adjusted total of social security taxes (see instructions)	10	8,878	13
11	Backup withholding ▶	11	-0-	
12	Adjustment of backup withholding tax for preceding quarters of calendar year	12	-0-	
13	Adjusted total of backup withholding	13	-0-	
14	Total taxes (add lines 5, 10, and 13) ▶	14	18,348	13
15	Advance earned income credit (EIC) payments, if any (see instructions)	15	-0-	
16	Net taxes (subtract line 15 from line 14). **This must equal line IV below** (plus line IV of Schedule A (Form 941) if you have treated backup withholding as a separate liability.)	16	18,348	13
17	Total deposits for quarter, including overpayment applied from a prior quarter, from your records ▶	17	18,348	13
18	Balance due (subtract line 17 from line 16). This should be less than $500. Pay to IRS ▶	18	-0-	
19	If line 17 is more than line 16, enter overpayment here ▶ $ ______ and check if to be: ☐ Applied to next return or ☐ Refunded.			

Record of Federal Tax Liability (Complete if line 16 is $500 or more) See the instructions under rule 4 for details before checking these boxes.
Check only if you made eighth-monthly deposits using the 95% rule ▶ ☐ Check only if you are a first time 3-banking-day depositor ▶ ☐

Date wages paid		Tax liability (**Do not show Federal tax deposits here.**) First month of quarter		Second month of quarter		Third month of quarter
1st through 3rd	A	1,413.60	I		Q	
4th through 7th	B	1,417.32	J	1,418.09	R	1,412.52
8th through 11th	C		K		S	
12th through 15th	D	1,382.45	L	1,410.50	T	1,404.30
16th through 19th	E		M		U	
20th through 22nd	F	1,393.45	N	1,415.15	V	1,413.60
23rd through 25th	G		O		W	
26th through the last	H	1,402.75	P	1,413.60	X	1,450.80
Total liability for month	*I*	7,009.57	*II*	5,657.34	*III*	5,681.22

IV Total for quarter (add lines *I*, *II*, and *III*) ▶ 18,348.13

Under penalties of perjury, I declare that I have examined this return, including accompanying schedules and statements, and to the best of my knowledge and belief it is true, correct, and complete.

Signature ▶ Albert Napier Title ▶ Manager Date ▶ 4/30/88

Employer's Quarterly Federal Tax Return and Quarterly Report (Form 941)

deposit is necessary, but this amount must be added to the amount subject to deposit for the next quarter. When a federal unemployment tax deposit is made, the employer should submit to the bank a completed copy of the Federal Tax Deposit of Unemployment Taxes, Form 508. This form is similar to Form 8109, which was illustrated on page 114.

In addition to these quarterly reports and deposits, employers are required to submit an annual report of federal unemployment tax on Form 940 to the District IRS Center by the end of the month following the close of the calendar year. Form 940 is not illustrated here. Any federal unemployment tax due for the last quarter or for other periods during the year would be submitted with Form 940.

To illustrate the accounting procedure for payment of federal unemployment tax, assume that a check for $149.45 was issued on January 29 in payment of federal unemployment tax on wages paid during the preceding three quarters ended December 26. This transaction would be entered in a two-column journal as follows:

		Debit	Credit
Jan. 29	FUTA Tax Payable	149.45	
	Cash		149.45
	Paid federal unemployment tax.		

BUILDING YOUR ACCOUNTING KNOWLEDGE

1. Why do employer payroll taxes represent an additional expense to the employer, whereas the various employee payroll taxes do not?
2. What is the purpose of the FUTA tax and who must pay it?
3. Why is most of the total amount of the tax levied under the FUTA program typically paid to the state governments?
4. Describe how a state merit-rating system works to reduce an employer's unemployment tax rate.
5. Identify all items that are debited or credited to the FICA Tax Payable account.
6. What accounts are affected when employer payroll tax expenses are properly recorded?
7. Explain why an employee whose gross salary is $20,000 costs an employer more than $20,000 to employ.
8. What is the purpose of the Employer's Quarterly Federal Tax Return Form 941?

APPLYING ACCOUNTING CONCEPTS

Exercise 4-3. Karen Shumate operates a business in a state with a state unemployment tax rate of 2.7%, but she qualifies for a 1.2% rate because of her merit rating. The gross payroll for the period ending February 14 is $4,500, all of which is subject to state and federal unemployment taxes.

Compute **(a)** the state unemployment tax and **(b)** the federal unemployment tax for Shumate's payroll for the period ending February 14. (Assume a total FUTA tax rate of 6.2%.)

Exercise 4-4. Mason Company's gross payroll for the period ending June 6 is $8,500. All of the earnings are subject to FICA tax at a rate of 7.5%. Only $1,800 of the earnings are subject to state unemployment tax at a rate of 2.7% and FUTA tax at a rate of 0.8%.

Prepare the two-column journal entry for Mason Company's employer payroll taxes expense for wages paid on June 6.

Exercise 4-5. Delores Reed employs James McCarthy at a salary of $22,500 a year. Reed is subject to employer FICA taxes at a rate of 7.5% on the salary. In addition Reed must pay state unemployment tax at a rate of 2.7% and federal unemployment tax at a rate of 0.8% on the first $7,000 of McCarthy's salary.

Compute the total cost to Reed of employing McCarthy for the year.

Exercise 4-6. On December 15, Zimmer Company paid the following taxes imposed on wages paid on the November weekly payrolls:

Employees' income tax withheld from wages		$ 914.56
FICA tax:		
Withheld from employees' wages	$428.70	
Imposed on employer	428.70	857.40
Amount of check		$1,771.96

Prepare the two-column journal entry for the payment of these taxes.

Report No. 4-2

Complete Report No. 4-2 in the study assignments and submit your working papers to the instructor for approval.

MASTERY PROBLEMS

Problem 4-A Payroll register

Following is a summary of the hours worked, rates of pay, and other relevant information concerning the employees of the Davidson Motors Company, Richard S. Davidson, owner, for the week ended Saturday, December 5. Employees are paid at the rate of time and one half for all hours worked in excess of 8 in any day or 40 in any week.

No.	Name	Allow. Claimed	Hours Worked M	T	W	T	F	S	Regular Hourly Rate	Cumulative Earnings Jan. 1-Nov. 28
1	Cohen, John S.	4	8	8	8	8	9	5	$12.00	$25.454.00
2	Evans, Marie	2	8	9	8	8	8	4	16.00	33,336.00
3	McDonald, Stanley	3	8	8	9	8	8	6	14.00	30,186.00
4	Petersen, Brenda	1	8	8	8	8	8	4	12.00	22,821.00
5	Reinhart, Paul	5	8	8	10	8	0	4	13.00	28,539.00
6	Wallace, James	1	8	8	8	8	0	0	18.00	34,234.00

Cohen and Reinhart each have $5 withheld this payday for group life insurance. Each employee has $20 withheld this payday for health insurance. Evans has $4 withheld this payday as a contribution to the United Fund.

Required: (1) Using the payroll register enter the payroll for the week ended Saturday December 5. Refer to the weekly Income Tax Table on page 96 to determine the amounts to be withheld from the wages of each employee for income tax purposes. All of Davidson's employees are married. Seven and one half percent of the taxable wages of all the employees should be withheld for FICA tax. Checks Nos. 819 through 824 were issued to the employees. Complete the payroll register by footing the amount columns, proving the footings, entering the totals, and ruling. **(2)** Assuming that the wages were paid on December 7, record the payment on the journal paper.

Problem 4-B **Payroll taxes**

The Ramirez store employs 12 people. They are paid by checks on the day nearest to the 15th and last day of each month. The entry to record each payroll includes the liabilities for the amounts withheld. The expense and liabilities arising from the employer's payroll taxes are recorded on each payday. Following is a narrative of the transactions completed during the month of January and on February 2 that relate to payrolls and payroll taxes.

Jan. 5 Paid $3,221.80 for payroll taxes for the second half of December:
  FICA tax, $1,558.80.
  Employees' income tax withheld, $1,663.00.

15 Payroll for first half of month:

Total salaries		$10,468.00
Less amounts withheld:		
FICA tax	$ 785.10	
Employees' income tax	1,675.00	2,460.10
Net amount paid		$ 8,007.90

15 Social security taxes imposed on employer:
  FICA tax, 7.5%.
  FUTA tax, 0.8%.
  State unemployment tax, 2.7%.

19 Paid FICA tax and employees' income tax for the first half of January.

29 Paid FUTA tax for quarter ended December 31, $19.20.

29 Paid state unemployment tax for quarter ended December 31, $64.80.

31 Payroll for last half of month:

Total salaries		$10,445.00
Less amounts withheld:		
FICA tax	$ 783.38	
Employees' income tax	1,671.00	2,454.38
Net amount paid		$ 7,990.62

31 Social security taxes imposed on employer:
  All salaries taxable; rates same as on January 15.

Feb. 2 Paid FICA tax and employees' income tax for the second half of January.

***Required:* (1)** Journalize the foregoing transactions using the journal paper. **(2)** Foot the debit and credit columns as a means of proof.

CHALLENGE PROBLEM 4

Angelo Donato, Paul Chang, and Donald Weber are employed by the Meyer Floral Shop. Their monthly salaries are $1,800, $1,750, and $1,675 respectively. All of the employees are entitled to time and one half for all hours worked in excess of 40 hours a week. During the week ended April 18, 1987, the employees worked the following hours:

Angela Donato	44 hours
Paul Chang	47 hours
Donald Weber	48 hours

Required: Using the ruled paper, calculate the wages earned by each of the three employees in the week ended April 18, 1987.

EXPANDING YOUR BUSINESS VOCABULARY

What is the meaning of each of the following terms?

additional withholding allowances **(p. 94)**
automated systems **(p. 97)**
direct deposit **(p. 100)**
electronic system **(p. 97)**
employee **(p. 90)**
employee's earning's record **(pp. 97, 101)**
employer's identification number **(p. 103)**
fee **(p. 90)**
FICA taxes **(p. 92)**
FUTA tax **(p. 109)**
gross pay **(p. 92)**
independent contractor **(p. 90)**
manual system **(p. 97)**
mechanical system **(p. 97)**
merit-rating system **(p. 110)**
net pay **(p. 92)**
payroll register **(pp. 97, 99)**
salary **(p. 90)**
service bureaus **(p. 98)**
social security number **(p. 92)**
special withholding allowance **(p. 94)**
State Unemployment Tax **(p. 108)**
time sharing **(p. 98)**
Wage and Tax Statement **(p. 102)**
wage-bracket method **(p. 95)**
wages **(p. 90)**
withholding allowance **(p. 94)**
write-it-once principle **(p. 97)**
zero-bracket amounts **(p. 94)**

5
ACCOUNTING FOR PERSONAL SERVICE (ATTORNEYS)

CHAPTER OBJECTIVES

Careful study of this chapter should enable you to:

- Explain and use the cash basis of accounting.
- Understand the special characteristics of accounting for attorneys.
- Perform the tasks involved in accounting for attorneys.

In contrast to a manufacturing enterprise which manufactures and sells merchandise or a mercantile enterprise which buys merchandise for resale, a personal service enterprise is one in which service is rendered to a company or a person. There are two types of personal service enterprises:

1. Professional enterprises
2. Business enterprises

Professional enterprises include public accountants, attorneys, physicians, dentists, engineers, architects, artists, educators, and other professionals whose income is earned chiefly by performing personal services.

Business enterprises of the personal service type include insurance, brokerage, advertising, real estate, entertainment, storage, transportation, and dry cleaning.

This chapter relates to personal services performed by an attorney. An attorney may represent either a plaintiff or a defendant. A person or company instituting a suit against someone else is called the plaintiff. The person or company being sued is called the defendant.

In a personal service firm such as that conducted by attorneys, the most valuable asset the attorney has is "time." The significance of time to a professional firm cannot be overemphasized. Adequate time records must be maintained by each attorney, including the sole practitioner. Many legal firms believe that it is desirable for each attorney to account for a working day by analyzing the activities that cannot be charged to clients. An analysis of nonchargeable time will disclose the amount of time the firm is devoting to community affairs, research, and other desirable activities.

Time records may be kept in various ways; some attorneys maintain a daily diary, and the chargeable time is posted daily to the clients' records. In a large law firm, weekly reports of work for each client may be used to reduce paperwork. Another method of time reporting is to use a consolidated weekly report of all attorney time. Thus, a secretary posts the billable time to the clients' records on a weekly rather than a daily basis.

THE CASH BASIS OF ACCOUNTING FOR A PERSONAL SERVICE ENTERPRISE

Most law firms use the cash basis of accounting which means that revenue is not recognized until cash is received and expenses are not recorded until paid. Thus, services may be performed in one month, and the revenue may be accounted for the following month or several months later. The cash basis of accounting violates the matching principle which holds that revenues earned and expenses incurred during a period should be matched against each other in order to arrive at as accurate a figure of net income or net loss for the period as possible. In many cases, however, expenses such as rent or telephone bills may be approximately the same each month, so that only a slight distortion is caused by paying and recording an expense in November which actually was incurred in October. The cash basis of accounting is acceptable for federal and state income tax purposes.

It should be noted that accounting cannot be based completely on cash transactions. Property or service accepted in lieu of cash must be recorded as revenue at the fair market value of the property or service at the time it is received. Also, if revenue such as interest on a savings account is available for withdrawal by the owner of the account, the revenue is said to be constructively received and must be reported as revenue even though no cash is withdrawn from the account.

Another exception to the cash basis of accounting is made when depreciation is recorded. Assets which provide benefits for several years, such as automobiles or office equipment, will wear out or depreciate with the passage of time. When such assets are purchased, they must be debited to asset accounts. As the asset is used, expense is incurred which should be allocated over the estimated life of the asset. The purpose of depreciation is to charge the expense to the period in which it is actually incurred, in accordance with the matching principle explained above. The portion of cost assigned to each period is called depreciation expense.

For example, an automobile, possibly the largest item in the balance sheet of a legal firm, must be debited to the asset account Automobile. Depreciation of the automobile is based on the cost, less any residual or scrap value, and the estimated life of the automobile. Since the residual value and the expected useful life are estimates, the amount charged to depreciation expense each period is not entirely accurate; but an allocation of cost over the expected useful life of an asset results in a more equitable profit or loss measurement than charging such an asset to expense in the period it is purchased.

When an entry is made at the end of the period debiting Depreciation Expense, the credit is usually to an account called **Accumulated Depreciation**, such as Accumulated Depreciation—Automobile. Accumulated depreciation accounts are **contra accounts** (meaning "opposite" or "offsetting" accounts) and should be deducted from the related asset accounts in the balance sheet. The difference between the asset account and the accumulated depreciation account is known as the **book value** of the asset. Adjustments for depreciation will be explained further in Chapter 7.

Chart of Accounts

To illustrate the cash basis of accounting for an attorney, a chart of accounts for Jose Ortega, Attorney at Law, is reproduced on page 124. Note that asset accounts have account numbers beginning with 1 and 2; liability accounts begin with 3; owner's equity accounts begin with 5; revenue accounts begin with 6; and expense accounts begin with 7. New accounts may be added as needed without disturbing the numerical order of the existing accounts.

Many of the accounts in the following list have been explained and their uses illustrated in the previous chapters. Accounts appearing for the first time in this chapter will be discussed before the records of Ortega are presented.

Advances on Behalf of Clients, Account No. 130. Payments for items such as court filing fees, fees charged by accountants for making audits, and the cost of obtaining depositions are sometimes made for clients. Absorption of these expenses by the attorney would be equivalent to lowering fees for certain clients. To avoid unethical "fee cutting," payments made for clients are debited to the account Advances on Behalf of Clients and then billed to the clients on a monthly or quarterly basis. A record of the payments made and remittances received is also made in the client's account on an office docket (an auxiliary record which provides a complete record of each legal case). A minimum amount, usually 50 cents to $1, can be established below which the firm will absorb the expense to save clerical work.

Expense and Revenue Summary Account, Account No. 520. The expense and revenue summary account is a clearing account which is used only when the books are closed at the end of the accounting period. Use of this account will be explained further in Chapter 8.

JOSE ORTEGA, ATTORNEY AT LAW

CHART OF ACCOUNTS

Assets*

100 Cash
110 Petty Cash Fund
120 Clients' Trust Account
130 Advances on Behalf of Clients
200 Automobile
205 Accumulated Depreciation—Automobile
210 Office Equipment
215 Accumulated Depreciation—Office Equipment

Liabilities

300 Liability for Trust Funds
310 Employees' Income Tax Payable
320 FICA Tax Payable
330 FUTA Tax Payable
340 State Unemployment Tax Payable

Owner's Equity

500 Jose Ortega, Capital
510 Jose Ortega, Drawing
520 Expense and Revenue Summary

Revenue

600 Legal Fees Revenue
610 Collection Fees Revenue

Expenses

700 Automobile Expense
703 Charitable Contributions Expense
705 Depreciation Expense
708 Law Library Expense
710 Miscellaneous Expense
713 Office Supplies Expense
715 Payroll Taxes Expense
718 Rent Expense
720 Salary Expense
725 Telephone Expense

*Words in bold type represent headings and not account titles.

Legal Fees Revenue, Account No. 600. Legal Fees Revenue is a revenue account that is credited for cash received from clients in payment of legal work performed. When the accounts are kept on the cash basis, revenue is not recorded in the account until cash is received or until a note or other property is accepted in lieu of cash.

Since legal fees are usually not collected until they are billed, billing is very important. The more frequent the billing, the more frequent the collection. If bills are collected frequently, the firm can operate with a smaller cash investment, and in some cases may collect a larger total fee without impairing the client relationship than would be possible if the entire amount were billed at one time. Many clients of a law firm prefer to be billed on a monthly or quarterly basis even though the legal work is not completed, rather than to receive one large bill at the end of the engagement.

Clients' Trust Account, Account No. 120, Liability for Trust Funds, Account No. 300, and Collection Fees Revenue, Account No. 610. Funds received or collected by an attorney and held for a client must be deposited in a separate bank account promptly.[1] If money is collected on an account owed to a client, the lawyer will deduct a commission or fee before the money is deposited for the client in the special bank account. This transaction is then recorded as follows: Cash (Account No. 100) is debited for the lawyer's commission; Clients' Trust Account (Account No. 120) is debited for the amount that is in the special bank account; Liability for Trust Funds (Account No. 300) is credited to indicate the amount owed to the client; and Collection Fees Revenue (Account No. 610) is credited to indicate the commission or fee earned by the lawyer. The balance in Account No. 120 and in Account No. 300 will always be equal. When the amount in the special bank account is paid to the client, Liability for Trust Funds (Account No. 300) is debited, and Clients' Trust Account (Account No. 120) is credited.

To illustrate, Ortega undertakes to collect an account amounting to $600 for the Barnes Department Store on a commission basis of 33⅓%. When cash is received in payment of the account, the following entry should be made:

Date	Account	Debit	Credit
July 20	Cash	200	
	Clients' Trust Account	400*	
	Liability for Trust Funds		400
	Collection Fees Revenue		200
	Collected an account in the amount of $600 on behalf of the Barnes Department Store and recorded fee of $200.		

*The $400 is deposited in a special checking account.

When the amount collected for the Barnes Department Store ($400) is paid to them by the attorney, an entry should be made as follows:

Date	Account	Debit	Credit
July 21	Liability for Trust Funds	400	
	Clients' Trust Account		400*
	Payment to Barnes Department Store of collection made for them.		

*At this time a check is written for $400 from the special checking account and sent to the Barnes Department Store.

[1]For example, Rule 8-101 of the California Business and Professions Code entitled "Preserving Identity of Funds and Property of a Client," reads in part as follows:

(A) All funds received or held for the benefit of clients by a member of the State Bar or firm of which he is a member, including advances for costs and expenses, shall be deposited in one or more identifiable bank accounts labeled "Trust Account," "Client's Funds Account" or words of similar import. West's Annotated California Codes, Volume 3B (St. Paul, Minn. West Publishing Co. 1978) p. 91.

Books of Account

Ortega uses the following books of account:

1. General books
   (a) Cash receipts journal
   (b) Cash payments journal
   (c) General journal
   (d) General ledger
2. Auxiliary records
   (a) Petty cash payments record
   (b) Lawyer's office docket
   (c) Lawyer's collection docket
   (d) Employee's earnings record
   (e) Checkbook used with Account No. 100
   (f) Checkbook used with account No. 120

Cash Receipts Journal. The **cash receipts journal** is a special column journal which is used to record all receipts of cash. Ortega's cash receipts journal, reproduced on pages 140–141 contains six amount columns. The columnar arrangement follows:

1. General Credit
2. Revenue
   (a) Legal Fees 600 Cr.
   (b) Collection Fees 610 Cr.
3. Liability for Trust Funds 300 Cr.
4. Clients' Trust Account 120 Dr.
5. Cash 100 Dr.

The General Cr. column would be used to record payments made by clients for items charged to Advances on Behalf of Clients.

A law firm that does not collect accounts for clients would not need a column for Collection Fees Revenue in the cash receipts journal. The columns for Clients' Trust Account and Liability for Trust Funds would still be needed. A firm sometimes holds money for clients for reasons other than the collection of accounts.

Cash Payments Journal. The **cash payments journal** is a special column journal that is used to record all payments of cash. Ortega's cash payments journal, reproduced on pages 142–143, contains seven amount columns. The columnar arrangement follows:

1. General Debit
2. Liability for Trust Funds 300 Dr.
3. Salary Expense 720 Dr.
4. Employees' Income Tax Payable 310 Cr.
5. FICA Tax Payable 320 Cr.
6. Clients' Trust Account 120 Cr.
7. Cash 100 Cr.

The debits to Employees' Income Tax Payable and FICA Tax Payable should be entered in the General Dr. column when these taxes are paid.

Different law firms will want to have different special columns in their cash receipts and cash payments journals depending upon the nature of the practice and the size of the firm.

The cash payments journal contains a Check Number column to the left of the Cash 100 Cr. column to account for the law firm's cash account and a Check Number column to the left of the Clients' Trust Account 120 Cr. column to account for payment to the clients of their cash.

The account numbers in the headings in the cash receipts and cash payments journals are an aid in completing the summary posting at the end of the month.

General Journal. The **two-column general journal** is used to record items that do not go in the special columns of the cash receipts and cash payments journals.

The special journals are an alternative to the combination journal. As is explained in Chapter 3, having two or more persons handle cash transactions is one of the features of a system of internal control. If the number of employees is sufficiently large, one person could be responsible for making the entries in the cash receipts journal, another person could be responsible for making the entries in the cash payments journal, and a third person could reconcile the bank account. Entries in the general journal will probably be few and could be assigned to either the person in charge of the cash receipts or cash payments journals.

Another advantage of the special journals is that they permit more than one person to work on the journals. An additional person or persons could be employed, if necessary, to post the journals to the general ledger.

A narrative of transactions completed by Ortega during the month of December is given on pages 131–139. These transactions are recorded in the special journals and the general journal on pages 140–144. Note that before any December transactions were recorded in the journals, the bank balance at the start of the month, $60,786.89, would appear in the checkbook used with account No. 100 and also as the beginning balance in the cash account in the general ledger. Accounts No. 120 and No. 300 have no balance on December 1.

General Ledger. Ortega uses an account form, called a **balance-column-account form**, which has four amount columns: a debit column, a credit column, and two balance columns—one for debit and one for credit. Although the standard two-column account form illustrated to this point is still favored by some, the four-column form of balance-column account has the advantage of providing a place to record the balance of the account. The balance may be determined and recorded after each transaction or only at the end of the month.

The ledger is reproduced on pages 144–149. In each case, the balance as of December 1 has been entered. The accounts in the **general ledger** are arranged in the order given in the chart of accounts shown on page 124. All posting in the general ledger accounts is from the special journals and the general journal. A trial balance is taken at the end of each month to prove the equality of the general ledger account balances. The trial balance as of December 31 appears on page 139.

Auxiliary Records. **Auxiliary records** are used to record information not recorded in the regular accounting records. Ortega uses a petty cash payments record, an office docket, a collection docket, and two checkbooks as auxiliary records. An employee's earnings record similar to the one illustrated in Chapter 4, is maintained for each employee.

Petty Cash Payments Record. Ortega maintains a petty cash fund in the amount of $100. The petty cash payments record is similar to that illustrated in Chapter 3.

Lawyer's Office Docket. An **office docket** is a form used to maintain a memorandum record of each legal case with a client. A model filled-in office docket (reproduced on page 129) shows the history of the case of Tri-City Sales Co., plaintiff, vs. Virginia Steele, defendant. The legal information that may be needed in handling the case is recorded on the upper part of the form, and a memorandum account of the charges and credits to the account of the client is kept on the lower part of the form.

When an attorney's accounts are kept on the cash basis, there is no general ledger account for the client, but the information must be kept on the office docket. The client's account, as recorded on the office docket, should be charged for:

1. Fees for services rendered.
2. Payments on behalf of the client, such as filing fees and other expenses paid for the client.

The client's account should be credited for:

1. Payments received for services.
2. Reimbursements for advances made on behalf of the client.

In the illustration on page 129, the client, Tri-City Sales Co., is charged for the following:

November 24 Amount of the fee agreed upon at the time the case was taken, $1,000.

November 27 Amount advanced in payment of suit fee, $15.

The account is credited for the following:

CLIENT Tri-City Sales Co. ADDRESS 918 Delmar Rd., City No. 520

IN RE: TRI-CITY SALES CO.
vs.
VIRGINIA STEELE

COURT Common Pleas, Butler County
COURT FILE NO. 29836 19 87
CALENDAR NO. 912 ATTORNEY FOR Plaintiff
OTHER ATTORNEYS
NATURE OF MATTER Lawsuit
REMARKS

DATE		SERVICES RENDERED	FEES AND DISBURSEMENTS	MONEYS RECEIVED		BALANCE DUE
				PURPOSE	AMOUNT	
Nov.	24	Fee for preparing case	1000 00			1000 00
	27	Suit fee	15 00			1015 00
Dec.	1			Retainer	200 00	815 00
	28			Balance due	815 00	-0-
		CARRIED FORWARD				

Lawyer's Office Docket

December 1 Amount received as a retainer, $200.

December 28 Amount received in payment of balance due on account, $815.

DEBTOR Robert W. Matricia	DATE CLAIM REC'D. 12-3-87 NO. 85
ADDRESS 750 Hudson Avenue, City	DATE DISPOSED OF 1-23-88
BUSINESS	TOTAL AMOUNT $ 750
CREDITOR Johnson Fence Co.	AMOUNT COLLECTED $ 750
ADDRESS Seventh and Main Streets, City	FEE$ 250
REC'D CLAIM FROM	EXPENSE $
ATTORNEY FOR DEBTOR	AMOUNT REMITTED $ 500
CALLS ON DEBTOR	CHECK NO. 74 & 81

CORRESPONDENCE	RECEIVED FROM CREDITOR		
	DATE	FOR	AMOUNT
	12-22	Com.	100 00
	1-20	Com.	150 00

RECEIVED FROM DEBTOR				PAID TO CREDITOR			
DATE	AMOUNT	DATE	AMOUNT	CHECK NO.	AMOUNT	CHECK NO.	AMOUNT
12 22	300 00			74	200 00		
1 20	450 00			81	300 00		

REMARKS: Statement of account. Collection fee 33⅓%.
No suit without further instructions.

Lawyer's Collection Docket

Lawyer's Collection Docket. Lawyers who collect accounts for clients may use a form known as a **collection docket** to keep a record of the necessary information pertaining to collections. A model filled-in copy of a collection docket is shown on this page.

The docket provides a record of the case of the Johnson Fence Co., creditor, vs. Robert W. Matricia, debtor. It also furnishes a record of the amounts collected from the debtor and the amounts paid to the creditor.

Attorneys usually take most collection cases on a percentage basis. Any expenses incurred in making collections should be charged to the expense accounts of the attorney and not to the client. If, however, a client has agreed to pay any expenses incident to a lawsuit, such as court costs, the amounts paid by the attorney should be charged to the client's account just the same as payments made for clients in handling other legal cases.

In the illustration, the following transactions were recorded on the collection docket for the Johnson Fence Co.:

December 22 Collected $300 from Robert W. Matricia, debtor.
December 28 Paid $200 to the Johnson Fence Co.
January 20 Collected $450 from Robert W. Matricia, debtor.
January 23 Paid $300 to the Johnson Fence Co.

The amount of the commission of 33⅓% is deducted from the amounts collected from the debtor and is entered on the collection docket as follows:

December 22 $100.
January 20 $150.

Employee's Earnings Record. The employee's earnings record was discussed in Chapter 4.

Following is a narrative of the transactions completed by Jose Ortega during the month of December. These transactions are recorded in the journals on pages 140–144.

JOSE ORTEGA, ATTORNEY AT LAW

Narrative of Transactions

Tuesday, December 1

Issued Check No. 986 for $1,200, payable to Simpson Realty Co. for the December rent.

Received $200 from Tri-City Sales Co. as a retainer in the lawsuit of Tri-City Sales Co. against Virginia Steele, Case No. 520.

The amount received as a retainer constitutes revenue realized on the cash basis. Office Docket No. 520 is reproduced on page 129. This docket is an auxiliary record designed to supplement the information recorded in the regular accounting records and to facilitate the handling of the case.

The transaction was recorded in the cash receipts journal by debiting Cash, Account No. 100, and by crediting Legal Fees Revenue, Account No. 600. Since this entry was recorded in special columns, individual posting is not required, and a check mark was placed in the Posting Reference column.

Wednesday, December 2

Issued Check No. 987 for $61.30 to the Mid-States Electric Co. for electricity consumed during November.

Debit Miscellaneous Expense, Account No. 710.

Received $400 from Phyllis Turner for services rendered in preparation of a trust agreement.

Thursday, December 3

Issued Check No. 988 for $75.18 to the Bell Telephone Co. for November service.

Received a check for $2,000 from R. L. Santello in payment of the balance due on Case No. 515.

Received for collection from the Johnson Fence Company, Seventh and Main Streets, City, a statement of its account with Robert W. Matricia, 750 Hudson Avenue, City. Matricia's account is over 18 months past due. Collection fee 33⅓%; no suit without further instructions. Collection No. 85.

Inasmuch as Ortega's books are kept on the cash basis, no entry in the regular accounting records is required for this transaction. Collection docket No. 85 is reproduced on page 130. This docket is an auxiliary record of information designed to supplement the information recorded in the regular accounting records to facilitate handling the account.

Friday, December 4

Received a check for $1,785 from the Polaski Manufacturing Company in full payment of Case No. 513.

Issued Check No. 989 for $84.37 to the Callahan Service Station in payment of the December 1 statement for gasoline, oil, and services rendered during November.

Received a check for $400 from John Sanzere for participating in a financial planning conference with Sanzere's stockbroker and insurance agent.

End-of-Week Work

(1) Footed the cash receipts and cash payments journals and proved the footings. As was stated on page 127, the bank balance in the check book used with Account No. 100 was $60,786.89. The balance on December 4 was $64,151.04. Proved the balance in the checkbook as follows:

Checkbook balance, December 1	$60,786.89
Add cash received December 1–4	4,785.00
	$65,571.89
Deduct cash payments December 1–4	1,420.85
Checkbook balance, December 4	$64,151.04

Deposits of cash receipts have been made in the Security National Bank in Account No. 100 and the amounts of the deposits have been entered in the checkbook used with Account No. 100. (2) Completed the individual postings from the General Debit column of the cash payments journal to the ledger accounts. As each item was posted, the account number was entered in the Posting Reference column of the journal and the page number of the journal was entered in the Posting Reference column of the account. The page number of the cash receipts journal should be preceded by the letters "CR" and the page number of the cash payments journal should be preceded by the letters "CP."

Monday, December 7

Received a check for $300 from Nehring and Stewart, certified public accountants, for drafting a partnership agreement.

Tuesday, December 8

Ortega has been engaged to represent the Linda Gronefeld Photography Studio, Inc. in the purchase of a building owned by Charles Wolfe at a minimum fee of $825. Case No. 521. Received a check for $150 as a retainer.

Received an invoice for $123.35 from the Emerson Stationery Co., 418 Seventh Street, City, for office supplies.

Since Ortega's books are kept on the cash basis, invoices for expenses are not recorded until they are paid. When expense invoices are received, they are filed in an invoice file until they are paid. When payment is made, the proper entry is made in the cash payments journal.

Wednesday, December 9

Received a check for $528.15 from Katherine L. Carleton in payment of the amount due on Collection No. 82.

The collection docket shows that Ortega had agreed to handle this collection on a 33⅓% commission basis. The transaction was entered in the cash receipts journal by debiting Cash, Account No. 100, for $176.05, and by debiting Clients' Trust Account, Account No. 120, for $352.10, for the amount due to the Ralph Nieman Company. Liability for Trust Funds, Account No. 300, was credited for $352.10, and Collection Fees Revenue, Account No. 610, was credited for $176.05, the amount of the commission earned. A memorandum entry was also made in the collection docket for the amount received from the debtor.

Thursday, December 10

Issued Check No. 990 for $1,235.87 to the American Law Book Company for law books.

Friday, December 11

Issued Check No. 991 for $50 to the Christmas Bureau Fund.

The check is recorded in the cash payments journal by debiting Charitable Contributions Expense, Account No. 703, and crediting Cash, Account No. 100.

Received $100 from Modern Kitchens, Inc. for preparing and filing a mechanic's lien on the property of David Murdoch.

End-of-Week Work

(1) Proved the footings of the cash receipts and cash payments journals. (2) On December 11, the balance in the checkbook used with Account No. 100 was $63,591.22. Proved the balance in this checkbook as follows:

Checkbook balance, December 1	$60,786.89
Add cash received December 1–11	5,511.05
	$66,297.94
Deduct cash payments December 1–11	2,706.72
Checkbook balance, December 11	$63,591.22

(3) Compared the balance in the Clients' Trust Account, Account No. 120, $352.10, with the balance of $352.10 in the checkbook used with Account No. 120. (4) Completed the individual postings from the General Debit column in the cash payments journal to the ledger accounts.

Monday, December 14

Issued Check No. 992 for $100 to the State Bar Association for annual dues.

The amount of this check was debited to Miscellaneous Expense, Account No. 710.

Received $150 from Maria Salinas for preparing a lease on office space in a building owned by Salinas.

Issued Check No. 993 for $753.50 to the Security National Bank in payment of the following payroll taxes based on wages paid during the month of November.

Employees' income tax withheld from wages		$344.00
FICA tax:		
Withheld from employees' wages	$204.75	
Imposed on employer	204.75	409.50
Amount of check		$753.50

A Federal Tax Deposit Form, No. 8109, was filled out and sent with the check. Ortega will not be required to pay the balance in the FUTA tax payable account until January.

Ortega telephoned the Security National Bank and learned that the check for $528.15 received from Katherine L. Carleton had cleared. Issued Check No. 73 to the Ralph Nieman Company in the amount of $352.10 which represents the full amount of Collection No. 82 ($528.15 less a collection fee of $176.05).

The transaction was recorded in the cash payments journal by debiting Liability for Trust Funds, Account No. 300, for $352.10 and by crediting Clients' Trust Account, Account No. 120 for the same amount. The collection fee had been recorded at the time the remittance was received from the debtor. A memorandum entry, however, was made in the collection docket to record the amount paid to the creditor. Since the claim was settled in full, the following information was entered in the upper right corner of the collection docket: **(1)** the date the case was disposed of, **(2)** the total amount collected, **(3)** the total amount of the attorney's fees, **(4)** the amount sent to the client, and **(5)** the check number.

Tuesday, December 15

Issued the following checks in payment of salaries for the first half of the month:

No. 994 for $535.62 to Dolores Fernandez, part-time law clerk, in payment of her salary in the amount of $645.00 less $61.00 withheld for income tax and $48.38 withheld for FICA tax.

No. 995 for $616.00 to Rita Mullaney, the office secretary, in payment of her salary in the amount of $800.00, less $124.00 withheld for income tax and $60.00 withheld for FICA tax.

Received a check for $3,400 from the Hoffman Construction Company, 825 Buttermilk Pike, City, in full payment of Case No. 516.

This remittance is in payment of the balance due for legal fees $3,000, and $400 for payment for work done by an accountant paid by Ortega on November 18 and debited to Advances on Behalf of Clients.

The check was recorded in the cash receipts journal by debiting Cash, Account No. 100, for $3,400, by crediting Advances on Behalf of Clients, Account No. 130, for $400, and by crediting Legal Fees Revenue, Account No. 600 for $3,000.

Wednesday, December 16

Ortega withdrew $2,000 for personal use. Check No. 996.

The check was recorded in the cash payments journal by debiting Jose Ortega, Drawing, Account No. 510, and by crediting Cash.

Paid the Mason Equipment Company $414.21 for an office refrigerator. Check No. 997.

The check was recorded in the cash payments journal by debiting Office Equipment, Account No. 210, and by crediting Cash.

Thursday, December 17

Issued Check No. 998 for $123.35 to the Emerson Stationery Co. in payment of the invoice received on December 8.

Office Supplies Expense is debited.

Ortega completed the work he had been doing on the settlement of the estate of Luis Sarmiento, deceased, and received a check for $8,500 in payment for his services. Case No. 511.

Friday, December 18

Received $100 from Donna Wilson for drawing a will.

End-of-Week Work

(1) Proved the footings of the cash receipts and cash payments journals. (2) Checked the balance in the checkbook used with Account No. 100 ($71,198.54) by adding $17,661.05 from the Cash 100 column in the cash receipts journal to the December 1 balance of $60,786.89 and subtracting $7,249.40 from the Cash 100 column in the cash payments journal. (3) Completed the individual postings from the General Credit column of the cash receipts journal and from the General Debit column of the cash payments journal to the ledger accounts.

Monday, December 21

Ortega has been engaged to represent the Medrano Manufacturing Company in the purchase of a building owned by Raymond Kappas at a minimum fee of $1,500. Case No. 522. Received a check for $100 as a retainer and also received a check for $4,000 as a deposit on the purchase price.

This transaction was recorded by debiting Cash, Account No. 100, for $100, and by crediting Legal Fees Revenue, Account No. 600, for $100. Also Clients' Trust Account, Account No. 120, was debited for $4,000, and Liability for Trust Funds, Account No. 300, was credited for $4,000.

Issued Check No. 999 for $666.75 to Preston Office Equipment Company in payment for a new electric typewriter.

Tuesday, December 22

Received a check for $300 from Robert W. Matricia to apply on his account with the Johnson Fence Co. Collection No. 85.

This transaction was recorded in the cash receipts journal by debiting Cash, Account No. 100, for $100, and by debiting Clients' Trust Account, Account No. 120, for $200 for the amount due the Johnson Fence Co. Liability for Trust Funds, Account No. 300, was credited for $200, and Collection Fees Revenue, Account No. 610, was credited for $100, the amount of the commission earned. A memorandum entry was also made in the collection docket for the amount received.

Wednesday, December 23

Received a check for $675 from the Linda Gronefeld Photography Studio, Inc. in payment of the balance due for legal work done in connection with the purchase of a building. Case No. 521.

Thursday, December 24

Brenda Oliveri, 2926 Burdsall Avenue, City, has engaged Ortega to handle the incorporation of a temporary help agency. Minimum fee $750. A check for $100 was received as a retainer. Case No. 523.

Received an invoice for $110.15 from the Legal Supply Co., 530 Fifth Avenue, New York City, for legal forms.

Legal forms used by an attorney are an expense and invoices for expenses are recorded only when paid in cash.

End-of-Week Work

(1) Proved the footings in the cash receipts and cash payments journals. (2) Checked the balance in the checkbook used with Account No. 100 ($71,506.79) by adding $18,636.05 from the Cash 100 column in the cash receipts journal to the December 1 cash balance of $60,786.89 in Account No. 100 and subtracting $7,916.15 from the Cash 100 column in the cash payments journal. (3) Checked the balance in the checkbook used with Account No. 120 ($4,200.00) by subtracting the total of the Clients' Trust Account Credit column in the cash payments journal ($352.10) from the total of the Clients' Trust Account Debit column in the cash receipts journal ($4,552.10). (4) Completed the individual postings from the General Debit and Credit columns of the cash receipts and cash payments journals to the ledger accounts.

Monday, December 28

Received a check for $815 from Tri-City Sales Co. in payment of the balance due on account. Case No. 520.

The check was recorded in the cash receipts journal by debiting Cash, Account No. 100, for $815, by crediting Advances on Behalf of Clients, Account No. 130, for $15, and by crediting Legal Fees Revenue, Account No. 600, for $800.

Ortega directed that Check No. 1,000 for $235.30 be issued to the Porter Department Store in payment of his personal account.

Since this transaction is a payment of a personal account of Ortega, it was recorded in the cash payments journal by debiting Jose Ortega, Drawing, Account No. 510, and by crediting Cash, Account No. 100.

Received a check for $200 from Frances Santini for a title search of a house Santini wishes to buy.

Tuesday, December 29

Issued Check No. 1,001 for $625 to C. A. Reynolds, CPA, in payment of her statement covering accounting services rendered to Ortega's client, R. J. Ojeda. Case No. 512.

Received a check in the amount of $250 from S. R. Graue in settlement of account. Case No. 514.

Issued Check No. 74 for $200 to remit a partial collection from Robert W. Matricia in the amount of $300 less a 33⅓% collection fee. Collection No. 85.

This transaction was recorded in the cash receipts journal by debiting Liability for Trust Funds, Account No. 300, for $200 and by crediting Clients' Trust Account, Account No. 120, for $200. A memorandum entry was made in the collection docket to record the amount paid to the creditor.

Wednesday, December 30

Ortega withdrew $3,000 for personal use. Check No. 1,002.

Thursday, December 31

Issued the following checks in payment of salaries for the second half of the month:

No. 1,003 for $589.00 to Dolores Fernandez, part-time law clerk, in payment of her salary in the amount of $720.00 less $77.00 withheld for income tax and $54.00 withheld for FICA tax.

No. 1,004 for $656.24 to Rita Mullaney, office secretary, in payment of her salary in the amount of $855.40 less $135.00 withheld for income tax and $64.16 withheld for FICA tax.

Issued Check No. 1,005 for $88.19 to replenish the petty cash fund.

The following statement provided the information needed in recording this transaction in the cash payments journal:

STATEMENT OF PETTY CASH PAYMENTS FOR DECEMBER

Advances on Behalf of Clients	$15.00
Jose Ortega, Drawing	18.34
Automobile Expense	20.17
Charitable Contributions Expense	20.00
Miscellaneous Expense	4.26
Office Supplies Expense	10.42
Total payments	$88.19

Made an entry in the general journal for the employer's portion of the FICA tax for the month of December by debiting Payroll Taxes Expense and by crediting FICA Tax Payable for $226.54.

Made an entry in the general journal for the FUTA tax in the amount of $10.92 and for the state unemployment tax in the amount of $36.86 on Fernandez' December salary. Mullaney's salary has exceeded $7,000 in the current year and there is no expense in the month of December for federal or state unemployment taxes on her salary.

End-of-Month Work

(1) Proved the footings, entered the totals, and ruled the cash receipts, cash payments and general journals. (2) Checked the balance in the checkbook used with Account No. 100 ($67,578.06) by adding $19,901.05 to the December 1 cash balance of $60,786.89 and subtracting $13,109.88 from the Cash 100 column in the cash payments journal. (3) Totaled and ruled the columns in the general journal. (4) Compared the balance in the Clients' Trust Account, Account No. 120, ($4,000) with the balance in the checkbook used with Account No. 120 as follows:

Balance, December 1	$ –0–
Add the total of the Clients' Trust Account Debit column in the cash receipts journal	4,552.10
Deduct the total of the Clients' Trust Account Credit column in the cash payments journal	552.10
Checkbook balance, December 31	$4,000.00

(5) Completed the individual postings from the General Debit columns in the cash payments journal, from the General credit column in the cash receipts journal and from the Debit and Credit columns in the general journal to the ledger accounts.

Since this was the end of the month, the summary posting was completed and the account numbers were written immediately below the totals of the columns in the cash receipts and cash payments journals.

A trial balance of the general ledger accounts that have balances on December 31 appears below.

Jose Ortega, Attorney at Law
Trial Balance
December 31, 1987

Account	Acct. No.	Dr. Balance	Cr. Balance
Cash	100	67,578.06	
Petty Cash Fund	110	100.00	
Clients' Trust Account	120	4,000.00	
Advances on Behalf of Clients	130	775.00	
Automobile	200	15,895.00	
Accumulated Depreciation—Automobile	205		7,947.50
Office Equipment	210	10,042.96	
Accumulated Depreciation—Office Equipment	215		3,584.80
Liability for Trust Funds	300		4,000.00
Employees' Income Tax Payable	310		397.00
FICA Tax Payable	320		453.08
FUTA Tax Payable	330		122.92
State Unemployment Tax Payable	340		107.06
Jose Ortega, Capital	500		20,914.58
Jose Ortega, Drawing	510	60,900.82	
Legal Fees Revenue	600		184,638.00
Collection Fees Revenue	610		4,495.57
Automobile Expense	700	4,051.57	
Charitable Contributions Expense	703	1,195.00	
Law Library Expense	708	5,920.87	
Miscellaneous Expense	710	792.91	
Office Supplies Expense	713	4,066.43	
Payroll Taxes Expense	715	2,985.45	
Rent Expense	718	14,400.00	
Salary Expense	720	32,635.40	
Telephone Expense	725	1,321.04	
		226,660.51	226,660.51

CASH RECEIPTS JOURNAL

PAGE 25

	DATE		DESCRIPTION	POST. REF.	GENERAL CR.	REVENUE: LEGAL FEES CR.	REVENUE: COLL. FEES CR.	LIAB. FOR TRUST FUNDS CR.	CLIENTS' TRUST ACCT. DR.	CASH DR.	
1	1987 Dec.	1	Tri-City Sales Co. Case No. 520	✓		20000				20000	1
2		2	P. Turner-Trust Agreement	✓		40000				40000	2
3		3	R.L. Santello Case No. 515	✓		200000				200000	3
4		4	Polaski Mfg. Co. Case No. 513	✓		178500				178500	4
5		4	John Sanzere-Financial								5
6			Planning Conference	✓		40000 478500				40000 478500	6
7		7	Nehring and Stewart-Partner-								7
8			ship Agreement	✓		30000				30000	8
9		8	L. Gronefeld Photography								9
10			Studio, Inc. Case No. 521	✓		15000				15000	10
11		9	K.L. Carleton Collection No. 82	✓			17605	35210	35210	17605	11
12		11	Modern Kitchens, Inc.-Mechanics								12
13			Lien	✓		10000 533500	17605	35210	35210	10000 551105	13
14		14	Maria Salinas - Lease	✓		15000				15000	14
15		15	Hoffman Const. Co. Case No. 516	✓							15
16			Advances on Behalf of Clients	130	40000	300000				340000	16
17		17	L. Sarmiento Case No. 511	✓		850000				850000	17
18		18	Donna Wilson-Will	✓	40000	10000 1708500	17605	35210	35210	10000 1766105	18
19		21	Medrano Mfg. Co. Case No. 522	✓		10000		400000	400000	10000	19
20		22	R.W. Matricia Collection No. 85	✓			10000	20000	20000	10000	20
21		23	L. Gronefeld Photography Studio,								21
22			Inc. Case No. 521	✓		67500				67500	22
23		24	Brenda Oliveri Case No. 523	✓	40000	10000 1796000	27605	455210	455210	10000 1863605	23
24											24

Date	Account	P.R.						
28	Tri-City Sales Co. Case No. 520	✓						
	Advances on Behalf of Clients	130	1500	80000				81500
28	F. Santini - Title Search	✓		20000				20000
29	S. R. Grave Case No. 514	✓		25000				25000
			41500	1921000	27605	455210	455210	1990105
			(✓)	(600)	(610)	(300)	(120)	(100)

Cash Receipts Journal

CASH PAYMENTS JOURNAL PAGE 23

	DATE		DESCRIPTION	POST. REF.	GENERAL DR.	LIAB. FOR TRUST FUNDS DR.	SALARY EXPENSE DR.	EMP. INC. TAX PAY. CR.	FICA TAX PAY. CR.	CK. NO.	CLIENTS' TRUST ACCT. CR.	CK. NO.	CASH CR.	
1	1987 Dec.	1	Rent Expense	718	120000							986	120000	1
2		2	Miscellaneous Expense	710	6130							987	6130	2
3		3	Telephone Expense	725	7518							988	7518	3
4		4	Automobile Expense	700	8437							989	8437	4
5		10	Law Library Expense	708	142085 123587							990	142085 123587	5
6		11	Charitable Contributions Exp.	703	5000							991	5000	6
7		14	Miscellaneous Expense	710	270672 10000							992	270672 10000	7
8		14	Employees' Income Tax Pay.	310	34400									8
9			FICA Tax Payable	320	40950							993	75350	9
10		14	Collection No. 82	✓		35210				73	35210			10
11		15	Dolores Fernandez	✓			64500	6100	4838			994	53562	11
12		15	Rita Mullaney	✓			80000	12400	6000			995	61600	12
13		16	Jose Ortega, Drawing	510	200000							996	200000	13
14		16	Office Equipment	210	41421							997	41421	14
15		17	Office Supplies Expense	713	12335							998	12335	15
16		21	Office Equipment	210	609778 66675	35210	144500	18500	10838		35210	999	724940 66675	16
17		28	Jose Ortega, Drawing	510	676453 23530	35210	144500	18500	10838		35210	1000	791615 23530	17
18		29	Advances on Behalf of Clients											18
19			Case No. 512	130	62500							1001	62500	19
20		29	Collection No. 85	✓		20000				74	20000			20
21		30	Jose Ortega, Drawing	510	300000							1002	300000	21
22		31	Dolores Fernandez	✓			72000	7700	5400			1003	58900	22
23		31	Rita Mullaney	✓			85540	13500	6416			1004	65624	23

24	31	Advances on Behalf of Clients	130	1500									24
25		Jose Ortega, Drawing	510	1834									25
26		Automobile Expense	700	2017									26
27		Charitable Contributions Exp.	703	2000									27
28		Miscellaneous Expense	710	426									28
29		Office Supplies Expense	713	1042							1005	8819	29
30				1071302	55210	302040	39700	22654		55210		1310988	30
31				(✓)	(300)	(720)	(310)	(320)		(120)		(100)	31
32													32
33													33
34													34
35													35
36													36
37													37
38													38
39													39
40													40

Cash Payments Journal

JOURNAL PAGE 12

	DATE		DESCRIPTION	POST. REF.	DEBIT	CREDIT	
1	1987 Dec.	31	Payroll Taxes Expense	715	22654		1
2			FICA Tax Payable	320		22654	2
3			Employer's portion of FICA				3
4			tax for December.				4
5		31	Payroll Taxes Expense	715	4778		5
6			FUTA Tax Payable	330		1092	6
7			State Unemployment Tax Payable	340		3686	7
8			FUTA and State unemployment				8
9			taxes on December payroll.				9
10					27432	27432	10
11					(✓)	(✓)	11

Jose Ortega — General Journal

ACCOUNT *Cash* ACCOUNT NO. 100

DATE		ITEM	POST. REF.	DEBIT	CREDIT	BALANCE DEBIT	BALANCE CREDIT
1987 Dec.	1	Balance	✓			6078689	
	31		CR25	1990105			
	31		CP23		1310988	6757806	

ACCOUNT *Petty Cash Fund* ACCOUNT NO. 110

DATE		ITEM	POST. REF.	DEBIT	CREDIT	BALANCE DEBIT	BALANCE CREDIT
1987 Dec.	1	Balance	✓			10000	

ACCOUNT *Clients' Trust Account* ACCOUNT NO. 120

DATE		ITEM	POST. REF.	DEBIT	CREDIT	BALANCE DEBIT	BALANCE CREDIT
1987 Dec.	31		CR25	455210			
	31		CP23		55210	400000	

General Ledger Accounts *(continued)*

ACCOUNT *Advances on Behalf of Clients* ACCOUNT NO. 130

DATE		ITEM	POST. REF.	DEBIT	CREDIT	BALANCE DEBIT	BALANCE CREDIT
1987 Dec.	1	Balance	✓			55000	
	15		CR25		40000		
	28		CR25		1500		
	29		CP23	62500			
	31		CP23	1500		77500	

ACCOUNT *Automobile* ACCOUNT NO. 200

DATE		ITEM	POST. REF.	DEBIT	CREDIT	BALANCE DEBIT	BALANCE CREDIT
1987 Dec.	1	Balance	✓			1589500	

ACCOUNT *Accumulated Depreciation-Automobile* ACCOUNT NO. 205

DATE		ITEM	POST. REF.	DEBIT	CREDIT	BALANCE DEBIT	BALANCE CREDIT
1987 Dec.	1	Balance	✓				794750

ACCOUNT *Office Equipment* ACCOUNT NO. 210

DATE		ITEM	POST. REF.	DEBIT	CREDIT	BALANCE DEBIT	BALANCE CREDIT
1987 Dec.	1	Balance	✓			896200	
	16		CP23	41421			
	21		CP23	66675		1004296	

ACCOUNT *Accumulated Depreciation-Office Equipment* ACCOUNT NO. 215

DATE		ITEM	POST. REF.	DEBIT	CREDIT	BALANCE DEBIT	BALANCE CREDIT
1987 Dec.	1	Balance	✓				358480

ACCOUNT *Liability for Trust Funds* ACCOUNT NO. 300

DATE		ITEM	POST. REF.	DEBIT	CREDIT	BALANCE DEBIT	BALANCE CREDIT
1987 Dec.	31		CR25		455210		
	31		CP23	55210			400000

General Ledger Accounts *(continued)*

ACCOUNT Employees' Income Tax Payable ACCOUNT NO. 310

DATE		ITEM	POST. REF.	DEBIT	CREDIT	BALANCE DEBIT	BALANCE CREDIT
1987 Dec.	1	Balance	✓				34400
	14		CP23	34400			
	31		CP23		39700		39700

ACCOUNT FICA Tax Payable ACCOUNT NO. 320

DATE		ITEM	POST. REF.	DEBIT	CREDIT	BALANCE DEBIT	BALANCE CREDIT
1987 Dec.	1	Balance	✓				40950
	14		CP23	40950			
	31		CP23		22654		
	31		GJ12		22654		45308

ACCOUNT FUTA Tax Payable ACCOUNT NO. 330

DATE		ITEM	POST. REF.	DEBIT	CREDIT	BALANCE DEBIT	BALANCE CREDIT
1987 Dec.	1	Balance	✓				11200
	31		GJ12		1092		12292

ACCOUNT State Unemployment Tax Payable ACCOUNT NO. 340

DATE		ITEM	POST. REF.	DEBIT	CREDIT	BALANCE DEBIT	BALANCE CREDIT
1987 Dec.	1	Balance	✓				7020
	31		GJ12		3686		10706

ACCOUNT Jose Ortega, Capital ACCOUNT NO. 500

DATE		ITEM	POST. REF.	DEBIT	CREDIT	BALANCE DEBIT	BALANCE CREDIT
1987 Dec.	1	Balance	✓				2091458

General Ledger Accounts *(continued)*

ACCOUNT *Jose Ortega, Drawing* ACCOUNT NO. *510*

DATE		ITEM	POST. REF.	DEBIT	CREDIT	BALANCE DEBIT	BALANCE CREDIT
1987 Dec.	1	Balance	✓			5564718	
	16		CP23	200000			
	28		CP23	23530			
	30		CP23	300000			
	31		CP23	1834		6090082	

ACCOUNT *Expense and Revenue Summary* ACCOUNT NO. *520*

DATE		ITEM	POST. REF.	DEBIT	CREDIT	BALANCE DEBIT	BALANCE CREDIT

ACCOUNT *Legal Fees Revenue* ACCOUNT NO. *600*

DATE		ITEM	POST. REF.	DEBIT	CREDIT	BALANCE DEBIT	BALANCE CREDIT
1987 Dec.	1	Balance	✓				16542800
	31		CR25		1921000		18463800

ACCOUNT *Collection Fees Revenue* ACCOUNT NO. *610*

DATE		ITEM	POST. REF.	DEBIT	CREDIT	BALANCE DEBIT	BALANCE CREDIT
1987 Dec.	1	Balance	✓				421952
	31		CR25		27605		449557

ACCOUNT *Automobile Expense* ACCOUNT NO. *700*

DATE		ITEM	POST. REF.	DEBIT	CREDIT	BALANCE DEBIT	BALANCE CREDIT
1987 Dec.	1	Balance	✓			394703	
	4		CP23	8437			
	31		CP23	2017		405157	

General Ledger Accounts *(continued)*

ACCOUNT *Charitable Contributions Expense* ACCOUNT NO. 703

DATE		ITEM	POST. REF.	DEBIT	CREDIT	BALANCE DEBIT	BALANCE CREDIT
1987 Dec.	1	Balance	✓			1125 00	
	11		CP23	50 00			
	31		CP23	20 00		1195 00	

ACCOUNT *Depreciation Expense* ACCOUNT NO. 705

DATE		ITEM	POST. REF.	DEBIT	CREDIT	BALANCE DEBIT	BALANCE CREDIT

ACCOUNT *Law Library Expense* ACCOUNT NO. 708

DATE		ITEM	POST. REF.	DEBIT	CREDIT	BALANCE DEBIT	BALANCE CREDIT
1987 Dec.	1	Balance	✓			4685 00	
	10		CP23	1235 87		5920 87	

ACCOUNT *Miscellaneous Expense* ACCOUNT NO. 710

DATE		ITEM	POST. REF.	DEBIT	CREDIT	BALANCE DEBIT	BALANCE CREDIT
1987 Dec.	1	Balance	✓			627 35	
	2		CP23	61 30			
	14		CP23	100 00			
	31		CP23	4 26		792 91	

ACCOUNT *Office Supplies Expense* ACCOUNT NO. 713

DATE		ITEM	POST. REF.	DEBIT	CREDIT	BALANCE DEBIT	BALANCE CREDIT
1987 Dec.	1	Balance	✓			3932 66	
	17		CP23	123 35			
	31		CP23	10 42		4066 43	

General Ledger Accounts *(continued)*

ACCOUNT *Payroll Taxes Expense* ACCOUNT NO. 715

DATE		ITEM	POST. REF.	DEBIT	CREDIT	BALANCE DEBIT	BALANCE CREDIT
1987 Dec.	1	Balance	✓			271113	
	31		GJ12	22654			
	31		GJ12	4778		298545	

ACCOUNT *Rent Expense* ACCOUNT NO. 718

DATE		ITEM	POST. REF.	DEBIT	CREDIT	BALANCE DEBIT	BALANCE CREDIT
1987 Dec.	1	Balance	✓			1320000	
	1		CP23	120000		1440000	

ACCOUNT *Salary Expense* ACCOUNT NO. 720

DATE		ITEM	POST. REF.	DEBIT	CREDIT	BALANCE DEBIT	BALANCE CREDIT
1987 Dec.	1	Balance	✓			2961500	
	31		CP23	302040		3263540	

ACCOUNT *Telephone Expense* ACCOUNT NO. 725

DATE		ITEM	POST. REF.	DEBIT	CREDIT	BALANCE DEBIT	BALANCE CREDIT
1987 Dec.	1	Balance	✓			124586	
	3		CP23	7518		132104	

General Ledger Accounts *(concluded)*

BUILDING YOUR ACCOUNTING KNOWLEDGE

1. Why is time the most valuable asset an attorney has?
2. What is meant by nonchargeable time?
3. Why does the cash basis of accounting violate the matching principle?

4. Why cannot accounting be based completely on cash transactions?
5. What is meant by constructive receipt of revenue?
6. What is the purpose of depreciation?
7. Will the balance in the Clients' Trust Account, Account No. 121, and the balance in Account No. 321, Liability for Trust Funds, always be the same?
8. Why will special columns for specific items in a special column journal save time and labor in the bookkeeping process?

APPLYING ACCOUNTING CONCEPTS

Exercise 5-1. A blank lawyer's office docket used by Rebecca Randolph, an attorney, is reproduced in the study assignments. Enter the following information concerning the case of Robert Michaels vs. Hart Home Builders on the office docket.

Client—Robert Michaels
Address—740 Kennedy Avenue, City.
Number—785
IN RE:—Robert Michaels
vs.
Hart Home Builders
Court—Hancock County District
Court File—No. 78349 1987
Calendar No.—456
Attorney for—Plaintiff
Nature of matter—Lawsuit

June 3 Fee for preparing case $500.
June 4 Retainer $100.
June 10 Suit fee $15.
June 22 Payment on account $200.
June 29 Balance due $215 is paid on this date.

Exercise 5-2. Refer to Exercise 5-1 and prepare the entries in general journal form that would be made in the cash receipts and cash payments journals for these transactions. Use the journal paper.

Exercise 5-3. Harold Watson, an attorney, has been engaged to collect a debt owed by Jean Wagner to the Adams Department Store. Watson's collection docket is reproduced in the study assignments. Enter the following information in the collection docket.

Debtor — Jean Wagner
Address — 7892 Columbus Avenue, City.
Creditor — Adams Department Store.
Address — Sixth and Central Avenues, City.
Date claim received — 10-14-87
No. 110
Date disposed of — 12-17-87
Total amount — $735
Amount collected — $735
Fee — $245
Amount remitted — $490
Check No. — 78, 82, 88

Received from creditor

DATE	FOR	AMOUNT
10-28	Com.	$66.67
11-13	Com.	$100.00
12-11	Com.	$78.33

Received from debtor

DATE	AMOUNT
10-28	$200
11-13	$300
12-11	$235

Paid to creditor

CHECK NO.	AMOUNT
78	$133.33
82	$200.00
88	$156.67

Remarks: Statement of account. Collection fee 33⅓%. No suit without further instructions.

Exercise 5-4. Refer to Exercise 5-3 and prepare the entries in general journal form that would be made in the cash receipts and cash payments journals. Use the journal paper.

Report No. 5-1

Complete Report No. 5-1 in the study assignments and submit your working papers to the instructor for approval.

MASTERY PROBLEMS

Problem 5-A Journalizing payroll taxes

The law firm of Hale and Tyler has 19 employees. The employees are paid by check on the 15th and last business day of each month. The entry to record each payroll includes the liabilities for the amounts withheld. The employer's payroll taxes are recorded on each payday. The social security and withheld income taxes exceed $3,000 on each payday, and it is therefore necessary for Hale and Tyler to deposit the taxes within three banking days of each payday. Thus the taxes for salaries paid on April 15 and April 30 must be paid within three banking days following April 15 and April 30.

Following is a narrative of the transactions completed during the month of April of the current year that relate to payrolls and payroll taxes.

April	1	Paid $4,273.23 for March 31 payroll taxes:		
		Employees' income tax withheld		$1,824.00
		FICA tax		2,449.23
	15	Payroll for the first half of month:		
		Total salaries		$16,574.46
		Less amounts withheld:		
		Employees' income tax	$1,881.00	
		FICA tax	1,243.08	3,124.08
		Net amount paid		$13,450.38
	15	Social security taxes imposed on employer:		
		FICA tax, 7.5%		
		State Unemployment tax, 2.5%		
		FUTA tax, 0.8%		
	30	Payroll for the second half of month:		
	30	Total salaries		$16,945.34
		Less amounts withheld:		
		Employees' income tax	$1,957.00	
		FICA tax	1,270.90	3,227.90
		Net amount paid		$13,717.44
	30	Social security taxes imposed on employer:		
		All salaries taxable; rates same as on April 15.		
	30	Paid first quarter state unemployment taxes, $2,513.99.		
	30	Paid first quarter FUTA tax, $804.48.		

***Required:* (1)** Journalize the foregoing transactions using the journal paper provided in the study assignments. **(2)** Foot the debit and credit columns as a means of proof.

Problem 5-B Journalizing; posting; trial balance

Anita Markham and Patricia Ferguson are partners engaged in the practice of law. They employ a secretary-bookkeeper and a secretary. The books, which are kept on the cash basis, consist of a cash receipts journal, a cash payments journal, a general journal, and a general ledger. The April 1 balances of the accounts have been entered in the general ledger.

Narrative of Transactions for April

April 1 Paid rent for April, $2,000. Check No. 845.

2 Paid the following bills:

Telephone bill, $178.23. Check No. 846.

Bill for electricity, $52.94. Check No. 847.

3 Received $2,000 from the U.S. Government. Ferguson acted as an expert witness before a government committee.

4 Paid garage bill for March, $162.30. Check No. 848.

6 Received $4,860 from Jason Silverstein for the balance due on Case No. 348.

7 Paid $1,256.85 for a legal size fireproof filing cabinet. Check No. 849.

9 Received $1,100 in connection with the incorporation of the Maloney Manufacturing Corporation.

13 Paid $863 for March payroll taxes:

Employees' income tax withheld	$398.00
FICA tax	465.00
	$863.00

Check No. 850.

15 Paid wages of employees for first half of the month as follows:

15 Darlene Johnson, $869.25, less income tax payable, $99, and FICA tax payable, $65.19. Check No. 851.

Robert Trenkamp, $750, less income tax payable, $110, and FICA tax payable, $56.25. Check No. 852.

17 Received $3,250 from D'Amico and Malinofski for balance due on Case No. 345.

18 Paid for additions to the law library, $782.48. Check No. 853.

21 Received $750 for participation in a financial planning conference for Ezra Solomon.

23 On March 12, Markham and Ferguson received $4,500 from Samuel Mullins as a deposit on a building Mullins wished to buy from Margaret Hoskins. The $4,500 was charged to Account No. 120, Clients' Trust Account. The transaction was completed today, April 23, and Mullins directed that the $4,500 be paid to Hoskins, Check No. 25. (Debit Liability for Trust Funds, Account No. 310, and credit Clients' Trust Account, Account No. 120, for $4,500.)

23 Received a fee of $1,500 from Mullins for legal work in connection with the above transaction. Case No. 350.

25 Received $162.50 for a law book purchased in March and received in damaged condition. (Law Library Expense, Account No. 715, had been debited for the amount of the invoice.)

28 Received $3,500 for work in connection with preparing a pension plan for the Griffin Manufacturing Company.

29 Paid state unemployment tax for the first quarter of the year, $251.10. Check No. 854.

30 Paid wages of employees for the second half of the month as follows:

Darlene Johnson, $800, less income tax payable, $89, and FICA tax payable, $60. Check No. 855.

30 Robert Trenkamp, $801.92, less income tax payable, $124, and FICA tax payable, $60.14. Check No. 856.

30 Markham withdrew $3,000 for personal use. Check No. 857.

April 30 Ferguson withdrew $3,000 for personal use. Check No. 858.

30 Replenished the petty cash fund. Check No. 859. The following payments had been made:

Anita Markham, Drawing	$35.00
Automobile Expense	10.50
Stationery and Supplies Expense	22.36
Total payments	$67.86

30 Made an entry in the general journal for the employer's portion of the FICA tax, for the state unemployment tax, and for the FUTA tax for the month of April by debiting Payroll Taxes Expense for $354.32 and crediting FICA Tax Payable for $241.58, State Unemployment Tax Payable for $86.97, and FUTA Tax Payable for $25.77.

***Required:* (1)** Record the transactions in the cash receipts journal, the cash payments journal, and the general journal provided in the study assignments. Foot, enter the totals, and rule the journals. **(2)** Post from these journals to the general ledger accounts in the study assignments. In posting from the cash receipts journal, the page number preceded by the letters "CR" should be inserted in the Posting Reference column of the ledger. In posting from the cash payments journal, the page number should be preceded by the letters "CP." In posting from the general journal, the page number should be preceded by the letters "GJ." **(3)** Determine and record the account balances where necessary. **(4)** Take a trial balance of the accounts that have balances using the paper provided in the study assignments.

EXPANDING YOUR BUSINESS VOCABULARY

What is the meaning of each of the following terms:

accumulated depreciation **(p. 123)**
auxiliary records **(p. 128)**
balance column account form **(p. 127)**
book value **(p. 123)**
business enterprises **(p. 121)**
cash basis of accounting **(p. 122)**
cash payments journal **(p. 126)**
cash receipts journal **(p. 126)**
collection docket **(p. 130)**
constructively received **(p. 122)**
contra accounts **(p. 123)**
defendant **(p. 121)**
depreciate **(p. 122)**
depreciation expense **(p. 122)**
general ledger **(p. 127)**
manufacturing enterprise **(p. 121)**
matching principle **(p. 122)**
mercantile enterprise **(p. 121)**
office docket **(p. 128)**
personal service enterprise **(p. 121)**
plaintiff **(p. 121)**
professional enterprises **(p. 121)**
time records **(p. 121)**
two-column general journal **(p. 127)**

APPENDIX
THE PROFESSIONAL CORPORATION

Organizing a Professional Corporation

In Chapter 5, Ortega's legal practice is operated as a sole proprietorship, but the practice could have been incorporated. The designation of the corporate practice will vary with the state in which the practice is conducted. In one state the name of the corporation might be Jose Ortega, P.S.C. The letters P.S.C. stand for Professional Service Corporation. If attorneys Michael Senora, Pauline Murphy, and John Hensley decided to form a corporation for the practice of law in another state, the firm might be known as Senora, Murphy, and Hensley Co., LPA. The letters LPA stand for Lawyers Professional Association.

In 1819 in the Dartmouth College case, John Marshall, then Chief Justice of the United States Supreme Court, described a corporation as follows:

"A corporation is an artificial being, invisible, intangible, and existing only in contemplation of law."

The definition draws attention to the fact that corporations possess legal entity which means that they are separate and distinct from their owners. All corporations operate under a grant of authority from a state or other political unit in the form of articles of incorporation. The articles of incorporation is the document prepared by the person or persons establishing a corporation in the United States and filed with state authorities. One copy, returned with a certificate of incorporation, becomes the corporate charter, and enables the corporation to function. In the United States, each of the states, territories, and possessions has its own general- or business-corporation act and also an act which permits some or all licensed professional persons to form professional associations or corporations.

In many states the form of the certificate of incorporation for a professional corporation is essentially the same as that required for a business corporation, but in other states specific forms are required for professional corporations. In all states, the articles of incorporation must spell out the corporation's purpose, and in most states a professional corporation can be created only for the purpose of conducting a specific professional practice. Usually, a law corporation cannot carry on an engineering practice, and a medical practice cannot operate an accounting practice. Most states require that a professional corporation be incorporated in the state in which it is to carry on its practice. A business corporation, however, may be incorporated under the laws of one state and operate exclusively in another state.

The articles of incorporation must indicate the location of the corporate office and must designate the corporate name which in professional corporations usually includes the name of one or more of the professionals involved.

In many states, the use of fictitious names by professional corporations is prohibited. Before the articles of incorporation are filed with the state, the corporate name should be checked, because the name must not be the same as the name used by any other business organization.

Another item that must be included in the articles of incorporation is the number of shares of capital stock that the corporation is authorized to issue. Ownership of a corporation is represented by shares of capital stock each share of which might be assigned a par value such as $100 or there might be no par value at the time the corporation is formed. Authorization of more shares than will be issued immediately upon formation of the corporation may be requested. The unissued shares can be held in the corporate treasury for future use.

A small corporation with one or two or three stockholders does not need a board of directors, but the articles of incorporation of a large medical practice, for example, should provide that a board of directors is to be responsible for the management of the affairs of the corporation. The board of directors is a group of persons elected by the stockholders to determine corporate policies and select the officers who will manage the corporation.

In some states cumulative voting by the stockholders for directors of the corporation is mandatory and even if it is not required, it may be provided for in the articles of incorporation. Under cumulative voting, a stockholder is permitted to cast all of his or her votes for a single director. For example, if a stockholder has 100 shares of stock and there are seven directors to be elected, he or she can cast 700 votes for just one director. An advantage of cumulative voting is that it may enable a minority stockholder to elect a director. A minority stockholder is one who owns less than a majority of the number of shares of stock of the corporation.

The articles of incorporation should list the basic powers of the corporation. Among those usually stated are that the corporation will have the power to conduct its business or practice and carry on its operations; to elect or appoint officers and fix compensation; to sue and be sued; and to make and alter bylaws.

A professional corporation may have bylaws, but they may not be required by state law. The authority to adopt or amend bylaws may be given to the board of directors by the certificate of incorporation. In other cases, the bylaws must be adopted or amended by the stockholders.

The purpose of bylaws is to provide details concerning how the practice is to be operated. Some items such as the location of the principal office will be included in both the articles of incorporation and in the bylaws but such items as the date and location of the annual stockholders' meeting will be found only in the bylaws. The bylaws should identify the officers of the corporation and state their qualifications. If the corporation consists of only one person, he or she may serve as the president and treasurer of the corporation.

A small corporation having more than one stockholder may need only a president, secretary, and treasurer. A larger corporation may have a chairman of the board of directors, one or more vice presidents, a recording secretary, a controller, and an attorney who serves as general counsel.

The certificate of incorporation which has been approved by the state granting it is a matter of public record, and if it later becomes necessary to change the certificate, approval must be given by the state. The bylaws of the corporation are private records and any of the details in them can be changed or repealed through the use of a procedure usually stated in the bylaws themselves.

Characteristics of the Corporate Form of Organization

Some of the characteristics of the corporate form of organization are described in the following paragraphs.

Limited Liability of Owners. The owners of a corporation invest in the corporation by purchasing shares of stock. The stockholders cannot be compelled to contribute additional capital to the corporation if the stock is fully paid for at the time of issuance. The stockholders have no personal liability for the debts of the corporation. A sole proprietor such as Jose Ortega has unlimited personal liability for the debts of his legal practice.

Transferable Ownership Units. In a business corporation any stockholder can usually transfer stock to another person or company without the knowledge or the consent of the other stockholders and without disturbing the normal activities of the corporation. In most states, however, trading of the capital stock of a professional corporation is strictly limited. The limitations are necessary to permit the stockholders to control their future associates and to insure that no stockholder will sell his or her stock to an individual who is not a licensed member of the profession. An engineer or a certified public accountant, for example, would not be permitted to buy the capital stock of the firm incorporated as Senora, Murphy, and Hensley Co., LPA.

Unlimited Life. Most corporations are chartered either with a perpetual life or with provision for renewal if the charter specifies a limit, irrespective of the deaths of any stockholders or disposal of their stock. In some states, the duration of a professional corporation is limited; in others the duration may be perpetual. If the duration of the corporation is to be perpetual, this should be stated in the articles of incorporation.

Suitability for Large Scale Operations. Certain businesses such as large manufacturing companies must be operated on a large scale. The corporate form of organization makes it possible to secure substantial amounts of capital through the sale of stock. Large numbers of investors in the stock of corporations provide much of the capital required for their operation. The corporate form of organization is also suitable in many cases for persons who desire to form professional corporations.

Access to Stockholder and Employee Fringe Benefits. Some of the benefits that a professional person or persons may obtain by incorporating are being able to obtain group term life insurance, health and accident insurance, wage continuation, and medical reimbursement plans.

Taxation of Corporate Earnings. With regard to income taxes, there are advantages and disadvantages in the corporate form of organization. Corporations must pay income taxes on their earnings, and the individual stockholders of corporations are subject to personal income tax on the dividends they receive from their companies. A dividend is usually paid in cash and, in most cases, represents taxable income. A tax advantage of a corporation is that dividends do not have to be declared and paid and the earnings may be allowed to accumulate in the corporation within certain limits. Sole proprietorships and partnerships, as such, do not pay income taxes. Instead, the owner or partner reports his or her share of the net income or the net loss from the business or practice in his or her personal income tax return.

Lack of the Drawing Account. In accounting for a sole proprietorship the owner has both a capital account and a drawing account. In lieu of a salary paid by the enterprise, the owner can withdraw funds from the business or practice at will. Since the corporation is a legal entity separate from the owner or owners, professional persons who incorporate their practices become employees of the corporation. They are paid salaries that are subject to all the payroll taxes to which an employee who is not a stockholder is subject. If a professional person wishes to withdraw funds from the practice in excess of his or her salary, the transaction would have to be either in the form of a loan or of a sale of all or a part of the individual's stock in the practice. The sale of the stock in a professional corporation would be subject to the legal requirements of the state in which the corporation is located.

Government Regulation. A further disadvantage of the corporate form of organization is the restriction of freedom to act. Federal, state, and local governments may restrict the corporation's ownership of real property, the purchase of its own stock, and the excessive retention of its earnings.

The following paragraphs are presented to illustrate the accounting for a firm of three attorneys who have chosen to operate their practice as a professional corporation.

Attorneys Michael Senora, Pauline Murphy, and John Hensley combined their individual practices and applied for a certificate of incorporation. The certificate was received from the state on January 6, 1986, and permits them to practice law as a professional corporation to be known as Senora, Murphy, and Hensley Co., LPA. At a meeting on January 6, 1986, it was agreed that Michael Senora would be president of the corporation; Pauline Murphy would be the treasurer; and John Hensley would be the secretary. The fiscal year will be the calendar year. The firm will operate on the cash basis of accounting with the following exceptions. Property or service received in lieu of cash will be recorded at the fair market value of the property or service at the time it is received. Revenue constructively received will be reported as revenue in the period in which it is earned even though no cash is withdrawn from the account, and long-term assets will be depreciated.

The authorized capital stock of the firm on January 6, 1986, consists of 3,000 shares with a value of $25 each for a total of $75,000. The following number of shares have been issued to the incorporators:

Michael Senora	1,000 shares at $25 =	$25,000
Pauline Murphy	800 shares at $25 =	20,000
John Hensley	700 shares at $25 =	17,500
	2,500	$62,500

The remaining 500 shares are unissued and do not appear in the firm's accounts.

Accounts used only in a corporation are discussed in the following paragraphs.

Dividends Payable, Account No. 300. Earnings of a corporation are transmitted to the stockholders through the declaration of dividends. The declaration must state the amount of dividend per share to be paid. Payment may be made immediately upon declaration, or it may be deferred until a later date. When the payment is deferred, a current liability called Dividends Payable is created.

Corporation Income Tax Payable, Account No. 310. If a corporation operates at a profit, it must pay a tax on its earnings. Unpaid corporation income taxes are a liability of the corporation.

Common Stock, Account No. 500. All corporations operated for profit have capital stock. If there is only one class of stock, it is called common. Note that even though there are three stockholders in the firm of Senora, Murphy, and Hensley Co., LPA, there is only one common stock account. The firm keeps a subsidiary ledger which contains an account for each stockholder in number of shares only. Michael Senora's account is shown on page 160.

Retained Earnings, Account No. 510. At the end of the fiscal year, the earnings of the corporation are determined and credited in the retained earnings account. When dividends are declared, the retained earnings account is debited. The account is also debited for a net loss.

Income Tax Expense, Account No. 700. The 1981 Economic Recovery Tax Act requires that corporations make quarterly estimated tax payments totaling at least 80 percent of the tax due for the year or face penalties for underpayments. Senora, Murphy, and Hensley Co., LPA, has estimated the 1987 earnings and has paid three-fourths of the amount prior to December 1, 1987.

Following is a narrative of selected transactions completed by Senora, Murphy, and Hensley Co., LPA, during the months of January 1986 and March 1987. These transactions are recorded in the cash receipts journal, the cash payments journal, and the general journal on pages 162–164.

STOCKHOLDERS LEDGER

STOCKHOLDER Michael Senora

ADDRESS 875 Misty Creek Drive, City

DATE		CERTIFICATE NOS.		RECEIVED FROM	TRANSFERRED TO	NO. OF SHARES	BALANCE
		OLD	NEW				
1986 Jan.	6		1	Original Issue		1,000	1,000

Stockholder's Ledger

SENORA, MURPHY, AND HENSLEY CO., LPA

Narrative of Transactions

Monday, January 6, 1986

Received cash from the incorporators as follows: Michael Senora, $25,000; Pauline Murphy, $20,000; John Hensley, $17,500.

The transaction was recorded in the cash receipts journal by debiting Cash, Account No. 100, for $62,500 and crediting Common Stock, Account No. 500, for $62,500.

Monday, March 2, 1987

The firm voted to pay a cash dividend of $5 per share to be paid on March 25 to stockholders of record on March 16.

The entry was recorded in the general journal by debiting Retained Earnings, Account No. 510, for $12,500 and crediting Dividends Payable, Account No. 310, for $12,500. There are 2,500 shares in the hands of the stockholders and 2,500 × $5 = $12,500. The record date, March 16, means that the dividend will be paid to the persons who own the stock on that date. Dividends may also be paid on the date of declaration.

Wednesday, March 25, 1987

Issued the following checks in payment of the dividend declared on March 2:

No. 726 for $5,000 to Michael Senora (1,000 shares × $5).
No. 727 for $4,000 to Pauline Murphy (800 shares × $5).
No. 728 for $3,500 to John Hensley (700 shares × $5).

The checks were recorded in the cash payments journal by debiting Dividends Payable, Account No. 310, and crediting Cash, Account No. 100.

Friday, March 27, 1987

Received $2,500 from Michael Senora for the purchase of 100 of the 500 shares of unissued stock at $25 a share.

This transaction was recorded in the cash receipts journal by debiting Cash, Account No. 100, for $2,500 and by crediting Common Stock, Account No. 500, for $2,500. One hundred shares was entered in Senora's account in the stockholders' ledger.

Tuesday, March 31, 1987

Issued the following checks in payment of the salaries for the month of March:

No. 729 for $1,232.00 to Janice Costello in the amount of $1,600.00 less $248.00 withheld for income tax and $120.00 withheld for FICA tax.

No. 730 for $1,231.50 to Gertrude Zerhusen in the amount of $1,500.00 less $156.00 withheld for income tax and $112.50 withheld for FICA tax.

No. 731 for $1,000.00 to Lawrence Spencer in the amount of $1,200.00 less $110.00 withheld for income tax and $90.00 withheld for FICA tax.

No. 732 for $1,963.50 to Michael Senora in the amount of $2,500.00 less $349.00 withheld for income tax and $187.50 withheld for FICA tax.

No. 733 for $1,735.00 to Pauline Murphy in the amount of $2,200.00 less $300.00 withheld for income tax and $165.00 withheld for FICA tax.

No. 734 for $1,847.50 to John Hensley, in the amount of $2,300.00 less $280.00 withheld for income tax and $172.50 withheld for FICA tax.

CASH RECEIPTS JOURNAL PAGE 1

	DATE		DESCRIPTION	POST. REF.	GENERAL CR.	REVENUE LEGAL FEES CR.	REVENUE COLL. FEES CR.	LIAB. FOR TRUST FUNDS CR.	CLIENTS' TRUST ACCT. DR.	CASH DR.	
1	1986 Jan.	6	Common Stock	500	6250000					6250000	1
2											2
3											3

CASH RECEIPTS JOURNAL PAGE 15

	DATE		DESCRIPTION	POST. REF.	GENERAL CR.	REVENUE LEGAL FEES CR.	REVENUE COLL. FEES CR.	LIAB. FOR TRUST FUNDS CR.	CLIENTS' TRUST ACCT. DR.	CASH DR.	
1	1987 Mar.	27	Common Stock	500	250000					250000	1
2											2
3											3

Senora, Murphy, and Hensley — Cash Receipts Journals

CASH PAYMENTS JOURNAL PAGE 30

DATE	DESCRIPTION	POST. REF.	GENERAL DR.	LIAB. FOR TRUST FUNDS DR.	SALARY EXPENSE DR.	EMP. INC. TAX PAY. CR.	FICA TAX PAY. CR.	CK. NO.	CLIENTS' TRUST ACCT. CR.	CK. NO.	CASH CR.
1987 Mar. 25	Dividends Payable	310	500000							726	500000
25	Dividends Payable	310	400000							727	400000
25	Dividends Payable	310	350000							728	350000
31	Janice Costello	✓			160000	24800	12000			729	123200
31	Gertrude Zerhusen	✓			150000	15600	11250			730	123150
31	Lawrence Spencer	✓			120000	11000	9000			731	100000
31	Michael Senora	✓			250000	34900	18750			732	196350
31	Pauline Murphy	✓			220000	30000	16500			733	173500
31	John Hensley	✓			230000	28000	17250			734	184750
			1250000		1130000	144300	84750				2150950
			(✓)		(700)	(320)	(330)				(100)

Senora, Murphy, and Hensley — Cash Payments Journals

JOURNAL PAGE 15

DATE		DESCRIPTION	POST. REF.	DEBIT	CREDIT
1987 Mar.	2	Retained Earnings	510	1250000	
		Dividends Payable	310		1250000
		Declared dividends of $5 per share to stockholders of record on March 16, 1987. The dividend is to be paid on March 25, 1987.			

Senora, Murphy, and Hensley—General Journal

ACCOUNT Cash ACCOUNT NO. 100

DATE		ITEM	POST. REF.	DEBIT	CREDIT	BALANCE DEBIT	BALANCE CREDIT
1986 Jan.	6		CR1	6250000		6250000	
1987 Mar.	1	Balance	✓			6474285	
	27		CR15	250000			
	31		CP30		2150950	4573335	

ACCOUNT Dividends Payable ACCOUNT NO. 310

DATE		ITEM	POST. REF.	DEBIT	CREDIT	BALANCE DEBIT	BALANCE CREDIT
1987 Mar.	2		GJ15		1250000		1250000
	25		CP30	500000			
	25		CP30	400000			
	25		CP30	350000			- 0 -

General Ledger Accounts *(continued)*

ACCOUNT *Employees' Income Tax Payable* ACCOUNT NO. 320

DATE		ITEM	POST. REF.	DEBIT	CREDIT	BALANCE DEBIT	BALANCE CREDIT
1987 Mar.	31		CP30		144300		144300

ACCOUNT FICA *Tax Payable* ACCOUNT NO. 330

DATE		ITEM	POST. REF.	DEBIT	CREDIT	BALANCE DEBIT	BALANCE CREDIT
1987 Mar.	31		CP30		84750		84750

ACCOUNT *Common Stock* ACCOUNT NO. 500

DATE		ITEM	POST. REF.	DEBIT	CREDIT	BALANCE DEBIT	BALANCE CREDIT
1986 Jan.	6		CR1		6250000		6250000
1987 Mar.	27		CR15		250000		6500000

ACCOUNT *Retained Earnings* ACCOUNT NO. 510

DATE		ITEM	POST. REF.	DEBIT	CREDIT	BALANCE DEBIT	BALANCE CREDIT
1987 Mar.	1	Balance	✓				3042689
	2		GJ15	1250000			1792689

ACCOUNT *Salary Expense* ACCOUNT NO. 700

DATE		ITEM	POST. REF.	DEBIT	CREDIT	BALANCE DEBIT	BALANCE CREDIT
1987 Mar.	31		CP30	1130000		1130000	

General Ledger Accounts *(concluded)*

CHALLENGE PROBLEM 5

On May 1, 1986, Sylvia Murray and Karl Schadler received a certificate of incorporation for their individual law practices. The new firm will be known as Murray and Schadler, P.S.C. Jennifer Turner and Carol Chen have been hired as a secretary-bookkeeper and a secretary respectively. The records will be kept on the cash basis, and will consist of a cash receipts journal, a cash payments journal, a general journal, and a general ledger.

The corporation has been authorized to issue 1,500 shares of common capital stock with a value of $50 per share. The incorporators hold the following number of shares:

Sylvia Murray	500 shares at $50 =	$25,000
Karl Schadler	500 shares at $50 =	$25,000
Total	1,000	$50,000

The following selected transactions were completed during the month of June, 1987. The June 1 balances of the accounts have been entered in the general ledger in the study assignments.

June 1 Issued Check No. 321 for $2,000 to the Star Realty Company for rent of office for the month of June.

2 Issued Check No. 32 for $1,750 to the Carlisle Manufacturing Company to remit a collection from the Jarvis Tool Company in the amount of $2,500 less a 30% collection fee. Collection No. 26.

4 Purchased office supplies for cash, $113.56. Check No. 322.

4 Declared a dividend of $10 a share to be paid to the stockholders on this date. Issued Check No. 323 for $5,000 ($10 × 500 shares) to Sylvia Murray. Issued Check No. 324 for $5,000 ($10 × 500 shares) to Karl Schadler.

Debit Retained Earnings, Account No. 515, for $5,000 and credit Cash, Account No. 110, for $5,000 for each check. Since the dividends are being paid on the date of declaration, it is not necessary to credit Dividends Payable when Retained Earnings is debited.

8 Received a check for $20,000 from the Doherty Sales Co. in full payment of the balance due for legal fees. Case No. 37.

10 Issued Check No. 325 for $1,312.50 in payment of an invoice received from the Central Publishing Co. for law books.

11 The firm has been engaged to represent the Carson Heating Co. against Donald Hauck. Received retainer, $200. Case No. 46.

11 Received a check for $250 for drafting a partnership agreement for Dalton and Horwitz, certified public accountants.

12 Issued Check No. 326 for $67.28 to the City Service Co. for electricity consumed during the month of May.

12 Issued Check No. 327 in the amount of $2,212 to the Southern Hills National Bank in payment of the following payroll taxes on wages paid during the month of May:

Employees' income tax withheld from wages......		**$1,087.00**
FICA tax:		
Withheld from employees' wages	**$562.50**	
Imposed on employer	**562.50**	**1,125.00**
Amount of check		**$2,212.00**

June 15 Nancy Whitmore, an attorney, invested $10,000 in the firm of Murray and Schadler by purchasing 200 of the unissued shares of common stock at $50 a share. Whitmore will begin work with the firm on July 1. (It would be possible to change the name of the firm to include Whitmore's name, but it is not necessary to do so.)

17 Work has been completed on the settlement of the estate of Daniel LaRosa, deceased, and a check for $8,000 in payment for services rendered has been received. Case No. 40.

19 Paid the State Bar Association for annual dues for the members of the firm, $300. Check No. 328.

25 Received a check for $1,800 from Heather Clark in payment of the amount due on Collection No. 24.

The collection docket shows that the firm had agreed to handle this collection on a 33⅓% commission basis.

30 Issued the following salary checks for the month of June:

No. 329 for $1,209.53 to Jennifer Turner in payment of salary $1,564.90 less $238.00 withheld for income tax and $117.37 withheld for FICA tax.

No. 330 for $1,101.12 to Carol Chen in payment of salary, $1,345.00 less $143.00 withheld for income tax and $100.88 withheld for FICA tax.

No. 331 for $1,843.50 in payment of salary, $2,500.00, less $469.00 withheld for income tax and $187.50 withheld for FICA tax.

No. 332 for $1,773.00 to Karl Schadler in payment of salary, $2,200.00, less $262.00 withheld for income tax and $165.00 withheld for FICA tax.

30 Made an entry in the general journal for the employer's portion of the FICA tax for the month of June by debiting Payroll Taxes Expense and crediting FICA Tax Payable for $570.75.

30 Made an entry in the general journal by debiting Payroll Taxes Expense for $17.50 and crediting FUTA Tax Payable for $4.00 and crediting State Unemployment Tax Payable for $13.50.

The FUTA tax is figured at 0.8% of salaries earned up to $7,000 in a year. By the end of May, all of the salaries had exceeded $7,000 except the salary of Carol Chen. Chen's taxable wages for the FUTA tax in June are $500.

The state unemployment tax is figured at 2.7% of the first $7,000 of wages earned during the year, or $13.50 for June.

Required: **(1)** Record the transactions in the cash receipts journal, the cash payments journal, and the general journal in the study assignments. Foot, enter the totals, and rule the journals. **(2)** Post the summary columns and the General columns from the journals to the ledger accounts in the study assignments. In posting from the cash receipts journal, the page number preceded by the letters "CR" should be inserted in the Posting Reference column of the ledger. In posting from the cash payments journal, the posting reference should be the page number preceded by the letters "CP". In posting from the general journal, the posting reference should be the page number preceded by the letters "GJ". **(3)** Determine and record the account balances where necessary. **(4)** Take a trial balance as of June 30 using the paper provided in the study assignments.

6

ACCOUNTING FOR PERSONAL SERVICE (PHYSICIANS AND DENTISTS)

CHAPTER OBJECTIVES

Careful study of this chapter should enable you to:

- Define terms used in accounting for a physician or dentist who uses the cash basis of accounting.
- Understand the special characteristics of accounting for physicians and dentists.
- Perform the tasks involved in accounting for physicians and dentists.
- Be familiar with other accounting systems used in accounting for physicians and dentists.

Accounting for the medical and dental professions has much in common with the accounting for attorneys that was illustrated in Chapter 5. Indeed, there are many similarities in accounting for any type of personal service, whether professional or business. Each type of service, however, tends to have its own special requirements. Some of the items characteristic of accounting for physicians and dentists will be explained in this chapter.

As with attorneys, the most valuable assets the physician or dentist has are time and expertise in the profession. An auxiliary record that serves as a daily log of services performed, charges made, and payments received is used to summarize the time spent with each patient. This auxiliary record is called a **daily service record** or a **day sheet**. The daily service record, which provides data for cash receipts journal entries, will be explained in detail on page 174.

This chapter illustrates the basic system of accounting for cash receipts and payments for the medical and dental professions. Special journals similar to those illustrated in Chapter 5 are used. The one-write system for recording cash receipts and cash payments for a dental office as well as computerized systems are explained in the Appendix.

THE CASH BASIS OF ACCOUNTING FOR PHYSICIANS AND DENTISTS

Most physicians and dentists use a modified cash basis of accounting similar to that used by attorneys. With the **pure cash basis** of accounting, income is not recognized until cash is received and expenses are not entered until they are actually paid. For example, the revenue for services performed in one month may not be collected immediately and, thus, would not be accounted for until actually received in a later month. Similarly, expenses incurred in one month may not be paid until the following month or perhaps several months later. These expenses would not be recognized until they were paid.

Under the modified cash basis, some exceptions are allowed to the pure cash basis of accounting. For example, depreciation expense for plant assets is recognized for the useful life of the asset, prepaid expenses are allocated to the accounting periods in which they provide benefit, and some long-term and payroll-related liabilities are recognized when incurred. A cash basis of accounting that incorporates these exceptions is referred to as **modified cash basis** and is acceptable for use by personal service companies such as medical and dental practices.

BASIC SYSTEM OF ACCOUNTING

To illustrate some of the characteristics of accounting for the medical and dental professions, a basic system of accounting for Angeline Weinberg and Lael Himmo, Physicians and Surgeons, is presented.

Chart of Accounts

The chart of accounts, which is similar to those presented in previous chapters, appears on page 171. Asset accounts have numbers which begin with 1 and 2; liability accounts begin with 3; owner's equity accounts begin with 5; revenue accounts begin with 6; and expense accounts begin with 7. If new accounts are needed, they may be added to the appropriate category without disturbing the numerical order of the existing accounts.

Most of the accounts shown in the chart of accounts for Weinberg and Himmo have been explained and illustrated in previous chapters. New accounts that will be used in this chapter are discussed in the following paragraphs.

Prepaid Insurance, Account No. 115; Insurance Expense, Account No. 710. The balance in the prepaid insurance account represents premiums paid in advance for such items as automobile insurance, fire and casualty insurance on the equipment, and medical liability insurance. Prepaid insurance is an asset that is a prepaid expense similar to equipment items. With the passage of time the premiums expire and this asset gradually becomes an expense. Accounts that represent both an asset and an expense, such as Prepaid Insurance, are referred to as **mixed accounts**. Just as an adjustment is needed to allocate the cost of the equipment over the time benefited, an adjustment is necessary to transfer the expired premiums to the insurance Expense account.

Professional Fees, Account No. 600. Weinberg and Himmo use only one general ledger revenue account, Professional Fees, in which all fees from professional services are entered. The Daily Service Record for Weinberg and Himmo is shown on page 175 and includes several special columns. Office Visits and Surgery are used to identify the type of service performed by the doctors. Separate revenue accounts could be kept for each doctor, and each type of service rendered could also be entered in separate revenue accounts. For example, Office Visits might be assigned the number 601, Surgery the number 602, and Laboratory Work the number 603. In the dental profession, a dentist might use only one account in which all professional fees are entered or separate accounts for diagnostic, preparative, reconstructive, restoration, preventive, and other types of services rendered to patients could be used.

Other Income, Account Number 610. Weinberg and Himmo have leased the entire office building in which their practice is located. This will enable them to expand their practice in the future and remain in the same location. Terms of their lease permit them to sublease unused office space to other professionals until the space is needed by Weinberg and Himmo. They currently sublease to John Williams, an optometrist, Eleanor Delwood, an electrologist, Buddy Glasen, a chiropractor, and Robert Able, a pharmacist and owner of Able Pharmacy. Other sources of income in addition to the rent income include interest on the checking account and miscellaneous income from such activities as speaking engagements. All sources of income other than that from professional fees are credited to the other income account.

Medical Library Expense, Account No. 715. Depending upon the needs of the doctor, most medical and dental offices maintain some kind of medical library for reference. The number of reference books a professional person may have in a personal library will vary according to the doctor's needs. For example, if a nearby hospital has a complete reference library to which doctors have access, only a limited number of references would need to be kept in a personal library. On the other hand, if such resources are not readily accessible, the doctor would need to maintain an extensive library. In the illus-

WEINBERG AND HIMMO, PHYSICIANS AND SURGEONS

CHART OF ACCOUNTS

Assets*
- 100 Cash
- 110 Petty Cash Fund
- 115 Prepaid Insurance
- 200 Automobiles
- 205 Accumulated Depreciation—Automobiles
- 210 Laboratory Equipment
- 215 Accumulated Depreciation—Laboratory Equipment
- 220 Medical Equipment
- 225 Accumulated Depreciation—Medical Equipment
- 230 Office Equipment
- 235 Accumulated Depreciation—Office Equipment

Liabilities
- 310 Employees Income Tax Payable
- 320 FICA Tax Payable
- 330 FUTA Tax Payable
- 340 State Unemployment Tax Payable

Owner's Equity
- 500 Angeline Weinberg, Capital
- 510 Angeline Weinberg, Drawing
- 520 Lael Himmo, Capital
- 530 Lael Himmo, Drawing
- 540 Expense and Revenue Summary

Revenues
- 600 Professional Fees
- 610 Other Income

Expenses
- 700 Automobile Expense
- 703 Charitable Contributions Expense
- 705 Depreciation Expense
- 706 Dues and Subscriptions Expense
- 708 Electricity Expense
- 710 Insurance Expense
- 712 Laundry Expense
- 713 Legal Expense
- 715 Medical Library Expense
- 716 Medical Supplies Expense
- 717 Miscellaneous Expense
- 719 Office Supplies Expense
- 720 Payroll Taxes Expense
- 722 Postage Expense
- 725 Rent Expense
- 727 Repairs and Maintenance Expense
- 729 Salary Expense
- 730 Surgical Instruments Expense
- 732 Surgical Supplies Expense
- 735 Telephone Expense
- 738 Traveling and Meetings Expense

*Words in bold type represent headings and not account titles.

tration for Weinberg and Himmo, medical reference books are charged to the medical library expense account when payment is made.

Medical Supplies Expense, Account No. 716; Surgical Instruments Expense, Account No. 730; Surgical Supplies Expense, Account No. 732. Because of the frequent need to be restocked or replaced, medical supplies and instruments are charged to these expense accounts when payment is made.

Other expense accounts introduced in this chapter and their uses include **Dues and Subscriptions Expense, Account No. 706** (for dues paid to professional organizations and for subscriptions to trade journals and office magazines); Laundry Expense, Account No. 712 (for medical gowns, sheets, towels, etc.); Legal Expense, Account No. 713 (for professional legal advice, collection of patients accounts, and other services); Postage Expense, Account No. 722 (for mailing monthly statements, insurance claims, and other outgoing mail); and Repairs and Maintenance Expense, Account No. 727 (for repairs and maintenance of the automobiles, equipment, and building).

Books of Account

The illustration for Weinberg and Himmo uses the following books of account:

1. General books
   (a) Cash receipts journal
   (b) Cash payments journal
   (c) General journal
   (d) General ledger
2. Auxiliary records
   (a) Petty cash payments record
   (b) Daily service record
   (c) Patients ledger
   (d) Employee's earnings record
   (e) Checkbook

Three books of original entry—cash receipts journal, cash payments journal, and general journal—and a general ledger are used by Weinberg and Himmo.

Cash Receipts Journal. A cash receipts journal is used as the book of original entry for all cash that is received by the business. The cash receipts journal, reproduced on page 189, contains two credit columns and two debit columns to the right of the Date and Account Debited columns. The column headings for amounts are as follows:

1. Other Income 610 Cr.
2. Professional Fees 600 Cr.
3. General Dr.
4. Cash 100 Dr.

Every entry in the cash receipts journal includes:

1. Date of the cash receipt
2. Account and amount to be debited if the General Dr. column is used
3. Amounts to be credited if the special columns are used
4. Amount of the cash receipt, entered in the Cash Dr. column

Posting from this journal includes summary and individual posting. The General and special columns for Cash, Other Income, and Professional Fees are totaled at the end of the month, or sooner if desired. Special columns are posted in summary. This **summary posting** requires one debit entry to be posted to the Cash account, one credit entry to be posted to the Other Income account and one credit entry to be posted to the Professional Fees account in the general ledger. Account numbers are written in parentheses below the column totals to indicate that the totals have been posted to the general ledger. Each time the General Dr. column is used to enter a transaction, the Account Debited column must include the account title to which the amount is to be debited. Account numbers identifying these individual accounts are entered in the Post Reference column of the cash receipts journal, and **individual posting** of each of these amounts is made in the appropriate account in the general ledger. To indicate that the total of the General Dr. column is not posted, a check mark (✔) is written in parentheses below the total. As a proof of the journal, the total of the two debit columns must equal the total of the two credit columns.

Cash Payments Journal. The cash payments journal is used as the book of original entry for all payments of cash. The cash payments journal used by Weinberg and Himmo is shown on pages 190–191. It contains two debit columns and three credit columns to the right of the Date, Check Number, and Account Debited columns. The column headings for amounts are as follows:

1. Debits
   - **(a)** General Dr.
   - **(b)** Salary Expense 729 Dr.
2. Credits
   - **(a)** Employees Income Tax Payable 310 Cr.
   - **(b)** FICA Tax Payable 320 Cr.
   - **(c)** Cash 100 Cr.

Every entry in the cash payments journal includes:

1. Date and check number of the cash payment
2. Account and amount to be debited if the General Dr. column is used
3. Amounts to be debited and/or credited if the special columns are used
4. Amount of the cash payment, entered in the Cash Cr. column

Summary and individual posting from this journal is similar to that from the cash receipts journal.

General Journal. The third book of original entry used by Weinberg and Himmo is the two-column general journal. All transactions which cannot be entered in the cash receipts journal or the cash payments journal are entered in the general journal. Posting from the general journal is done individually to the general ledger.

Advantages of using special journals to enter business transactions were presented and discussed in Chapter 5. Generally these journals assist with internal control, provide for division of labor, improve accuracy, and save time.

General Ledger. Weinberg and Himmo use a **balance-column** or **four-column-account** form for the general ledger accounts. The ledger is reproduced on pages 192–201. In each account, the balance as of February 1 has been entered. The accounts in the general ledger are arranged in the order listed in the chart of accounts on page 171. Posting to the general ledger is from the cash receipts journal, cash payments journal, and general journal. The posting references used are CR for cash receipts journal, CP for cash payments journal, and GJ for general journal. The trial balance as of February 28 appears on page 202.

Auxiliary Records. To enter information not entered in the journals and ledger, auxiliary records are used. Weinberg and Himmo use a petty cash payments record, daily service record, patients ledger, employees' earnings record, and checkbook as auxiliary records. The employee's earnings record kept for each employee is similar to the one illustrated in Chapter 4 on pages 102 and 103 and is not shown in this chapter.

Petty Cash Payments Record. Weinberg and Himmo maintain a petty cash fund of $100. The petty cash payments record, not shown in this chapter, is similar to that illustrated in Chapter 3 on pages 64 and 65.

Daily Service Record. A portion of the daily service record is illustrated on page 175. Note that the daily service record is not set up as a double-entry record where debit entries equal the credit entries. Nothing offsets the Payments column under Patients' Accounts, but the total of the Office Visits and Surgery columns must equal the total of the Patients' Charges and the Cash Services columns. This proof of the Daily Service Record can be done daily, weekly, or monthly, depending upon the volume of transactions. The February proof for the end of the month is shown below:

Office Visits..........	$ 3,045	Patients' Accounts Charges..........	$38,100
Surgery..............	37,535	Cash Services...........................	2,480
	$40,580		$40,580

Each entry in the appropriate Kinds of Services column must also be entered in either the Patients' Accounts Charges or the Cash Services column. This information is posted to the appropriate patient's account in the patients ledger as explained in the next paragraph. A daily or weekly bank deposit is made, and the total cash received is entered in the cash receipts journal by debiting Cash and crediting Professional Fees. The flowchart on page 176 summarizes the flow of accounting data through the Daily Service Record.

DAILY SERVICE RECORD FOR MONTH OF FEBRUARY 19--

Day	Name of Patient	KINDS OF SERVICES				PATIENTS' ACCOUNTS				Cash Services	
		Office Visits		Surgery		Charges		Payments			
1	Angela Humphrey			1,175	00	1,175	00				
1	Chris Brennan	35	00							35	00
1	Carl Lomax	30	00							30	00
1	Larry Reeves			1,800	00	1,800	00				
1	Dalton Jones	40	00			40	00				
1	Blue Shield—C. Falco							1,800	00		
1	Jerry Ingram			750	00	750	00				
1	Pamela Knight	30	00							30	00
1	Larry Locke	35	00							35	00
1	Winnie Maas	40	00							40	00
2	Robert Lyons			1,350	00	1,350	00				
2	Jay Natalie			825	00	825	00				
2	Mary James	40	00							40	00
2	Mark Johnson			500	00	500	00				
2	Frank Lyssy	35	00							35	00
2	Gregg Schuler	30	00							30	00
2	Thomas Scillian	40	00							40	00
2	Lois Lennox			1,500	00	1,500	00				
3	Robert Magee	30	00							30	00
3	Medicare—A. Latimer							2,900	00		
3	James Woolsey	35	00							35	00
3	Prudential—F. Woos							1,585	00		
3	Jim Young							650	00		
3	Eva Zuniga			300	00	300	00				
3	James Yates	40	00							40	00
3	Stanley Biers							500	00		
3	Robert Bridges	35	00			35	00				
3	Mack Dickey	30	00			30	00				
4	Glenn Ecord			1,200	00	1,200	00				
4	Champus—B. Easterly							2,435	00		
4	Kenneth Foley	35	00							35	00
4	Jennifer Gibbons			200	00	200	00				
28	Jaime Garza	40	00							40	00
28	MONY—Norma Kamp							2,200	00		
28	Kelly Madrid			170	00	170	00				
28	Bonnie McKenney			90	00	90	00				
	Totals	3,045	00	37,535	00	38,100	00	36,014	00	2,480	00

Daily Service Record for Month of February

Patients Ledger. The patients' accounts are kept on ledger cards and collectively they are known as the patients' ledger. The patients ledger is generally not in a bound book but is kept as loose cards. This permits using a copying machine to reproduce the accounts with outstanding balances. The copies are then mailed as monthly statements. Having the accounts on loose cards also allows new accounts to be inserted and the ledger continually kept in alphabetical order. Charges and payments from the daily service record are usually posted daily or weekly to the patients' accounts. Information in the

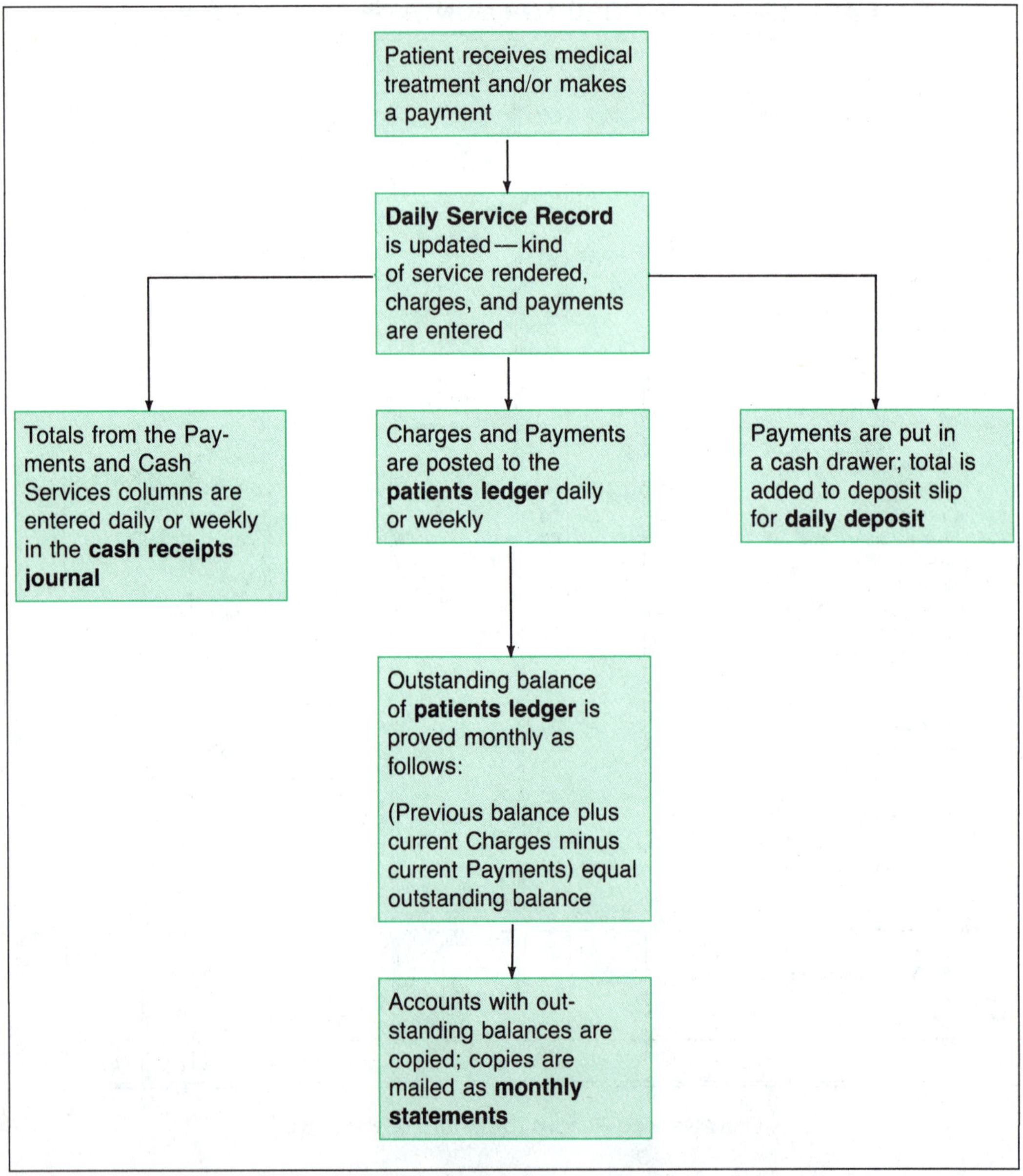

Flow of Data Through the Daily Service Record

Charges column is posted as a charge, and payments to the patients' accounts are posted from the Payments column. Information from the Cash Services column of the daily service record is also posted to the patients' accounts in both the Charges and Payments columns. This shows that service was

STATEMENT

WEINBERG AND HIMMO, PHYSICIANS AND SURGEONS
2478 Spencer Drive
Pasadena, TX 77505-5999

Jennifer Collins
6904 Shady Lane
Pasadena, TX 77505-5999

DATE	PROFESSIONAL SERVICE	CHARGE	PAID	BALANCE
2/10	OV; LAB	105 00		105 00
2/13	OV	25 00		130 00
2/15	M	75 00	100 00	105 00
2/18	OV; X	65 00	130 00	40 00
2/20	Check — Blue Shield		136 00	(96 00)
2/25	OV	25 00		(71 00)
2/25	Refund		(71 00)	-0-

PAY LAST AMOUNT IN THIS COLUMN ⇧

1603

HV—Hospital Visit
OV—Office Visit
LAB—Laboratory
M—Medical
S—Surgical
X—X-ray
MISC—Miscellaneous

Illustration of Patient's Account

rendered and payment was immediately received. A patient's account for Jennifer Collins is reproduced on this page. A description of the type of service performed is shown in the Professional Service column. Frequent types of services are listed on the bottom of the account form along with codes for each. To save space, instead of writing the complete description, only the code or a combination of codes for multiple services is written in the Professional Service column.

At the end of the month, the patients' ledger is totaled to show the balance of the outstanding accounts. The outstanding balance from the previous month, plus current charges from the daily service record, minus payments from the daily service record should equal the current total of the patients' ledger. This is called proving the patients' ledger and is helpful in identifying and correcting errors.

The accounts may also be aged. To age the patients' accounts, each account is listed and its balance is recorded in one of several columns, depending upon the age of the balance (how long it has been due). A listing of this information for Weinberg and Himmo is shown on this page. Aging the patients' accounts is helpful in identifying the delinquent accounts so that special attempts to collect these accounts may be made. While patients' accounts receivable are not formally recorded in the general books under the modified cash basis system, having this information available improves cash collections and assists with internal control over cash.

WEINBERG AND HIMMO, PHYSICIANS AND SURGEONS
PATIENT ACCOUNTS RECEIVABLE
February 28, 19--

	Balance Owed	Age of Balance in Days			
		Less than 30	31 – 60	61 – 90	90+
Anderson, Alice	$ 300				$300
Antonelli, Jane	250				250
Auerbach, Margaret	100	$ 100			
Baker, Roberta	1,300	1,300			
Brown, Margaret	800	800			
Crowell, James	75	75			
Goldstein, Daniel	1,300	1,300			
Huneke, Kathy	1,700	1,700			
Lauber, Dan	25	25			
Massarelli, Louis	1,750	1,750			
Meridith, Mike	250		$250		
Pratt, Evelyn	625	625			
Russell, Linda	25	25			
Silvers, Rachael	25	25			
Simmons, Tara	150			$150	
Skidmore, Robert	100			100	
Smith, Mary	20	20			
Williams, Barbara	325				325
Wu, James	300	300			
Totals	$9,420	$8,045	$250	$250	$875

Aging the Accounts Receivable

Other Payments for Services

In the last few years, much of the burden of payment for services rendered by the medical and dental professions has shifted from the patient to private commercial insurance companies, company health plans, health maintenance organizations (HMOs), and government programs such as Medicare, Medicaid, and Champus. As a result, keeping the accounts in the patients' ledger has become much more complex.

Some patients pay their accounts in full and have their insurance carrier reimburse them for covered charges. On the other hand, the doctor or dentist may accept an assignment of the amounts due. Accepting **assignment** means that the patient will pay only those amounts due that are not covered by insurance. The balance will be paid by the insurance company to the doctor. For example, Jackie Johnson's bill for services rendered totals $1,500 for illness that is covered by the insurance company. The terms of his insurance policy specify that the patient must pay the first $75, a **deductible**, and the insurance company will pay 80% of the remaining charges for covered illnesses. The patient is responsible for the remaining 20%, any charges for illnesses not covered, and charges deemed unreasonable by the insurance carrier. In this example, the insurance company will pay $1,140 ($1,500 − $75 = $1,425 × 80%) and Jackie Johnson must pay $360 ($1,500 − $1,140). Whether the patient pays the account and is reimbursed by the insurance company or the doctor accepts assignment, the patient needs to be provided with special information related to the charges so that a claim can be filed.

Weinberg and Himmo have agreed to accept assignments and to complete the necessary insurance forms. In order to process the insurance claims as efficiently as possible, one person in an office is usually given the responsibility for preparing the claims forms. A supply of forms may be kept on hand, but usually a standard form is prepared at the time service is rendered. This form is then given to the patient to attach to the insurance claim.

Weinberg and Himmo use the **Universal Health Insurance Claim Form** that was developed by the American Medical Association. This form has been adopted by most insurance carriers and programs. Special coding is used on the forms. Insurance companies have generally adopted the American Medical Association's Current Procedural Terminology, Fourth Edition (**CPT-4**), codes as the standard identification for medical procedures and treatments. The International Classification of Diseases, Revision Nine (**ICD-9CM**) has been adopted as the industry standard for diagnosis coding on forms. Hospital patients' illnesses are also classified into several groups. **DRGs**, Diagnosis-Related Groups, are codes to identify these illness groupings. A completed Universal Health Insurance Claim Form is shown on page 180.

HEALTH INSURANCE CLAIM FORM

READ INSTRUCTIONS BEFORE COMPLETING OR SIGNING THIS FORM

[ ] MEDICAID [ ] MEDICARE [ ] CHAMPUS [X] OTHER

FORM APPROVED
OMB NO. 66-R0012

PATIENT & INSURED (SUBSCRIBER) INFORMATION

1. PATIENT'S NAME *(First name, middle initial, last name)*: John S. Hammond
2. PATIENT'S DATE OF BIRTH: 08 | 15 | 41
3. INSURED'S NAME *(First name, middle initial, last name)*: John S. Hammond
4. PATIENT'S ADDRESS *(Street, city, state, ZIP code)*: 5168 Oak Grove Terrace, Pasadena, TX 77505-5999; TELEPHONE NO.
5. PATIENT'S SEX: MALE [X] FEMALE [ ]
6. INSURED'S I.D., MEDICARE AND/OR MEDICAID NO. *(Include any letters)*: 283-58-6871
7. PATIENT'S RELATIONSHIP TO INSURED: SELF [X] SPOUSE [ ] CHILD [ ] OTHER [ ]
8. INSURED'S GROUP NO. *(Or Group Name)*: TN 75281
9. OTHER HEALTH INSURANCE COVERAGE - Enter Name of Policyholder and Plan Name and Address and Policy or Medical Assistance Number: John Hammond; United Surgical Plan; 53 Taft Road, Nashville, TN 37206-1293; Group No. 6248
10. WAS CONDITION RELATED TO: A. PATIENT'S EMPLOYMENT YES [ ] NO [X]; B. ACCIDENT AUTO [ ] OTHER [X]
11. INSURED'S ADDRESS *(Street, city, state, ZIP code)*: 5168 Oak Grove Terrace, Pasadena, TX 77505-5999
12. PATIENT'S OR AUTHORIZED PERSON'S SIGNATURE *(Read back before signing)*
I Authorize the Release of any Medical Information Necessary to Process this Claim and Request Payment of MEDICARE Benefits Either to Myself or to the Party Who Accepts Assignment Below
SIGNED *John S. Hammond* DATE 6/16/--
13. *I AUTHORIZE PAYMENT OF MEDICAL BENEFITS TO UNDERSIGNED PHYSICIAN OR SUPPLIER FOR SERVICE DESCRIBED BELOW*
John S. Hammond
SIGNED *(Insured or Authorized Person)*

PHYSICIAN OR SUPPLIER INFORMATION

14. DATE OF ILLNESS (FIRST SYMPTOM) OR INJURY (ACCIDENT) OR PREGNANCY (LMP): 2/25/--
15. DATE FIRST CONSULTED YOU FOR THIS CONDITION: 4/14/--
16. HAS PATIENT EVER HAD SAME OR SIMILAR SYMPTOMS? YES [X] NO [ ]
16a. IF AN EMERGENCY CHECK HERE [ ] DNA
17. DATE PATIENT ABLE TO RETURN TO WORK: DNA
18. DATES OF TOTAL DISABILITY: FROM DNA THROUGH DNA
DATES OF PARTIAL DISABILITY: FROM DNA THROUGH DNA
19. NAME OF REFERRING PHYSICIAN OR OTHER SOURCE *(e.g., public health agency)*: Ann Kirkpatrick, M.D.
20. FOR SERVICES RELATED TO HOSPITALIZATION GIVE HOSPITALIZATION DATES: ADMITTED DNA DISCHARGED DNA
21. NAME & ADDRESS OF FACILITY WHERE SERVICES RENDERED *(If other than home or office)*: DNA
22. WAS LABORATORY WORK PERFORMED OUTSIDE YOUR OFFICE? YES [ ] NO [X] CHARGES DNA
23. DIAGNOSIS OR NATURE OF ILLNESS OR INJURY. RELATE DIAGNOSIS TO PROCEDURE IN COLUMN D BY REFERENCE NUMBERS 1, 2, 3, ETC. OR DX CODE
A
1. Unstable arteriosclerotic heart disease, recent
2. heart irregularity (412.9)
3. Type II hypoglycemia (251.0)
4.

B. EPSDT YES [DNA] NO [ ]; FAMILY PLANNING YES [DNA] NO [ ]
PRIOR AUTHORIZATION NO. ____

24.

A DATE OF SERVICE	B* PLACE OF SERVICE	C PROCEDURE CODE (IDENTIFY)	FULLY DESCRIBE PROCEDURES, MEDICAL SERVICES OR SUPPLIES FURNISHED FOR EACH DATE GIVEN (EXPLAIN UNUSUAL SERVICES OR CIRCUMSTANCES)	D DIAGNOSIS CODE	E CHARGES	F DAYS OR UNITS	G* T O S	H LEAVE BLANK
4/14/--	3	90060	Intermediate service	412.9 251.0	25 00			
4/14/--	3	71020	Chest X ray	412.9	30 00			
4/14/--	3	93000	Electrocardiogram	412.9	30 00			
4/14/--	3	80003	Blood sugar check	251.0	15 00			

25. SIGNATURE OF PHYSICIAN OR SUPPLIER *(I certify that the statements on the reverse apply to this bill and are made a part hereof.)*
SIGNED *Angelina Weinberg, M.D.* DATE 6/16/--
26. ACCEPT ASSIGNMENT (GOVERNMENT CLAIMS ONLY) (SEE BACK): YES [ ] NO [X]
27. TOTAL CHARGE: 100.00
28. AMOUNT PAID: None
29. BALANCE DUE: $100 00
30. YOUR SOCIAL SECURITY NO.: 238-54-1345
31. PHYSICIAN'S OR SUPPLIER'S NAME, ADDRESS, ZIP CODE & TELEPHONE NO.: Weinberg and Himmo, Physicians and Surgeons, 2478 Spencer Drive, Pasadena, TX 77505-5999, (713)476-1841
32. YOUR PATIENT ACCOUNT NO.: 839
33. YOUR EMPLOYER I.D. NO.: 2083899022

*PLACE OF SERVICE AND TYPE OF SERVICE (T.O.S.) CODES ON THE BACK

REMARKS

APPROVED BY AMA COUNCIL ON MEDICAL SERVICE 5-80
APPROVED BY THE HEALTH CARE FINANCING ADMINISTRATION & CHAMPUS

Form **AMA-OP-407**
Form **HCFA-1500 (4-80)**
Form **CHAMPUS-501**

Universal Health Insurance Claim Form

Reference: *The Modern Medical Office: A Reference Manual,* Doris Humphrey and Kathie Sigler, South-Western Publishing Co., Cincinnati, Ohio, 1986, page 159.

Accounting Procedure

Following is a narrative with explanations of transactions completed by Weinberg and Himmo during the month of February. These transactions have been entered in either the cash receipts journal, cash payments journal, or general journal illustrated on pages 189–192. The general ledger and trial balance as of February 28 are also shown.

WEINBERG AND HIMMO, PHYSICIANS AND SURGEONS

Narrative of Transactions

Tuesday, February 1

Issued Check No. 900 for $4,000 payable to Space Area Realtors for rent of the office building for the month of February.

Weinberg and Himmo have leased the entire office building from Space Area Realtors and terms of their lease agreement permit them to sublease to other professionals. This transaction was entered in the cash payments journal by debiting Rent Expense, Account No. 725, in the General Dr. column and crediting Cash, Account No. 100.

Issued Check No. 901 for $136.40 payable to Nasa Road Garage for business automobile repairs for January.

The transaction was entered in the cash payments journal by debiting Automobile Expense, Account No. 700, and crediting Cash, Account No. 100.

Wednesday, February 2

Received a check for $650 from John Williams, an optometrist, for the February rent payment.

Williams subleases from Weinberg and Himmo, and his check was entered in the cash receipts journal by debiting Cash, Account No. 100, and crediting Other Income, Account No. 610.

Thursday, February 3

Received a check for $600 payable to the partnership for serving as speakers on the program at a professional meeting.

Receipt of the check was entered in the cash receipts journal by debiting Cash, Account No. 100, and crediting Other Income, Account No. 610.

Issued Check No. 902 for $250.67 to The Electric Company for electricity consumed during January.

This expenditure was entered in the cash payments journal by debiting Electricity Expense, Account No. 708, and by crediting Cash, Account No. 100.

Issued Check No. 903 for $125.30 to S-W Telephone Company for January service.

This transaction was entered in the cash payments journal by debiting Telephone Expense, Account No. 735, and by crediting Cash, Account No. 100.

Issued Check No. 904 for $215.40 to Queen Oaks Laundry for laundry service for the month of January.

This check was entered in the cash payments journal by debiting Laundry Expense, Account No. 712, and by crediting Cash, Account No. 100.

Issued Check No. 905 for $150.75 to Medical Supply Corporation for medical supplies purchased in January.

This transaction was entered in the cash payments journal by debiting Medical Supplies Expense, Account No. 716, and by crediting Cash, Account No. 100.

Friday, February 4

Issued Check No. 906 for $75 to Webster Medical Equipment Company for equipment repair.

This check was entered in the cash payments journal by debiting Repairs and Maintenance Expense, Account No. 727, and by crediting Cash, Account No. 100.

Issued Check No. 907 for $4,200 to Bay Area Insurance Agency for a physicians' liability insurance policy for Weinberg and Himmo.

Payment of this check was entered in the cash payments journal by debiting Prepaid Insurance, Account No. 115, and by crediting Cash, Account No. 100.

Weinberg and Himmo have given the account of Robert Amason in the amount of $1,581 and the account of Tara Simmons in the amount of $600 to Cindi McCaghren, an attorney, for collection. If McCaghren collects all or part of these amounts, her fee will be 33⅓%. No entry is needed at this time.

Completed the End-of-the-Week Procedures

(a) Footed the amount columns in the daily service record and obtained the following totals:

Kind of service:	
Office visits	$ 750
Surgery	9,860
Total	$10,610
Patients' Accounts—Charges	$10,080
Cash Services	530
Total	$10,610

(b) Posted all entries in the Patients' Accounts Charges and Payments columns and Cash Services to the appropriate individual accounts in the patients ledger.

(c) The total cash received from patients for the week was found to be:

Payments	$8,645
Cash Services	530
Total	$9,175

(d) Recorded the total cash received ($9,175) in the cash receipts journal by entering the words "Total receipts" in the Account Debited column and the amount in both the Cash Dr. column and the Professional Fees Cr. column.

(e) Footed the amount columns of the cash receipts and cash payments journals, proved the journals by comparing total debits with total credits, and checked the cash balance in the checkbook ($76,696.78) by starting with the checkbook balance on February 1 ($75,425.30) and adding the total of the Cash Dr. column ($10,425.00) from the cash receipts journal and subtracting the total of the Cash Cr. column ($9,153.52) from the cash payments journal.

(f) Completed the individual postings from the General Dr. columns of the cash receipts and cash payments journals and from the general journal. As each item was posted, the account number of the account to which each item from the journal was posted was entered in the Posting Reference column of the journal.

Monday, February 7

Issued Check No. 908 for $250.48 to Gulfcoast Surgical Supply Company for surgical instruments purchased in January.

This transaction was entered in the cash payments journal by debiting Surgical Instruments Expense, Account No. 730, and by crediting Cash, Account No. 100.

Tuesday, February 8

Issued Check No. 909 for $85 to American Medical Association for the subscription to a professional journal.

Payment of the subscription was entered in the cash payments journal by debiting Dues and Subscriptions Expense, Account No. 706, and by crediting Cash, Account No. 100.

Wednesday, February 9

Issued Check No. 910 to Wilson Supply Company for surgical supplies, $126.80.

This check was entered in the cash payments journal by debiting Surgical Supplies Expense, Account No. 732, and crediting Cash, Account No. 100.

Thursday, February 10

Issued Check No. 911 for $211.47 to Western Publishing Company for medical books.

This transaction was entered in the cash payments journal by debiting Medical Library Expense, Account No. 715, and by crediting Cash, Account No. 100.

Issued Check No. 912 for $65 to Aikens Department Store in payment of Weinberg's personal account.

Since this transaction is a personal expense, it was entered in the cash payments journal by debiting Angeline Weinberg, Drawing, Account No. 510, and by crediting Cash, Account No. 100.

Friday, February 11

Weinberg withdrew $2,500 for personal use. Check No. 913.

Himmo withdrew $2,500 for personal use. Check No. 914.

Issued the following checks in payment of salaries for the first half of the month:

Check No. 915 for $714.75 to Evelin Riley, R.N., in payment of salary in the amount of $950, less $164 withheld for federal income tax and $71.25 withheld for FICA tax.

Check No. 916 for $649 to Michael Tummins, office manager, in payment of salary in the amount of $800, less $91 withheld for federal income tax and $60 withheld for FICA tax.

Check No. 917 for $612 to Sandy Touchstone, secretary, in payment of salary in the amount of $800, less $128 withheld for federal income tax and $60 withheld for FICA tax.

Check No. 918 for $759.75 to Barbara Simmons, laboratory technologist, in payment of salary in the amount of $950, less $119 withheld for federal income tax and $71.25 withheld for FICA tax.

Weinberg and Himmo are subject to the federal unemployment tax (.8%) and state unemployment tax (2.7%). These taxes are collected entirely from the employer on the first $7,000 of each employee's earnings during the year. No deductions are made from the salaries of the employees for unemployment taxes. The liability for these taxes is entered at the end of each month.

Completed End-of-the-Week Procedures

(a) Footed the amount columns in the daily service record and obtained the following totals:

Kind of service:	
Office Visits	$ 775
Surgery	9,350
Total	$10,125

Patients' Accounts—Charges	$ 9,365
Cash Services	760
Total	$10,125

(b) Posted all entries in the Patients' Accounts Charges and Payments columns to the appropriate individual accounts in the patients ledger.

(c) The total cash received from patients for the week was found to be:

Payments	$8,964
Cash Services	760
Total	$9,724

(d) Entered the total cash received ($9,724) in the cash receipts journal.

(e) Footed the amount columns of the cash receipts and cash payments journals and checked the cash balance in the checkbook ($75,425.30 + $20,149.00 − $17,627.77 = $77,946.53).

(f) Completed the individual postings from the General Dr. columns of the cash receipts and cash payments journals.

Monday, February 14

Issued Check No. 919 for $189.60 to Top Office Furniture Company in payment of a new filing cabinet.

This payment was entered in the cash payments journal by debiting Office Equipment, Account No. 230, and crediting Cash, Account No. 100.

Tuesday, February 15

Issued Check No. 920 to Clear Lake National Bank in payment of the following payroll taxes based on wages paid during the month of January.

Employees income tax withheld from wages		$1,004.00
FICA tax:		
Withheld from employees' wages	$525.00	
Imposed on employer	525.00	1,050.00
Amount of check		$2,054.00

Issued Check No. 921 for $75.18 to Zepata Office Supplies Company for stationery and office supplies.

Issued Check No. 922 for $198.35 to Medical Supply Company for medical supplies.

Received a check for $900 for rent payment from Eleanor Delwood, an electrologist who subleases from Weinberg and Himmo.

Wednesday, February 16

Issued Check No. 923 for $600 to United Fund.

This transaction was entered in the cash payments journal by debiting Charitable Contributions Expense, Account No. 703, and by crediting Cash, Account No. 100.

Received a check for $850 for rent payment from Buddy Glasen, a chiropractor who subleases from Weinberg and Himmo.

Thursday, February 17

Issued Check No. 924 for $630 to Austin Insurance Agency in payment of the renewal premium on an insurance policy for Weinberg's car, which is used exclusively for business purposes.

Since the car is used exclusively for business purposes, the cost of the policy is debited to Prepaid Insurance, Account No. 115, and credited to Cash, Account No. 100, in the cash payments journal.

Friday, February 18

Issued Check No. 925 for $35 to Clear Lake National Bank in payment of the annual rental of a safe deposit box for use by the partnership.

This transaction was entered in the cash payments journal by debiting Miscellaneous Expense, Account No. 717, and by crediting Cash, Account No. 100.

Completed the End-of-the-Week Procedures

(a) Footed the amount columns in the daily service record and obtained the following totals:

Kind of service:	
Office Visits	$ 725
Surgery	8,700
Total	$9,425
Patients' Accounts—Charges	$9,100
Cash Services	325
Total	$9,425

(b) Posted all entries in the Patients' Accounts Charges and Payments columns to the appropriate individual accounts in the patients ledger.

(c) The total cash received from patients for the week was found to be:

Payments	$8,865
Cash Services	325
Total	$9,190

(d) Entered the total cash received ($9,190) in the cash receipts journal.

(e) Footed the amount columns of the cash receipts and cash payments journals and checked the cash balance in the checkbook ($75,425.30 + 31,089.00 − 21,409.90 = $85,104.40).

(f) Completed the individual postings from the General Dr. columns of the cash receipts and cash payments journals.

Monday, February 21

Issued Check No. 926 for $400 to American Cancer Society.

Entered $65 of interest earned on the partnership checking account.

This transaction was entered in the cash receipts journal by debiting Cash, Account No. 100, and crediting Other Income, Account No. 610.

Issued Check No. 927 for $225.18 to Express Service Center for oil and gas used during the month of January by the business automobiles.

Tuesday, February 22

Issued Check No. 928 for $2,532.95 to Collins Medical Equipment Company for medical equipment.

Received $1,054 from Cindi McCaghren representing collection of the account of Robert Amason in the amount of $1,581. McCaghren deducted the fee of $527 and remitted the balance, $1,054.

This transaction was entered in the cash receipts journal by debiting Cash, Account No. 100, for $1,054 and Legal Expense, Account No. 713, for $527, and by crediting Professional Fees, Account No. 600, for $1,581. In order to avoid a duplication of the $1,581 credit to Professional Fees, this payment was not entered in the daily service record. An entry was made, however, in Amason's account in the patients ledger crediting the account for $1,581.

Wednesday, February 23

Issued Check No. 929 for $63.70 to Janack Office Equipment Company for typewriter repairs.

Thursday, February 24

Issued Check No. 930 for $875.60 to Himmo for reimbursement of expenses incurred in attending a medical convention earlier this month.

This transaction was recorded in the cash payments journal by debiting Traveling and Meetings Expense, Account No. 738, and crediting Cash, Account No. 100.

Friday, February 25

Received $300 from Cindi McCaghren to apply on the account of Tara Simmons. McCaghren collected $450 from Simmons and remitted $300 after deducting the fee of $150.

Since the next workday is the end of the month, the usual end-of-the-week procedures were not completed.

Monday, February 28

Weinberg withdrew $2,500 for personal use. Check No. 931.

Himmo withdrew $2,500 for personal use. Check No. 932.

Issued the following checks in payment of salaries for the second half of the month:

Check No. 933 for $714.75 to Evelin Riley, R.N., in payment of salary in the amount of $950, less $164 withheld for federal income tax and $71.25 withheld for FICA tax.

Check No. 934 for $649 to Michael Tummins, office manager, in payment of salary in the amount of $800, less $91 withheld for federal income tax and $60 withheld for FICA tax.

Check No. 935 for $612 to Sandy Touchstone, secretary, in payment of salary in the amount of $800, less $128 withheld for federal income tax and $60 withheld for FICA tax.

Check No. 936 for $759.75 to Barbara Simmons, laboratory technologist, in payment of salary in the amount of $950, less $119 withheld for federal income tax and $71.25 withheld for FICA tax.

Received a check for $1,200 for rent payment from Able Pharmacy, which subleases from Weinberg and Himmo.

Completed End-of-the-Month Procedures

(a) Footed the amount columns in the daily service record and obtained the following totals:

Kind of service:	
Office Visits	$ 795
Surgery	9,625
Total	$10,420
Patients' Accounts—Charges	$ 9,555
Cash Services	865
Total	$10,420

(b) Posted all entries in the Patients' Accounts Charges and Payments columns to the appropriate individual accounts in the patients ledger.

(c) The total cash received from patients for the week was found to be:

Payments	$ 9,540
Cash Services	865
Total	$10,405

(d) Entered the total cash received ($10,405) in the cash receipts journal.

(e) Made an entry in the general journal for the payroll taxes imposed on Weinberg and Himmo for the month of February by debiting Payroll Taxes Expense, Account No. 720, for $770 and by crediting FICA Tax Payable, Account No. 320, for $525, FUTA Tax Payable, Account No. 330, for $56, and State Unemployment Tax Payable, Account No. 340, in the amount of $189.

(f) Issued Check No. 937 for $80.75 to replenish the petty cash fund. The following statement provided the information needed in entering this transaction in the cash payments journal:

Statement of Petty Cash Payments for February

Angeline Weinberg, Drawing	$15.00
Lael Himmo, Drawing	17.50
Automobile Expense	13.75
Office Supplies Expense	2.50
Postage Expense	22.00
Traveling and Meetings Expense	10.00
Total payments	$80.75

(g) Footed the amount columns of the cash receipts and cash payments journals and checked the cash balance in the checkbook ($75,425.30 + 44,113.00 − 33,323.58 = $86,214.72).

(h) Completed the individual postings from the General Dr. and Cr. columns of the cash receipts journal, cash payments journal, and the general journal. Completed the summary postings from the cash receipts and cash payments journals. A trial balance of the general ledger accounts that have balances on February 28 appears on page 202.

CASH RECEIPTS JOURNAL PAGE 2

DATE		DESCRIPTION	POST. REF.	OTHER INCOME 610 CR.	PROFESSIONAL FEES 600 CR.	GENERAL DR.	CASH 100 DR.
19-- Feb.	2	John Williams	✓	650 00			650 00
	3	Speaking engagement	✓	600 00			600 00
	4	Total receipts	✓	 1250 00	9175 00 9175 00		9175 00 10425 00
	11	Total receipts	✓	 1250 00	9724 00 18899 00		9724 00 20149 00
	15	Eleanor Delwood	✓	900 00			900 00
	16	Buddy Glasen	✓	850 00			850 00
	18	Total receipts	✓	 3000 00	9190 00 28089 00		9190 00 31089 00
	21	Interest on checking account	✓	65 00			65 00
	22	Legal Expense	713		1581 00	527 00	1054 00
	25	Legal Expense	713		450 00	150 00	300 00
	28	Able Pharmacy	✓	1200 00			1200 00
	28	Total receipts	✓		10405 00		10405 00
	28			4265 00	40525 00	677 00	44113 00
				(610)	(600)	(✓)	(100)

CASH PAYMENTS JOURNAL PAGE 3

	DATE		CK. NO.	DESCRIPTION	POST. REF.	GENERAL DR.	SALARY EXPENSE 729 DR.	EMP. INC. TAX PAY. 310 CR.	FICA TAX PAY. 320 CR.	CASH 100 CR.	
1	19-- Feb.	1	900	Rent Expense	725	400000				400000	1
2		1	901	Automobile Expense	700	13640				13640	2
3		2	902	Electricity Expense	708	25067				25067	3
4		2	903	Telephone Expense	735	12530				12530	4
5		3	904	Laundry Expense	712	21540				21540	5
6		3	905	Medical Supplies Expense	716	15075				15075	6
7		4	906	Repairs + Maintenance Expense	727	7500				7500	7
8		4	907	Prepaid Insurance	115	420000 915352				420000 915352	8
9		7	908	Surgical Instruments Expense	730	25048				25048	9
10		8	909	Dues + Subscriptions Expense	706	8500				8500	10
11		9	910	Surgical Supplies Expense	732	12680				12680	11
12		10	911	Medical Library Expense	715	21147				21147	12
13		10	912	Angeline Weinberg, Drawing	510	6500				6500	13
14		11	913	Angeline Weinberg, Drawing	510	250000				250000	14
15		11	914	Lael Himmo, Drawing	530	250000				250000	15
16		11	915	Evelin Riley	✓		95000	16400	7125	71475	16
17		11	916	Michael Tummins	✓		80000	9100	6000	64900	17
18		11	917	Sandy Touchstone	✓		80000	12800	6000	61200	18
19		11	918	Barbara Simmons	✓	1489227	95000 350000	11900 50200	7125 26250	75975 1762777	19
20		14	919	Office Equipment	230	18960				18960	20
21		15	920	FICA Tax Payable	320	105000				205400	21
22				Employees Income Tax Payable	310	100400					22
23		15	921	Office Supplies Expense	719	7518				7518	23
24		15	922	Medical Supplies Expense	716	19835				19835	24

Weinberg and Himmo Cash Payments Journal

(continued)

16	923	Charitable Contributions Expense	703	60000				60000
17	924	Prepaid Insurance	115	63000				63000
18	925	Miscellaneous Expense	717	3500				3500
				1867440	350000	50200	26250	2140990
21	926	Charitable Contributions Expense	703	40000				40000
21	927	Automobile Expense	700	22518				22518
22	928	Medical Equipment	220	253295				253295
23	929	Repairs & Maintenance Expense	727	6370				6370
24	930	Traveling & Meetings Expense	738	87560				87560
28	931	Angeline Weinberg, Drawing	510	250000				250000
28	932	Lael Himmo, Drawing	530	250000				250000
28	933	Evelin Riley	✓		95000	16400	7125	71475
28	934	Michael Tummins	✓		80000	9100	6000	64900
28	935	Sandy Touchstone	✓		80000	12800	6000	61200
28	936	Barbara Simmons	✓		95000	11900	7125	75975
28	937	Angeline Weinberg, Drawing	510	1500				8075
		Lael Himmo, Drawing	530	1750				
		Automobile Expense	700	1375				
		Office Supplies Expense	719	250				
		Postage Expense	722	2200				
		Traveling & Meetings Expense	738	1000				
28				2785258	700000	100400	52500	3332358
				(✓)	(729)	(310)	(320)	(100)

Weinberg and Himmo Cash Payments Journal

(concluded)

GENERAL JOURNAL PAGE 2

	DATE		DESCRIPTION	POST. REF.	DEBIT	CREDIT	
1	19-- Feb.	28	Payroll Taxes Expense	720	770 00		1
2			FICA Tax Payable	320		525 00	2
3			FUTA Tax Payable	330		56 00	3
4			State Unemployment Tax Pay.	340		189 00	4
5							5
6							6
7							7
8							8

Weinberg and Himmo General Journal

ACCOUNT Cash ACCOUNT NO. 100

DATE		ITEM	POST. REF.	DEBIT	CREDIT	BALANCE DEBIT	BALANCE CREDIT
19-- Feb.	1	Balance	✓			75,425 30	
	28		CR2	44,113 00		119,538 30	
	28		CP3		33,323 58	86,214 72	

ACCOUNT Petty Cash Fund ACCOUNT NO. 110

DATE		ITEM	POST. REF.	DEBIT	CREDIT	BALANCE DEBIT	BALANCE CREDIT
19-- Feb.	1	Balance	✓			100 00	

ACCOUNT Prepaid Insurance ACCOUNT NO. 115

DATE		ITEM	POST. REF.	DEBIT	CREDIT	BALANCE DEBIT	BALANCE CREDIT
19-- Feb.	4		CP3	4,200 00		4,200 00	
	17		CP3	630 00		4,830 00	

General Ledger *(continued)*

ACCOUNT *Automobiles* ACCOUNT NO. 200

DATE		ITEM	POST. REF.	DEBIT	CREDIT	BALANCE DEBIT	BALANCE CREDIT
19-- Feb.	1	Balance	✓			24000 00	

ACCOUNT *Accumulated Depreciation - Automobiles* ACCOUNT NO. 205

DATE		ITEM	POST. REF.	DEBIT	CREDIT	BALANCE DEBIT	BALANCE CREDIT
19-- Feb.	1	Balance	✓				6000 00

ACCOUNT *Laboratory Equipment* ACCOUNT NO. 210

DATE		ITEM	POST. REF.	DEBIT	CREDIT	BALANCE DEBIT	BALANCE CREDIT
19-- Feb.	1	Balance	✓			17635 00	

ACCOUNT *Accumulated Depreciation - Laboratory Equipment* ACCOUNT NO. 215

DATE		ITEM	POST. REF.	DEBIT	CREDIT	BALANCE DEBIT	BALANCE CREDIT
19-- Feb.	1	Balance	✓				3527 00

ACCOUNT *Medical Equipment* ACCOUNT NO. 220

DATE		ITEM	POST. REF.	DEBIT	CREDIT	BALANCE DEBIT	BALANCE CREDIT
19-- Feb.	1	Balance	✓			28600 00	
	22		CP3	2532 95		31132 95	

General Ledger *(continued)*

ACCOUNT Accumulated Depreciation-Medical Equipment ACCOUNT NO. 225

DATE		ITEM	POST. REF.	DEBIT	CREDIT	BALANCE DEBIT	BALANCE CREDIT
19-- Feb.	1	Balance	✓				572000

ACCOUNT Office Equipment ACCOUNT NO. 230

DATE		ITEM	POST. REF.	DEBIT	CREDIT	BALANCE DEBIT	BALANCE CREDIT
19-- Feb.	1	Balance	✓			450000	
	14		CP3	18960		468960	

ACCOUNT Accumulated Depreciation-Office Equipment ACCOUNT NO. 235

DATE		ITEM	POST. REF.	DEBIT	CREDIT	BALANCE DEBIT	BALANCE CREDIT
19-- Feb.	1	Balance	✓				112500

ACCOUNT Employees Income Tax Payable ACCOUNT NO. 310

DATE		ITEM	POST. REF.	DEBIT	CREDIT	BALANCE DEBIT	BALANCE CREDIT
19-- Feb.	1	Balance	✓				100400
	15		CP3	100400			- 0 -
	28		CP3		100400		100400

General Ledger *(continued)*

ACCOUNT FICA Tax Payable ACCOUNT NO. 320

DATE		ITEM	POST. REF.	DEBIT	CREDIT	BALANCE DEBIT	BALANCE CREDIT
19-- Feb.	1	Balance	✓				105000
	15		CP3	105000			-0-
	28		CP3		52500		52500
	28		GJ2		52500		105000

ACCOUNT FUTA Tax Payable ACCOUNT NO. 330

DATE		ITEM	POST. REF.	DEBIT	CREDIT	BALANCE DEBIT	BALANCE CREDIT
19-- Feb.	1	Balance	✓				5600
	28		GJ2		5600		11200

ACCOUNT State Unemployment Tax Payable ACCOUNT NO. 340

DATE		ITEM	POST. REF.	DEBIT	CREDIT	BALANCE DEBIT	BALANCE CREDIT
19-- Feb.	1	Balance	✓				18900
	28		GJ2		18900		37800

ACCOUNT Angeline Weinberg, Capital ACCOUNT NO. 500

DATE		ITEM	POST. REF.	DEBIT	CREDIT	BALANCE DEBIT	BALANCE CREDIT
19-- Feb.	1	Balance	✓				5582400

General Ledger *(continued)*

ACCOUNT *Angeline Weinberg, Drawing* ACCOUNT NO. 510

DATE		ITEM	POST. REF.	DEBIT	CREDIT	BALANCE DEBIT	BALANCE CREDIT
19-- Feb.	1	Balance	✓			533550	
	10		CP3	6500		540050	
	11		CP3	250000		790050	
	28		CP3	250000		1040050	
	28		CP3	1500		1041550	

ACCOUNT *Lael Himmo, Capital* ACCOUNT NO. 520

DATE		ITEM	POST. REF.	DEBIT	CREDIT	BALANCE DEBIT	BALANCE CREDIT
19-- Feb.	1	Balance	✓				5755600

ACCOUNT *Lael Himmo, Drawing* ACCOUNT NO. 530

DATE		ITEM	POST. REF.	DEBIT	CREDIT	BALANCE DEBIT	BALANCE CREDIT
19-- Feb.	1	Balance	✓			544420	
	11		CP3	250000		794420	
	28		CP3	250000		1044420	
	28		CP3	1750		1046170	

ACCOUNT *Expense and Revenue Summary* ACCOUNT NO. 540

DATE	ITEM	POST. REF.	DEBIT	CREDIT	BALANCE DEBIT	BALANCE CREDIT

General Ledger *(continued)*

ACCOUNT *Professional Fees* ACCOUNT NO. 600

DATE		ITEM	POST. REF.	DEBIT	CREDIT	BALANCE DEBIT	BALANCE CREDIT
19-- Feb.	1	Balance	✓				3766300
	28		CR2		4052500		7818800

ACCOUNT *Other Income* ACCOUNT NO. 610

DATE		ITEM	POST. REF.	DEBIT	CREDIT	BALANCE DEBIT	BALANCE CREDIT
19-- Feb.	1	Balance	✓				425882
	28		CR2		426500		852382

ACCOUNT *Automobile Expense* ACCOUNT NO. 700

DATE		ITEM	POST. REF.	DEBIT	CREDIT	BALANCE DEBIT	BALANCE CREDIT
19-- Feb.	1	Balance	✓			3500	
	1		CP3	13640		17140	
	21		CP3	22518		39658	
	28		CP3	1375		41033	

ACCOUNT *Charitable Contributions Expense* ACCOUNT NO. 703

DATE		ITEM	POST. REF.	DEBIT	CREDIT	BALANCE DEBIT	BALANCE CREDIT
19-- Feb.	16		CP3	60000		60000	
	21		CP3	40000		100000	

General Ledger *(continued)*

ACCOUNT *Depreciation Expense* ACCOUNT NO. 705

DATE		ITEM	POST. REF.	DEBIT	CREDIT	BALANCE DEBIT	BALANCE CREDIT

ACCOUNT *Dues and Subscriptions Expense* ACCOUNT NO. 706

DATE		ITEM	POST. REF.	DEBIT	CREDIT	BALANCE DEBIT	BALANCE CREDIT
19-- Feb.	8		CP3	8500		8500	

ACCOUNT *Electricity Expense* ACCOUNT NO. 708

DATE		ITEM	POST. REF.	DEBIT	CREDIT	BALANCE DEBIT	BALANCE CREDIT
19-- Feb.	2		CP3	25067		25067	

ACCOUNT *Insurance Expense* ACCOUNT NO. 710

DATE		ITEM	POST. REF.	DEBIT	CREDIT	BALANCE DEBIT	BALANCE CREDIT

ACCOUNT *Laundry Expense* ACCOUNT NO. 712

DATE		ITEM	POST. REF.	DEBIT	CREDIT	BALANCE DEBIT	BALANCE CREDIT
19-- Feb.	3		CP3	21540		21540	

General Ledger *(continued)*

ACCOUNT *Legal Expense* ACCOUNT NO. *713*

DATE		ITEM	POST. REF.	DEBIT	CREDIT	BALANCE DEBIT	BALANCE CREDIT
19-- Feb.	1	Balance	✓			53000	
	22		CR2	52700		105700	
	24		CR2	15000		120700	

ACCOUNT *Medical Library Expense* ACCOUNT NO. *715*

DATE		ITEM	POST. REF.	DEBIT	CREDIT	BALANCE DEBIT	BALANCE CREDIT
19-- Feb.	10		CP3	21147		21147	

ACCOUNT *Medical Supplies Expense* ACCOUNT NO. *716*

DATE		ITEM	POST. REF.	DEBIT	CREDIT	BALANCE DEBIT	BALANCE CREDIT
19-- Feb.	3		CP3	15075		15075	
	15		CP3	19835		34910	

ACCOUNT *Miscellaneous Expense* ACCOUNT NO. *717*

DATE		ITEM	POST. REF.	DEBIT	CREDIT	BALANCE DEBIT	BALANCE CREDIT
19-- Feb.	1	Balance	✓			9845	
	18		CP3	3500		13345	

General Ledger *(continued)*

ACCOUNT *Office Supplies Expense* ACCOUNT NO. 719

DATE		ITEM	POST. REF.	DEBIT	CREDIT	BALANCE DEBIT	BALANCE CREDIT
19-- Feb.	1	Balance	✓			6700	
	15		CP3	7518		14218	
	28		CP3	250		14468	

ACCOUNT *Payroll Taxes Expense* ACCOUNT NO. 720

DATE		ITEM	POST. REF.	DEBIT	CREDIT	BALANCE DEBIT	BALANCE CREDIT
19-- Feb.	1	Balance	✓			77000	
	28		GJ2	77000		154000	

ACCOUNT *Postage Expense* ACCOUNT NO. 722

DATE		ITEM	POST. REF.	DEBIT	CREDIT	BALANCE DEBIT	BALANCE CREDIT
19-- Feb.	1	Balance	✓			4400	
	28		CP3	2200		6600	

ACCOUNT *Rent Expense* ACCOUNT NO. 725

DATE		ITEM	POST. REF.	DEBIT	CREDIT	BALANCE DEBIT	BALANCE CREDIT
19-- Feb.	1	Balance	✓			400000	
	1		CP3	400000		800000	

ACCOUNT *Repairs and Maintenance Expense* ACCOUNT NO. 727

DATE		ITEM	POST. REF.	DEBIT	CREDIT	BALANCE DEBIT	BALANCE CREDIT
19-- Feb.	1	Balance	✓			3500	
	4		CP3	7500		11000	
	23		CP3	6370		17370	

General Ledger *(continued)*

ACCOUNT *Salary Expense* ACCOUNT NO. 729

DATE		ITEM	POST. REF.	DEBIT	CREDIT	BALANCE DEBIT	BALANCE CREDIT
19-- Feb.	1	Balance	✓			700000	
	28		CP3	700000		1400000	

ACCOUNT *Surgical Instruments Expense* ACCOUNT NO. 730

DATE		ITEM	POST. REF.	DEBIT	CREDIT	BALANCE DEBIT	BALANCE CREDIT
19-- Feb.	7		CP3	25048		25048	

ACCOUNT *Surgical Supplies Expense* ACCOUNT NO. 732

DATE		ITEM	POST. REF.	DEBIT	CREDIT	BALANCE DEBIT	BALANCE CREDIT
19-- Feb.	1	Balance	✓			9837	
	9		CP3	12680		22517	

ACCOUNT *Telephone Expense* ACCOUNT NO. 735

DATE		ITEM	POST. REF.	DEBIT	CREDIT	BALANCE DEBIT	BALANCE CREDIT
19-- Feb.	2		CP3	12530		12530	

ACCOUNT *Traveling and Meetings Expense* ACCOUNT NO. 738

DATE		ITEM	POST. REF.	DEBIT	CREDIT	BALANCE DEBIT	BALANCE CREDIT
19-- Feb.	1	Balance	✓			25500	
	24		CP3	87560		113060	
	28		CP3	1000		114060	

General Ledger *(concluded)*

Weinberg and Himmo, Physicians and Surgeons

Trial Balance
February 28, 19--

Account	Acct. No.	Dr. Balance	Cr. Balance
Cash	100	86,214.72	
Petty Cash Fund	110	100.00	
Prepaid Insurance	115	4,830.00	
Automobiles	200	24,000.00	
Accumulated Depr.—Automobiles	205		6,000.00
Laboratory Equipment	210	17,635.00	
Accumulated Depr.—Laboratory Equipment	215		3,527.00
Medical Equipment	220	31,132.95	
Accumulated Depr.—Medical Equipment	225		5,720.00
Office Equipment	230	4,689.60	
Accumulated Depr.—Office Equipment	235		1,125.00
Employees Income Tax Payable	310		1,004.00
FICA Tax Payable	320		1,050.00
FUTA Tax Payable	330		112.00
State Unemployment Tax Payable	340		378.00
Angeline Weinberg, Capital	500		55,824.00
Angeline Weinberg, Drawing	510	10,415.50	
Lael Himmo, Capital	520		57,556.00
Lael Himmo, Drawing	530	10,461.70	
Professional Fees	600		78,188.00
Other Income	610		8,523.82
Automobile Expense	700	410.33	
Charitable Contributions Expense	703	1,000.00	
Dues and Subscriptions Expense	706	85.00	
Electricity Expense	708	250.67	
Laundry Expense	712	215.40	
Legal Expense	713	1,207.00	
Medical Library Expense	715	211.47	
Medical Supplies Expense	716	349.10	
Miscellaneous Expense	717	133.45	
Office Supplies Expense	719	144.68	
Payroll Taxes Expense	720	1,540.00	
Postage Expense	722	66.00	
Rent Expense	725	8,000.00	
Repairs and Maintenance Expense	727	173.70	
Salary Expense	729	14,000.00	
Surgical Instruments Expense	730	250.48	
Surgical Supplies Expense	732	225.17	
Telephone Expense	735	125.30	
Traveling and Meetings Expense	738	1,140.60	
		219,007.82	219,007.82

BUILDING YOUR ACCOUNTING KNOWLEDGE

1. What are the most valuable assets that professionals employed in personal service business have?
2. How does the pure cash basis of accounting differ from the modified basis?
3. In what respect are prepaid insurance and office equipment similar?
4. Why must the total of the Kinds of Services columns equal the total of the Patients' Accounts Charges and the Cash Services columns on a daily service record?
5. How is the daily service record proved?
6. How are accounts receivable proved? Why is this important?
7. How are accounts receivable aged? What is the purpose of doing this?

APPLYING ACCOUNTING CONCEPTS

Exercise 6-1. Wanda Miers incurred medical expenses of $5,330. All the charges were covered by her insurance. The deductible on her policy is $75, and the coverage that her insurance company will pay is 80%.

1. How much of the debt must Wanda Miers pay?
2. How much of the debt will the insurance company pay?

Exercise 6-2. Complete a statement of account for Cindy Drewery, 3201 South Gregory Street, San Diego, CA 92111-5234, using the following information:

Date	Service Performed	Amount
July 7	Complete blood count	$ 35
July 9	Complete physical; electrocardiogram	150
July 16	Office visit	35
July 17	X-ray	85
July 23	Emergency room treatment	150
July 25	Hospital visit	25
July 26	Surgery	1,500
July 27	Hospital visit	25
August 1	Office visit	35

Payments were received as follows:

August 10 Check was received from Blue Shield for 80% of the balance owed by Ms. Drewery, less $100 deductible.

August 15 Check was received from Ms. Drewery for balance due on her account.

Exercise 6-3. Give the general journal entry to reimburse the petty cash fund. The following statement provides the information needed to enter this transaction.

LaCour and Caplen, Physicians
Statement of Petty Cash Payments for June 9, 19--

H. LaCour, Drawing	$ 15
B. Caplen, Drawing	26
Automobile Expense	37
Postage Expense	25
Traveling and Meetings Expense	9
Telephone Expense	17
Miscellaneous Expense	3
Total Payments	$132

Exercise 6-4. Dr. Clydette Collins is a practicing physician and surgeon. Enter the following transactions in general journal form:

Feb. 2 Footed the amount columns in the daily service record and obtained the following totals:

Kind of Service:

Office Visits	$ 367	Patients' Accounts Charges	$9,024
Surgery	9,007	Cash Services	350
Total	$9,374	Total	$9,374

The total cash received from patients for the week was found to be:

Payments	$8,577
Cash Services	350
Total	$8,927

Entered the total cash received.

3 Issued check for $55 to American Medical Association for subscription to a professional journal.

4 Issued check to Roberts Supply Company for surgical supplies, $110.

4 Issued check to Palais Center in payment of Clydette Collins' personal account, $115.

5 Issued check to Nassau Bay National Bank in payment of the following payroll taxes based on wages paid during the month of January:

Employees income tax withheld from wages		$ 754
FICA tax		
Withheld from employee's wages	$337	
Imposed on employer	337	674
Amount of check		$1,428

6 Issued check to David Koffi, laboratory technician, in payment of salary in the amount of $725, less $105 withheld for federal income tax and $54.38 withheld for FICA tax.

9 Received $420 from Marie Dalton, Attorney, representing collection of the account of Paul Amick in the amount of $630. Dalton deducted the fee of $210 and remitted the balance.

9 Issued check for $679 to Collins for reimbursement of expenses incurred in attending a medical convention earlier this month.

Report No. 6-1

Complete Report No. 6-1 in the study assignments and submit your working papers to the instructor for approval.

MASTERY PROBLEMS

Problem 6-A Journalizing; posting; trial balance

Dr. Marcus Reegan is a dentist. The books of original entry include a cash payments journal, cash receipts journal and general journal. The accounts are kept in a general ledger. Reegan has two employees: William Spitz, a dental hygienist, and Jorjanna Price, a secretary-bookkeeper. There is an auxiliary record for the patients seen by Reegan and for the patients seen by Spitz, but these records are not involved in this problem. The books are kept on the cash basis. Reegan requests that patients pay cash for the services of the hygienist, and most do. The trial balance as of March 31 is shown below.

Dr. Marcus Reegan, Dentist
Trial Balance
March 31, 19--

Account	Acct. No.	Debits	Credits
Cash	111	18,490.46	
Professional Equipment	221	29,206.11	
Accumulated Depr.—Professional Equip.	222		11,682.10
Office Equipment	231	14,352.84	
Accumulated Depr.—Office Equip.	232		954.85
Employees Income Tax Payable	311		464.00
FICA Tax Payable	321		562.52
FUTA Tax Payable	331		90.00
State Unemployment Tax Payable	341		303.75
Marcus Reegan, Capital	511		29,587.69
Marcus Reegan, Drawing	512	14,231.00	
Professional Fees—Dentistry	611		52,750.00
Professional Fees—Oral Hygiene	621		12,960.00
Laboratory Expense	700	12,340.67	
Laundry Expense	703	421.33	
Miscellaneous Expense	704	86.50	
Office Supplies Expense	705	650.25	
Payroll Taxes Expense	708	1,237.53	
Professional Supplies Expense	710	784.00	
Rent Expense	712	4,500.00	
Salary Expense	715	11,250.00	
Telephone Expense	720	591.38	
Utilities Expense	722	1,212.84	
		109,354.91	109,354.91

NARRATIVE OF TRANSACTIONS FOR APRIL

April 1 Paid rent for April, $1,500.

2 Paid water bill for March, $87.35.

5 Paid Wilson Professional Services for laboratory work performed in March, $2,918.

9 The amount columns in the daily service records kept by Reegan and Spitz for the week ended April 9 contained the following totals:

Kind of service:	
Dentistry—Reegan	$3,215
Oral hygiene—Spitz	890
Total	$4,105
Patients' Accounts—Charges	$1,119
Cash Services	2,986
Total	$4,105

The total cash received from patients during the week ended April 9 was:

Dentistry	$2,096
Oral hygiene	890
Total	$2,986

12 Paid laundry bill for March, $32.45.

13 Paid the following bills:
Electricity bill, $117.20
Gas bill, $54.96
(Issue check numbers 379 and 380 by debiting Utilities Expense twice.)

16 The amount columns in the daily service records kept by Reegan and Spitz for the week ended April 16 contained the following totals:

Kind of service:	
Dentistry—Reegan	$3,785
Oral hygiene—Spitz	830
Total	$4,615
Patients' Accounts—Charges	$1,800
Cash Services	2,815
Total	$4,615

The total cash received from patients during the week ended April 16 was:

Dentistry	$2,015
Oral hygiene	800
Total	$2,815

April 16 Paid salary to William Spitz for first half of month, $950, less income tax payable, $119, and FICA tax payable, $71.25; and to Jorjanna Price, $925, less income tax payable, $113, and FICA tax payable, $69.38.

16 Paid $1,026.52 for March payroll taxes:

Employees' income tax withheld	$ 464.00
FICA tax	562.52
Total	$1,026.52

19 Paid for professional supplies, $217.81.

20 Paid $200 for dues to the state dental society. (Debit Miscellaneous Expense.)

23 The amount columns in the daily service records kept by Reegan and Spitz for the week ended April 23 contained the following totals:

Kind of service:	
Dentistry—Reegan	$3,437
Oral hygiene—Spitz	832
Total	$4,269
Patients' Accounts—Charges	$1,419
Cash Services	2,850
Total	$4,269

The total cash received from patients during the week ended April 23 was:

Dentistry	$2,075
Oral hygiene	775
Total	$2,850

27 Paid for office supplies, $27.36.

28 Paid for subscriptions to magazines for the waiting room, $26. (Debit Miscellaneous Expense.)

28 Paid state unemployment tax for the first quarter of the year, $303.75.

30 The amount columns in the daily service records kept by Reegan and Spitz for the week ended April 30 contained the following totals:

Kind of service:	
Dentistry—Reegan	$3,185
Oral hygiene—Spitz	870
Total	$4,055
Patients' Accounts—Charges	$1,165
Cash Services	2,890
Total	$4,055

The total cash received from patients during the week ended April 30 was:

Dentistry	$2,010
Oral hygiene	880
Total	$2,890

April 30 Paid salary to William Spitz for second half of month, $950, less income tax payable, $119, and FICA tax payable, $71.25; and to Jorjanna Price, $925, less income tax payable, $113, and FICA tax payable, $69.38.

30 Reegan withdrew $2,500 for personal use.

30 Made an entry in the general journal for the employer's unemployment taxes and portion of the FICA tax for the month of April by debiting Payroll Taxes Expense for the total taxes and crediting FICA Tax Payable for $281.26, FUTA Tax Payable for $22 and State Unemployment Tax Payable for $74.25.

Required: **(1)** Record each transaction in the cash payments journal, cash receipts journal or general journal. Number the journal pages as follows: cash receipts, page 23; cash payments, page 31; and general, page 13. Number the checks issued beginning with check number 375. **(2)** At the end of the month, prove the cash receipts and cash payments journals by footing the amount columns and then totaling and ruling the journals. **(3)** Open the necessary general ledger accounts using the account forms provided. Record the April 1 balances as shown in the March 31 trial balance and complete the posting from the journals. All posting is done at the end of the month in order to simplify the problem. To keep most of the ledger entries in chronological order, post the General Dr. columns of the cash receipts and cash payments journals (if applicable) before posting the general journal and the special columns of the cash receipts and cash payments journals. Determine the balances of the accounts. **(4)** Take a trial balance as of April 30, using the two-column paper.

Problem 6-B Corrected trial balance

Dr. Elizabeth Hammond, a physician and surgeon, keeps her books on the cash basis. A trial balance taken as of June 30, 19--, does not balance. A check of the records reveals the following information:

(1) The correct total of the Cash Dr. column in the cash receipts journal is $8,734. This amount was posted in the cash account as $8,743.

(2) The cash payments journal was out of balance by $580 because a payment for prepaid insurance was debited to the proper account but was not entered in the Cash Cr. column.

(3) The correct total of the Professional Fees Cr. column in the cash receipts journal is $9,083. This amount was posted in the professional fees account as a debit.

(4) The balance in the professional equipment account was entered in the trial balance as $37,142.50 instead of $37,124.50.

(5) The utilities expense includes $96.30 that was a payment of Hammond's utility bill for her personal residence.

(6) A payment of $157.18 for medical supplies expense was entered in the office supplies expense account.
(7) The miscellaneous expense account in the amount of $179.81 was omitted from the trial balance.
(8) All accounts have normal balances.

Dr. Elizabeth Hammond
Trial Balance
June 30, 19--

Account	Dr. Balance	Cr. Balance
Cash	19,053.00	
Prepaid Insurance	2,417.00	
Professional Equipment	37,142.50	
Accumulated Depr.—Professional Equip.		16,246.20
Office Equipment	10,095.64	
Accumulated Depr.—Office Equip.		1,023.37
Employees Income Tax Payable		227.85
FICA Tax Payable		276.32
FUTA Tax Payable		47.65
Elizabeth Hammond, Capital		32,424.11
Elizabeth Hammond, Drawing	21,626.70	
Professional Fees		46,837.93
Payroll Taxes Expense		940.90
Medical Supplies Expense		1,352.05
Office Supplies Expense	764.15	
Rent Expense	12,000.00	
Salary Expense	8,900.00	
Utilities Expense	1,384.68	
Totals	113,383.67	99,376.38

Required: Prepare a corrected trial balance.

CHALLENGE PROBLEM 6

Fred Elliott has a dental practice and employs Mary Denovich as the office manager and Jill Barnes as the dental assistant. Below is the Chart of Accounts for Elliott's dental practice. The transactions for the first week of April along with the information to be entered in the daily service record are also shown.

FRED ELLIOTT, DENTIST

CHART OF ACCOUNTS

Assets
- 100 Cash
- 115 Prepaid Insurance
- 200 Automobile
- 205 Accumulated Depr.—Automobile
- 210 Equipment
- 215 Accumulated Depr.—Equipment

Liabilities
- 310 Employees Income Tax Payable
- 320 FICA Tax Payable
- 330 FUTA Tax Payable
- 340 SUTA Tax Payable

Owner's Equity
- 500 Fred Elliott, Capital
- 510 Fred Elliott, Drawing

Revenues
- 600 Professional Fees
- 610 Other Income

Expenses
- 701 Charitable Contributions Expense
- 703 Dues and Subscriptions Expense
- 704 Laboratory Expense
- 705 Laundry Expense
- 706 Legal Expense
- 707 Medical Supplies Expense
- 708 Miscellaneous Expense
- 709 Office Plants Expense
- 710 Payroll Taxes Expense
- 720 Rent Expense
- 724 Salary Expense
- 728 Utilities Expense

April 1 Issued check number 420 for $950 to University Property Management in payment of the monthly rent.

1 Issued check number 421 for $75 in payment of the annual subscription for a medical journal.

1 Received notice from First National Bank—West Region that $45 of interest had been added to the business checking account.

1 Entered and coded in the daily service record the following information related to services rendered:

Arthur Amick, Examination, Radiographs, $65; paid $65
David Hollings, Oral Surgery, $300; paid $50
Nina Chevalier, Root Canal, $295; paid $150
Maria Wise, Emergency Treatment, $275; paid $200
Keith Jackson, Study Models, $20; paid $20
Orajade Kiwi, Consultation, $10; paid $10

2 Issued check number 422 for $675 to Green and Scott Insurance Agency for the annual premium on Elliott's automobile which is used exclusively for business.

2 Issued check number 423 for $3,275.18 to Massey Office Equipment in payment for new copier for the office.

2 Received $765 from Ted Lutz, attorney. Lutz collected $1,147.50 from a delinquent patient and retained $382.50 for his fee.

2 Entered and coded in the daily service record the following information related to services rendered:

Sara Miles, Radiographs, Extraction, $40 each; no payment
John Anderson, Crown, $375; paid $300
Don Suggs, Partial Denture, $650; paid $350
Received check from Blue Shield for S. Joslyn for $275
Connie Brannon, Complete Denture, $1,900; paid $500
Chris Wilson, Partial Denture, $650; paid $100
Royce Holt, Root Canal, $325; paid $75

April 3 Issued check number 424 for $50 to Folies Department Store in payment of Elliott's personal charge account.

3 Issued check number 425 for $200 payable to the United Fund Charities.

3 Issued check number 426 for $683.25 to Lake Center Laboratories in payment of laboratory expense for the month.

3 Entered and coded in the daily service record the following information related to services rendered:

John Tims, Amalgam, $65; paid $65
Charles Johnson, Sealants, $25; paid $25
Norma Hidrova, Examination, $10, Radiographs, $40, Study Models, $10; paid $60
Omar Hemnu, Prophylaxis, $30, Fluoride, $15; paid $45
Claudia Henderson, Amalgam, $35; paid $35
Shelley Jenkins, Extraction, $55; paid $55
Jill Babola, Sealants, $25; paid $25

4 Issued check number 427 for $150.85 to United Laundry Service.

4 Issued check number 428 for $325.68 to Ocean Medical Supplies.

4 Issued check number 429 for $75 to Green Thumb Nursery for the monthly maintenance of the office plants.

4 Issued check number 430 for $196.12 to Central Lighting and Power in payment of the electricity bill.

4 Entered and coded in the daily service record the following information related to services rendered:

Helen Rubens, Space Retainer, $150; paid $100
Received check from Blue Shield for N. McCagh for $1,316
Helen Roberts, Control Visit, $15; paid $15
James Cook, Emergency Treatment, $20; paid $20
Lori Chauvelle, Pulpotomy, $30; paid $30
James Garza, Oral Surgery, $135; paid $50
Ashley Howard, Crown, $400; paid $100

5 Issued check number 431 for $1,000 to Fred Elliott for personal use.

5 Issued the following checks in payment of the weekly salaries:

Check number 432 to Mary Denovich for $325 less income tax payable, $65.00, and FICA tax payable, $24.38.

Check number 433 to Jill Barnes for $300 less income tax payable, $57.00, and FICA tax payable, $22.50.

April 5 Received $250 for Elliott's presentation at a professional meeting.

5 Issued check number 434 for $237.16 to Southern Bell for the telephone bill.

5 Entered and coded in the daily service record the following information related to services rendered:

Received check from Prudential Insurance for S. Besson for $1,600
Cindy Velazquez, Stainless Steel Crown, $250; paid $50
Paul Rea, Fluoride, $10; paid $10
Jeanie Sherrill, Examination, $10, Radiographs, $65, Control Visit, $15; paid $90
Kevin Goad, Extraction, $55; paid $55
Alan Palmer, Pulpotomy, $30; paid $30
Ron Spain, Post and Core, $85; paid $25
Roy Stuart, Emergency Treatment, $225; paid $50

5 Footed the daily service record and obtained the following totals:

Kind of Service	
Diagnostic	$ 270
Preparative	1,785
Reconstructive	4,060
Restoration	350
Preventive	285
Miscellaneous	–0–
Total	$6,750

Patients Accounts—Charges	$3,995
Cash Services	2,755
Total	$6,750

The total cash received from patients for the week was:

Payments	$3,191
Cash Services	2,755
Total	$5,946

Required: (1) Enter the transactions and information provided in the cash receipts journal, cash payments journal, and daily service record. The daily service record is to be completed daily and the total cash received will be entered in the cash receipts journal at the end of the week.

In entering data in the daily service record, the Charge column is used to record the amount of the current services for which payment was not made, and the Cash Services column is used to enter all cash paid for current services. All payments received for previous services (from insurance carriers and individuals) is recorded in the Payments column. The following codes are to be written in parentheses next to the patient's name to identify the procedure performed:

Diagnostic

EX Examination
R Radiographs
SM Study Models
CO Consultation

Reconstructive

C Crown
CB Crown & Bridge
PD Partial Denture
CD Complete Denture
RE Reline, Rebase, Repair
PC Post and Core

Preventive

CV Control Visit
P Prophylaxis
F Fluoride
S Sealants
SR Space Retainer

Preparative

OS Oral Surgery
PR Periodontal Treatment
PP Pulpotomy
RC Root Canal
OT Orthodontics
EC Extraction
ET Emergency Treatment

Restoration

AM Amalgam
CM Composite
GI Gold Inlay
SS Stainless Steel Crown
PT Pin Restoration

(2) Foot the journals and prove the balances.

EXPANDING YOUR BUSINESS VOCABULARY

What is the meaning of each of the following terms:

Aging accounts **(p. 178)**
Assignment **(p. 179)**
Balance-column account **(p. 174)**
CPT-4 **(p. 179)**
Day sheet **(p. 168, 174)**
Daily service record **(p. 168, 174)**
Deductible **(p. 179)**
DRGs **(p. 179)**
Four-column account **(p. 174)**
ICD-9CM **(p. 179)**
Individual posting **(p. 173)**
Mixed accounts **(p. 170)**
Modified cash basis **(p. 169)**
Patients ledger **(p. 175)**
Proving the patients ledger **(p. 178)**
Pure cash basis **(p. 169)**
Summary posting **(p. 173)**
Universal Health Insurance Claim Form **(p. 179)**

APPENDIX
OTHER ACCOUNTING SYSTEMS

The theory supporting a manual accounting system, such as that illustrated in the chapter, forms the foundation for other systems that might be used. This appendix will explain two types of systems that are rapidly being implemented in the medical and dental professions. These are the one-write and computerized systems.

ONE-WRITE ACCOUNTING SYSTEM

In order to decrease the time involved in recordkeeping, to reduce posting errors, and to maintain internal accounting controls, the **one-write** or **pegboard system** of accounting is being used in many professional services. It is a manual system which requires special forms that utilize special reproduction features.

The one-write system uses the basic accounting principles of the cash receipts, cash payments, and general journals. The procedures, however, are simplified. The special feature of this type of system is that an **accounting board** with pegs at the left permits several forms to be stacked and aligned. This allows entries to be recorded simultaneously on the different documents. Strategically located carbon strips or chemically treated pages permit this reproduction only in specific locations on the stacked forms. All forms are prenumbered. In the discussion that follows, the dental profession will be used to illustrate the journals and other features and procedures of a one-write system.

One-Write Accounts Receivable System

To record cash receipts, the one-write system uses an accounts receivable system as shown on page 215. Note that the forms are stacked in the following order on an accounting board: standard insurance form or transaction slip on the top, then the patient's account form, and finally the day sheet or daily service record. Features of these special documents are discussed below.

The Insurance Form

A standard three-part insurance form that is often called a **superbill** is shown on page 216. Each part serves a special function and shows specific information related to the patient's visit. The top copy is filed in the patient's chart as a permanent record for the office. The second copy contains the standard information required by insurance companies and is attached to the insurance claim. The third copy is the dentist's bill for services. It shows the services performed, date of the next appointment, previous balance of the

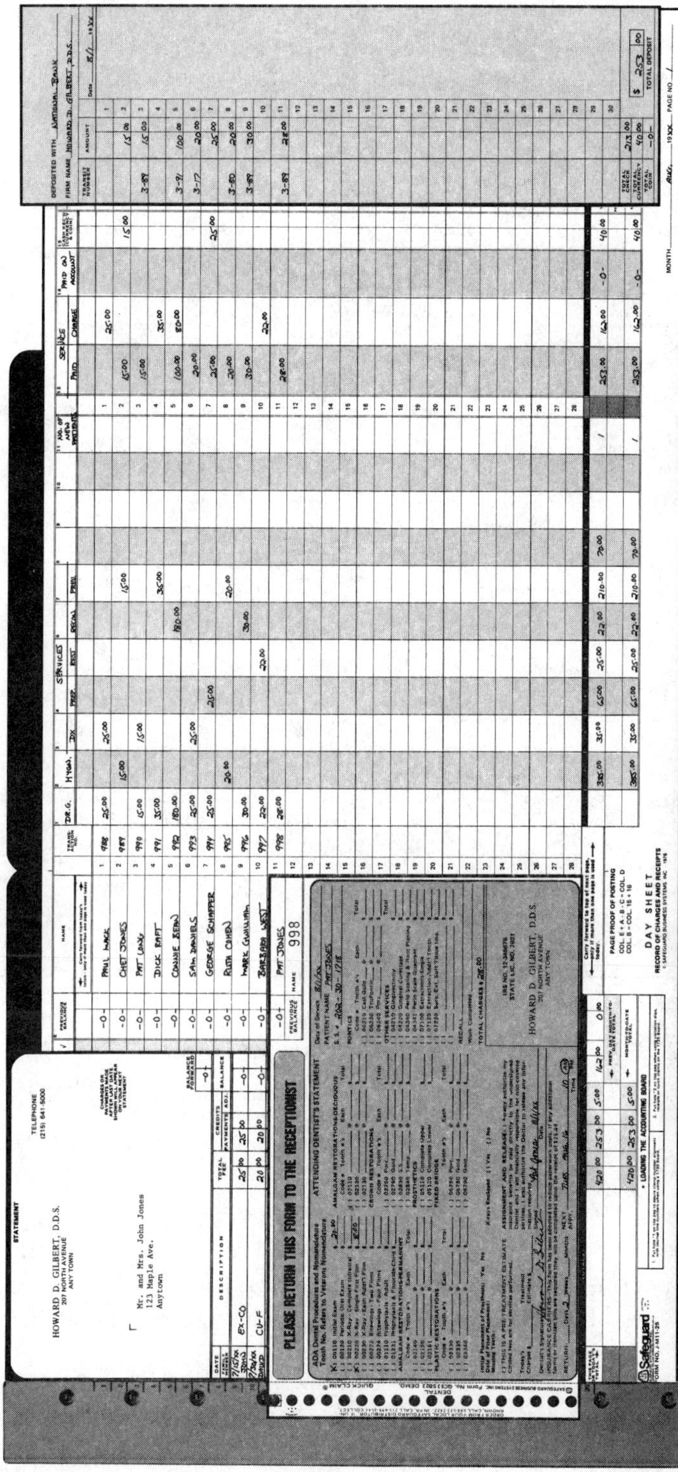

One-Write Accounts Receivable System

(Used by permission Safeguard Business Systems, Inc.)

account, current charge and payment, and current balance. The universal coding explained in this chapter is also used on these forms to identify a patient's diagnosis and the procedures performed by the dentist.

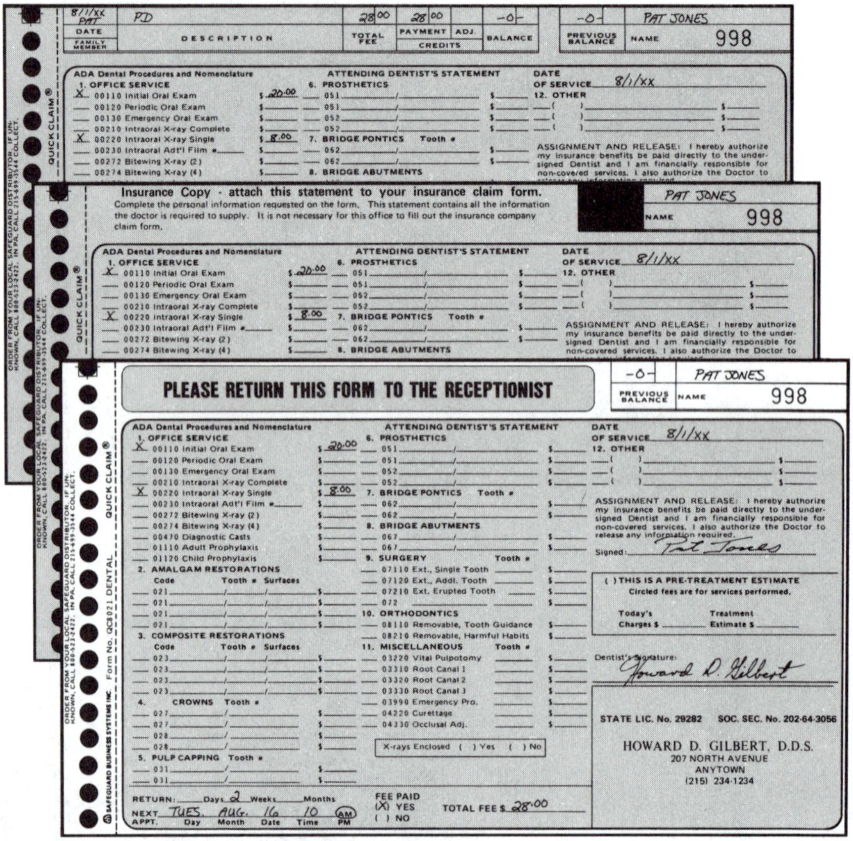

DATE / FAMILY MEMBER	DESCRIPTION	TOTAL FEE	PAYMENT	ADJ.	BALANCE	PREVIOUS BALANCE	NAME
8/1/xx PAT	PD	28.00	28.00		-0-	-0-	PAT JONES 998

Insurance Copy - attach this statement to your insurance claim form.
Complete the personal information requested on the form. This statement contains all the information the doctor is required to supply. It is not necessary for this office to fill out the insurance company claim form.

PLEASE RETURN THIS FORM TO THE RECEPTIONIST

PREVIOUS BALANCE -0- NAME PAT JONES 998

ADA Dental Procedures and Nomenclature

1. OFFICE SERVICE
X 00110 Initial Oral Exam $ 20.00
00120 Periodic Oral Exam $
00130 Emergency Oral Exam $
00210 Intraoral X-ray Complete $
X 00220 Intraoral X-ray Single $ 8.00
00230 Intraoral Adt'l Film # $
00272 Bitewing X-ray (2) $
00274 Bitewing X-ray (4) $
00470 Diagnostic Casts $
01110 Adult Prophylaxis $
01120 Child Prophylaxis $

2. AMALGAM RESTORATIONS — Code / Tooth # / Surfaces
021 / / $ (4 lines)

3. COMPOSITE RESTORATIONS — Code / Tooth # / Surfaces
023 / / $ (4 lines)

4. CROWNS Tooth #
027 / $
027 / $
028 / $
028 / $

5. PULP CAPPING Tooth #
031 / $
031 / $

ATTENDING DENTIST'S STATEMENT

6. PROSTHETICS
051 / $
051 / $
052 / $
052 / $

7. BRIDGE PONTICS Tooth #
062 / $
062 / $

8. BRIDGE ABUTMENTS
067 / $
067 / $

9. SURGERY Tooth #
07110 Ext., Single Tooth $
07120 Ext., Addl. Tooth $
07210 Ext. Erupted Tooth $
072 $

10. ORTHODONTICS
08110 Removable, Tooth Guidance $
08210 Removable, Harmful Habits $

11. MISCELLANEOUS Tooth #
03220 Vital Pulpotomy $
03310 Root Canal 1 $
03320 Root Canal 2 $
03330 Root Canal 3 $
03990 Emergency Pro. $
04220 Curettage $
04330 Occlusal Adj. $

X-rays Enclosed ( ) Yes ( ) No

DATE OF SERVICE 8/1/xx

12. OTHER
( ) $
( ) $
( ) $

ASSIGNMENT AND RELEASE: I hereby authorize my insurance benefits be paid directly to the undersigned Dentist and I am financially responsible for non-covered services. I also authorize the Doctor to release any information required.

Signed: Pat Jones

( ) THIS IS A PRE-TREATMENT ESTIMATE
Circled fees are for services performed.
Today's Charges $ Treatment Estimate $

Dentist's Signature: Howard D. Gilbert

STATE LIC. No. 29282 SOC. SEC. No. 202-64-3056

HOWARD D. GILBERT, D.D.S.
207 NORTH AVENUE
ANYTOWN
(215) 234-1234

RETURN: Days 2 Weeks Months
NEXT APPT. TUES. AUG. 16 10 AM (Day Month Date Time AM/PM)

FEE PAID (X) YES ( ) NO TOTAL FEE $ 28.00

QUICK CLAIM® Form No. QC8021 DENTAL
SAFEGUARD BUSINESS SYSTEMS INC.
ORDER FROM YOUR LOCAL SAFEGUARD DISTRIBUTOR. IF UNKNOWN, CALL 800-523-2422. IN PA. CALL 215-699-3544 COLLECT.

Three-Part Insurance Form

(Used by permission Safeguard Business Systems, Inc.)

Transaction Slip

A **transaction slip**, as shown on page 217, may be used instead of the insurance form. A perforation allows this form to be separated. The left part becomes the bill for services rendered and the right part is filed with the patient's chart and kept in the office files.

The patient's account form is similar to that shown in this chapter. The difference is that charges and payments are recorded in one operation at the same time the day sheet or daily service record is completed.

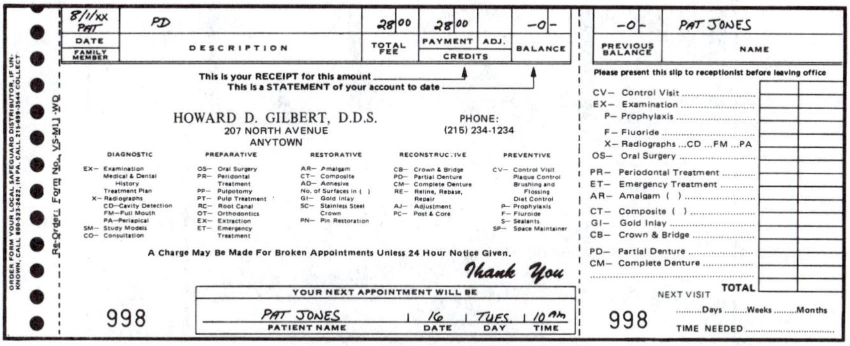

DATE / FAMILY MEMBER	DESCRIPTION	TOTAL FEE	CREDITS: PAYMENT	CREDITS: ADJ.	BALANCE	PREVIOUS BALANCE	NAME
8/1/xx PAT	PD	28 00	28 00		-0-	-0-	PAT JONES

This is your RECEIPT for this amount
This is a STATEMENT of your account to date

HOWARD D. GILBERT, D.D.S.
207 NORTH AVENUE
ANYTOWN
PHONE: (215) 234-1234

DIAGNOSTIC	PREPARATIVE	RESTORATIVE	RECONSTRUCTIVE	PREVENTIVE
EX– Examination, Medical & Dental History, Treatment Plan	OS– Oral Surgery	AR– Amalgam	CB– Crown & Bridge	CV– Control Visit, Plaque Control, Brushing and Flossing, Diet Control
X– Radiographs: CD–Cavity Detection, FM–Full Mouth, PA–Periapical	PR– Peridontal Treatment	CT– Composite	PD– Partial Denture	P– Prophylaxis
SM– Study Models	PP– Pulpotomy	AD– Adhesive	CM– Complete Denture	F– Fluroide
CO– Consultation	PT– Pulp Treatment	No. of Surfaces in ( )	RE– Reline, Rebase, Repair	S– Sealants
	RC– Root Canal	GI– Gold Inlay	AJ– Adjustment	SP– Space Maintainer
	OT– Orthodontics	SC– Stainless Steel Crown	PC– Post & Core	
	EX– Extraction	PN– Pin Restoration		
	ET– Emergency Treatment			

A Charge May Be Made For Broken Appointments Unless 24 Hour Notice Given.

Thank You

YOUR NEXT APPOINTMENT WILL BE

998 — PATIENT NAME: PAT JONES | DATE: 16 | DAY: TUES. | TIME: 10 am

Please present this slip to receptionist before leaving office

CV– Control Visit
EX– Examination
P– Prophylaxis
F– Fluoride
X– Radiographs ...CD ...FM ...PA
OS– Oral Surgery
PR– Periodontal Treatment
ET– Emergency Treatment
AR– Amalgam ( )
CT– Composite ( )
GI– Gold Inlay
CB– Crown & Bridge
PD– Partial Denture
CM– Complete Denture
TOTAL

998 NEXT VISIT ....Days ....Weeks ....Months
TIME NEEDED ....

ORDER FORM YOUR LOCAL SAFEGUARD DISTRIBUTOR, IF UNKNOWN, CALL 800-523-2422, IN PA. CALL 215-699-3544 COLLECT
Re-Order: Form No. VS-MIJ-WQ

Transaction Slip

(Used by permission Safeguard Business Systems, Inc.)

Day Sheet

The day sheet, or the daily service record, is shown on page 218 without the stacked forms. Much of the information previously discussed with the other forms is duplicated on this form. Special accounts receivable and cash control columns are included at the right. Across the bottom are columns for proving the entries on this page. By having all forms pre-numbered, internal controls are employed that account for all entries on the day sheet, money collected, and patients seen by the doctor.

A flowchart that summarizes the one-write accounts receivable system is shown on page 219.

One-Write Combination Payroll and Cash Payments System

The one-write cash payments system functions much like the accounts receivable system. It is called the combination payroll and cash payments system. Like the accounts receivable system, special forms are aligned and multiple entries are made in one writing. The special forms used with this system include payroll and regular checks, employee's earnings records, and the payroll and cash payments journal. Details related to the payroll deductions and other information are written on the payroll check as well as on the employee's earnings record and on the payroll and cash payments journal simultaneously. A duplicate copy of the payroll check is kept in the office file. Regular checks are also recorded in duplicate. Information related to the payment is concurrently recorded on the check and on the payroll and cash payments journal. The check copy is stapled to the invoice and filed. An illustration of this system is shown on page 220. This journal is somewhat similar to the cash payments journal shown in this chapter. It has special columns for recording to whom the check was issued and to what account the expenditure should be charged. A flowchart that summarizes the one-write combination and payroll and cash payments system is shown on page 221.

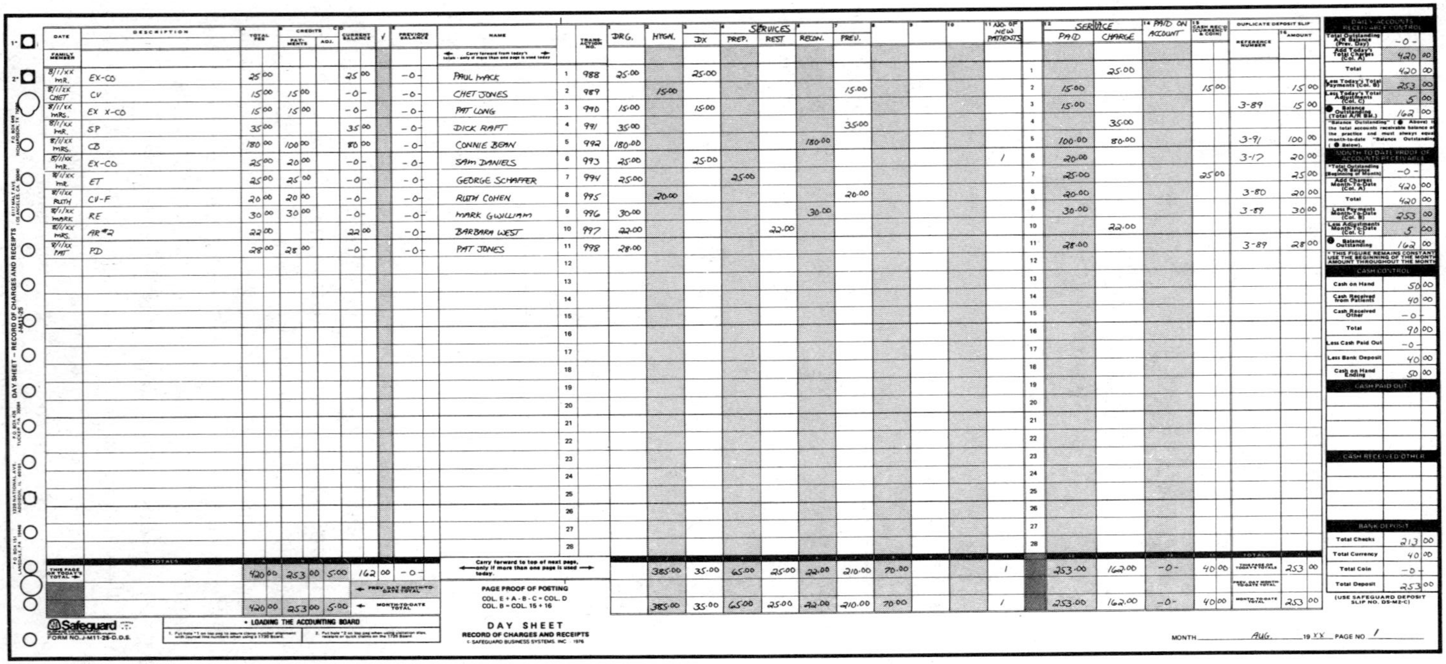

DAY SHEET — RECORD OF CHARGES AND RECEIPTS

Line	Date / Family Member	Description	Total Fee	Credits: Payments	Credits: Adj.	Current Balance	Previous Balance	Name	Trans. No.	Drg.	Hygn.	Dx	Prep.	Rest	Recon.	Prev.	No. of New Patients	Service Paid	Service Charge	Paid on Account	Cash Recd (Currency & Coin)	Reference Number	Amount
1	8/1/xx Mr.	EX-CO	25.00			25.00	-0-	Paul Mack	988	25.00		25.00							25.00				
2	8/1/xx Chet	CV	15.00	15.00		-0-	-0-	Chet Jones	989		15.00					15.00		15.00			15.00		15.00
3	8/1/xx Mrs.	EX X-CO	15.00	15.00		-0-	-0-	Pat Long	990	15.00		15.00						15.00				3-89	15.00
4	8/1/xx Mr.	SP	35.00			35.00	-0-	Dick Raft	991	35.00						35.00			35.00				
5	8/1/xx Mrs.	CB	180.00	100.00		80.00	-0-	Connie Bean	992	180.00					180.00			100.00	80.00			3-91	100.00
6	8/1/xx Mr.	EX-CO	25.00	20.00		-0-	-0-	Sam Daniels	993	25.00		25.00					1	20.00				3-17	20.00
7	8/1/xx Mr.	ET	25.00	25.00		-0-	-0-	George Schaffer	994	25.00			25.00					25.00			25.00		25.00
8	8/1/xx Ruth	CV-F	20.00	20.00		-0-	-0-	Ruth Cohen	995		20.00					20.00		20.00				3-80	20.00
9	8/1/xx Mark	RE	30.00	30.00		-0-	-0-	Mark Gwilliam	996	30.00					30.00			30.00				3-89	30.00
10	8/1/xx Mrs.	AR #2	22.00			22.00	-0-	Barbara West	997	22.00				22.00					22.00				
11	8/1/xx Pat	PD	28.00	28.00		-0-	-0-	Pat Jones	998	28.00								28.00				3-89	28.00
Totals (this page or today's total)			420.00	253.00	5.00	162.00	-0-			385.00	35.00	65.00	25.00	22.00	210.00	70.00	1	253.00	162.00	-0-	40.00		253.00
Month-to-date total			420.00	253.00	5.00					385.00	35.00	65.00	25.00	22.00	210.00	70.00	1	253.00	162.00	-0-	40.00		253.00

Page proof of posting: Col. E + A − B − C = Col. D; Col. B = Col. 15 + 16

Daily Accounts Receivable Control	
Total Outstanding A/R Balance (Prev. Day)	-0-
Add Today's Total Charges (Col. A)	420.00
Total	420.00
Less Today's Total Payments (Col. B1)	253.00
Less Today's Total Adjustments (Col. C)	5.00
Balance Outstanding (Total A/R Bal.)	162.00

Month-to-Date Proof of Accounts Receivable	
Total Outstanding A/R Balance (Beginning of Month)	-0-
Add Charges Month-To-Date (Col. A)	420.00
Total	420.00
Less Payments Month-To-Date (Col. B)	253.00
Less Adjustments Month-To-Date (Col. C)	5.00
Balance Outstanding	162.00

Cash Control	
Cash on Hand	50.00
Cash Received from Patients	40.00
Cash Received Other	-0-
Total	90.00
Less Cash Paid Out	-0-
Less Bank Deposit	40.00
Cash on Hand Ending	50.00

Bank Deposit	
Total Checks	213.00
Total Currency	40.00
Total Coin	-0-
Total Deposit	253.00

Month Aug. 19XX Page No. 1

Day Sheet

(Used by permission Safeguard Business Systems, Inc.)

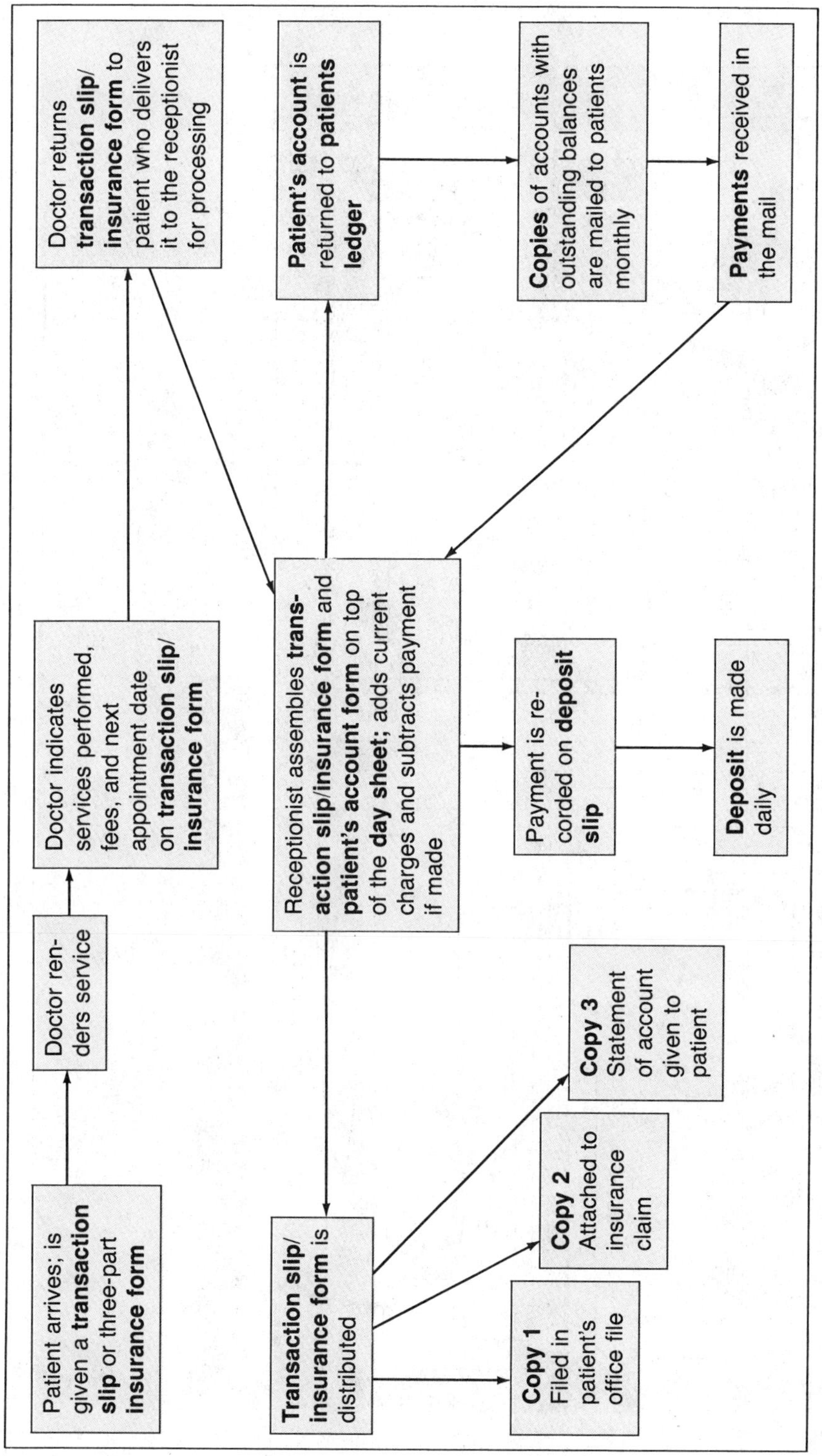

Flowchart for Accounts Receivable One-Write System

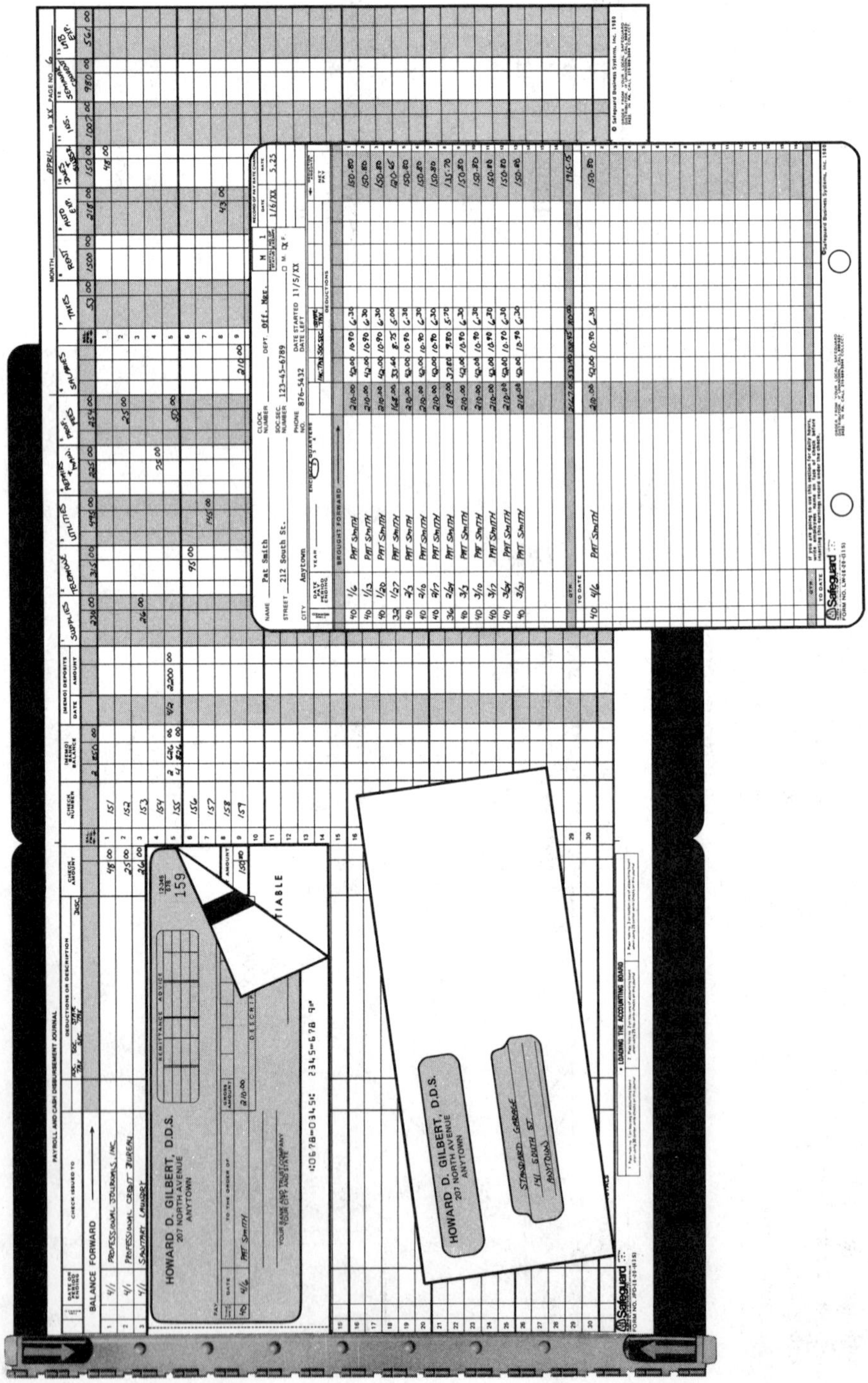

One-Write Combination Payroll/Disbursement (or Payments) System

(Used by permission Safeguard Business Systems, Inc.)

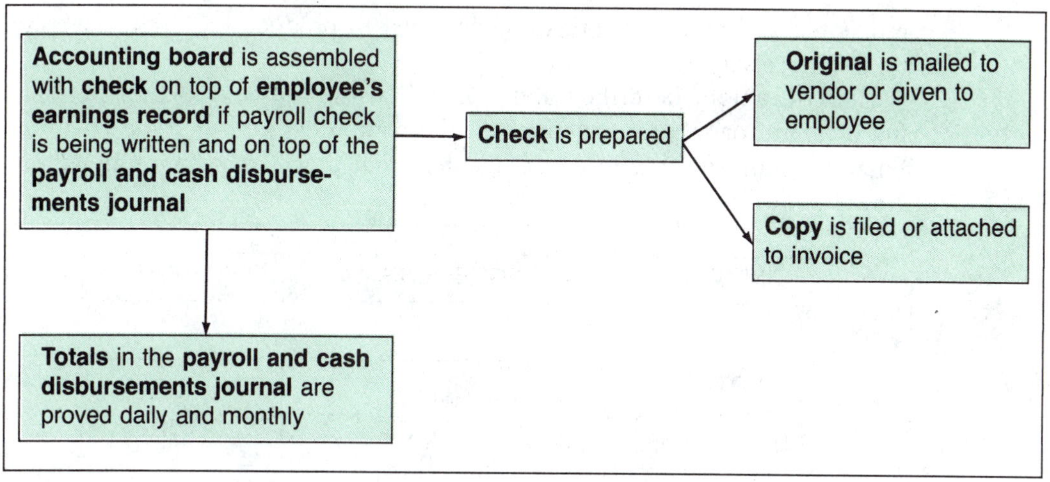

Flowchart for Combination Payroll/Cash Disbursements (or Payments) One-Write System

COMPUTER-BASED ACCOUNTING SYSTEMS

Manual accounting systems such as the one-write or those illustrated in the text are the most common systems found in medical and dental offices. A manual system is a good one if properly set up and maintained. Some physicians and dentists use a **computer service bureau**, an outside agency that processes their accounting data. Periodically, the office records are picked up by the agency or delivered to the agency by office personnel for processing. Reports, payroll checks, and other data are returned to the office.

The development of **microcomputers**, small computers with limited internal storage capacity, and their relatively low cost have made it possible for all professional persons to computerize their accounting systems. The accounting records may be processed and maintained on an integrated or partially computerized system. An integrated computer program is a tremendous time saver. A daily service record, a summary of the amounts owed the physician or dentist, a patients ledger, collection letters, monthly billing statements, and insurance reports can all be produced automatically. If an integrated system is not used, the major use of the computer is in maintaining accounts receivable. Charges and payments are entered via the computer keyboard. The computer automatically posts these entries and updates the patients' accounts. Depending upon the program used, a listing can be obtained of the patients with outstanding balances along with the ages of the balances. Monthly statements for accounts with balances can also be printed automatically by the system.

Basically what is needed for a computerized accounting system in a professional practice is a small computer consisting of a central processing unit **(CPU)** with the necessary storage capacity, a printer, a terminal **(CRT)**, and two disk drives. Computer disks on which programs and data can be recorded and stored and computer programs designed to produce the desired records are also necessary.

The equipment described above is called the **hardware**, and the disks and program, or set of instructions for the computer, are called the **software**. These function together to create a system that processes accounting data as shown below:

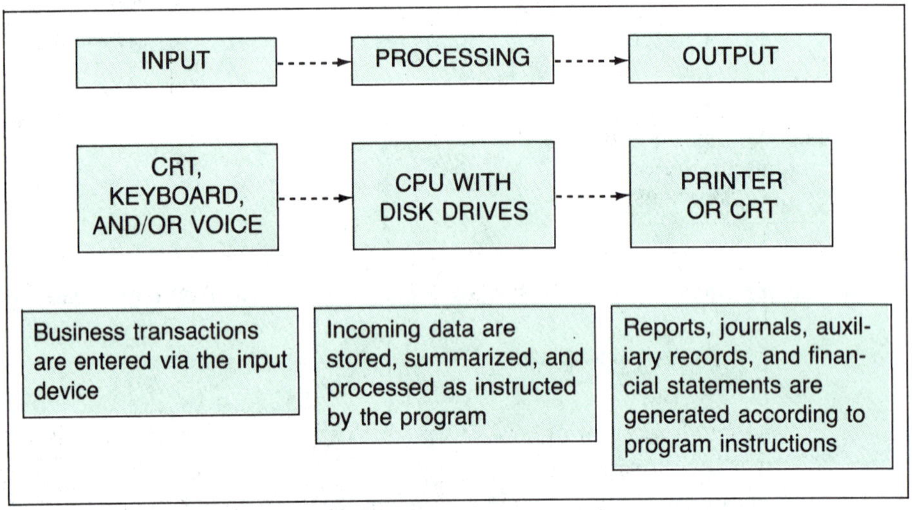

Computerized System for Processing Business Data

One-write and computerized systems improve the efficiency of an office in a number of ways. While one-write systems reduce the time spent in record-keeping and the number of errors made in posting, they are still manual systems and cannot give immediate, up-to-date information as can the computerized systems. The advantages associated with one-write systems are also the advantages of computerized systems—the computerized system simply speeds up the process and eliminates even more steps in the accounting process. Eliminating steps in the accounting process diminishes the opportunities for posting errors. Speed in getting the results of operations enables the professional person to make informed, up-to-date decisions about the practice.

BUILDING YOUR ACCOUNTING KNOWLEDGE

1. What are some advantages of using a one-write accounting system?
2. What are the multiple uses of the three-part insurance form?
3. What does stacking documents mean in a one-write system?
4. Summarize the procedure for recording data using a one-write accounts receivable system.
5. Summarize the procedure for recording data using a one-write payroll and cash payments journal.
6. Why are many personal service enterprises purchasing microcomputers for use in processing and maintaining their accounting records?
7. How does a manual system of accounting differ from a computerized system?

APPLYING ACCOUNTING CONCEPTS

Exercise 6A-1. Eugene A. Grasselli, D.D.S., uses the One-Write Systems for Accounts Receivable and for Payroll and Cash Disbursements. Indicate the system in which each of the following transactions would be recorded. Use an *A* for the Accounts Receivable System and a *D* for the Payroll and Cash Disbursements System. Indicate by an * entries that would be posted to the patients ledger.

1. _____ Paid $943 for monthly rent on office building
2. _____ Paid Sally Rogers $550, less $55 withheld for federal income tax and $41.25 withheld for FICA Tax.
3. _____ Withdrew $600 for personal use
4. _____ Reimbursed the petty cash fund for $67
5. _____ Received cash payment for services rendered $615
6. _____ Received $520 from the attorney to apply on James Byars' account; attorney deducted his fee from the $680 collected
7. _____ Received invoice for $110 for medical supplies purchased on account
8. _____ Paid payroll taxes for the quarter, $950 FICA, $115 FUTA and $215 SUTA
9. _____ Received cash payment of $250 on account
10. _____ Billed patient $25 for services rendered
11. _____ Collected cash of $750 from insurance company for patient's outstanding balance
12. _____ Reimbursed patient $25 for overpayment by insurance company

Exercise 6A-2. Using the following information related to Erica Beson's medical practice, prove the cash on hand balance:

Cash on hand at the beginning of the day	$ 100
Bank deposit made today	1,645
Cash received from patients today	1,620

Exercise 6A-3. Maureen Giacchino, M.D., uses the One-Write System of Payroll and Cash Disbursements. The balance of the accounts receivable for the previous day total $34,375. Totals from the Day Sheet for today are as follows:

Total Fees	$1,855
Payments (credit)	1,530
Adjustments (credit)	90

What is the current balance of the outstanding accounts receivable?

EXPANDING YOUR BUSINESS VOCABULARY

What is the meaning of each of the following terms:

Accounting board **(p. 214)**
Computer service bureau **(p. 221)**
CPU **(p. 221)**
CRT **(p. 221)**
Day sheet **(p. 217)**
Hardware **(p. 222)**
Microcomputer **(p. 221)**
One-write system **(p. 214)**
Pegboard system, **(p. 214)**
Software **(p. 222)**
Superbill **(p. 214)**
Transaction slip **(p. 216)**

7

The Periodic Summary

CHAPTER OBJECTIVES

Careful study of this chapter should enable you to:

- Prepare a ten-column end-of-year work sheet for an attorney.
- Prepare the financial statements for an attorney.

One of the major reasons for keeping accounting records is to accumulate information that will make it possible to prepare periodic summaries of both (1) the revenue and expenses of the business during a specified period and (2) the assets, liabilities, and owner's equity of the business at a specified date. A trial balance of the general ledger accounts will provide most of the information that is required for these summaries (the income statement and the balance sheet). However, the trial balance does not supply the data in a form that is easily interpreted, nor does it reflect changes in the accounting elements that have not been represented by ordinary business transactions. Therefore, at the end of a fiscal period it is necessary (1) to determine the kind and amounts of changes that the accounts do not reflect and to adjust the accounts accordingly and (2) to recast the information into the form of an income statement and a balance sheet. These two steps are often referred to as the **periodic summary**.

END-OF-PERIOD WORK SHEET

An end-of-period **work sheet** is a device that assists the accountant in three ways. It facilitates **(1)** the preparing of the financial statements, **(2)** the making of needed adjustments in the accounts, and **(3)** the closing of the temporary owner's equity accounts. When a number of adjustments are to be made at the end of a period, **end-of-period adjustments**, a work sheet is especially helpful in determining the balance of the accounts after adjustment.

Work sheets are not financial statements; they are devices used to assist the accountant in performing certain tasks. Ordinarily, it is only the accountant who uses or even sees a work sheet.

A Work Sheet for an Attorney

Although an end-of-period work sheet can be in any of several forms, a common and widely used arrangement involves ten amount columns. The amount columns are used in pairs. The first pair of amount columns is for the trial balance. The data to be recorded consist of the name, number, and debit or credit balance of each account. Debit balances should be entered in the left-hand column and credit balances in the right-hand column. The second pair of amount columns is used to record needed end-of-period adjustments. The third pair of amount columns is used to show that the debit and credit account balances as adjusted are equal in amount. The fourth pair of amount columns is for the adjusted balances of the expense and revenue accounts. This pair of columns is headed "Income Statement" since the amounts shown will be reported in that statement. The fifth, and last, pair of amount columns is headed "Balance Sheet" and shows the adjusted account balances that will be reported in that statement.

To illustrate the preparation and use of the end-of-period work sheet, the example of the accounts of Jose Ortega, Attorney at Law, will be continued. The journal and ledger for Ortega for the month of December were reproduced in Chapter 5. In this chapter, the income statement for the year and the balance sheet at the end of the year will be reproduced, showing the use of a work sheet as a device for summarizing the data to be presented in those statements.

The end-of-year work sheet for Ortega is reproduced on page 227. Following is a description and discussion of the steps that were followed in the preparation of the work sheet. Each step should be studied carefully with frequent reference to the work sheet.

Trial Balance Columns. The trial balance of the general ledger accounts as of December 31 was entered in the first pair of amount columns. This trial balance is the same as the one shown on page 227 except that all of the account titles were included in the work sheet even though certain accounts had no balance at this point.

The Trial Balance Debit and Credit columns were totaled. The totals should be equal. If not, the cause of any discrepancy must be found and corrected before the preparation of the work sheet can proceed.

Adjustments Columns. The second pair of amount columns on the work sheet was used to record certain entries necessary to reflect the depreciation that had occurred during the year.

Two entries were made in the Adjustments columns to reflect these changes. When the account was debited, the amount was entered in the Adjustments Debit column on the same horizontal line as the name of the account. Amounts credited were entered in the Credit column. Each entry made on the work sheet was identified by a small letter in parentheses to facilitate cross-reference. Following is an explanation of each of the entries.

Entry (a): This adjustment enters the depreciation expense on the automobile by debiting Depreciation Expense, Account No. 705, for $5,298.33 and crediting Accumulated Depreciation—Automobile, Account No. 205, for the same amount.

The automobile has been owned for the entire year. The original cost of the automobile was $15,895.00. The depreciation rate is 33⅓ percent; therefore, the depreciation expense is $5,298.33 ($15,895.00 × .33⅓).

Entry (b): This adjustment enters the depreciation expense for the year on office equipment by debiting Depreciation Expense, Account No. 705, for $1,792.40 and crediting Accumulated Depreciation—Office Equipment, Account No. 215, for the same amount. Office Equipment, Account No. 210, shows that an office refrigerator was purchased on December 16 at a cost of $414.21 and that on December 21 an electric typewriter was purchased at a cost of $666.75. Ortega follows the practice of not taking depreciation on assets that have been owned for less than a month. The debit to Depreciation Expense is therefore based on the December 1 balance of $8,962.00 in Account No. 210. The depreciation rate used for office equipment is 20 percent; therefore the depreciation expense is $1,792.40 ($8,962.00 × .20).

After making the required entries in the Adjustments columns of the work sheet, the columns were totaled to prove the equality of the debit and credit entries.

Adjusted Trial Balance Columns. The third pair of amount columns of the work sheet was used for the **adjusted trial balance**. To determine the balance of each account after making the required adjustments, it was necessary to take into consideration the amounts entered in the first two pairs of amount columns. When an account balance was not affected by entries in

Jose Ortega, Attorney at Law
Work Sheet
For the Year Ended December 31, 1987

	Account Title	Acct. No.	Trial Balance Debit	Trial Balance Credit	Adjustments Debit	Adjustments Credit	Adjusted Trial Balance Debit	Adjusted Trial Balance Credit	Income Statement Debit	Income Statement Credit	Balance Sheet Debit	Balance Sheet Credit	
1	Cash	100	6757806				6757806				6757806		1
2	Petty Cash Fund	110	10000				10000				10000		2
3	Clients' Trust Account	120	400000				400000				400000		3
4	Advances on Behalf of Clients	130	77500				77500				77500		4
5	Automobile	200	1589500				1589500				1589500		5
6	Accum. Depr.-Automobile	205		794750		(a) 529833		1324583				1324583	6
7	Office Equipment	210	1004296				1004296				1004296		7
8	Accum. Depr.-Office Equipment	215		358480		(b) 179240		537720				537720	8
9	Liability for Trust Funds	300		400000				400000				400000	9
10	Employees' Income Tax Pay.	310		39700				39700				39700	10
11	FICA Tax Payable	320		45308				45308				45308	11
12	FUTA Tax Payable	330		12292				12292				12292	12
13	State Unemployment Tax Pay.	340		10706				10706				10706	13
14	Jose Ortega, Capital	500		2091458				2091458				2091458	14
15	Jose Ortega, Drawing	510	6090082				6090082				6090082		15
16	Expense + Revenue Summary	520											16
17	Legal Fees Revenue	600		18463800				18463800		18463800			17
18	Collection Fees Revenue	610		449557				449557		449557			18
19	Automobile Expense	700	405157				405157		405157				19
20	Charitable Contrib. Expense	703	119500				119500		119500				20
21	Depreciation Expense	705			(a) 529833		529833		529833				21
22					(b) 179240		179240		179240				22
23	Law Library Expense	708	592087				592087		592087				23
24	Miscellaneous Expense	710	79291				79291		79291				24
25	Office Supplies Expense	713	406643				406643		406643				25
26	Payroll Taxes Expense	715	298545				298545		298545				26
27	Rent Expense	718	1440000				1440000		1440000				27
28	Salary Expense	720	3263540				3263540		3263540				28
29	Telephone Expense	725	132104				132104		132104				29
30			22666051	22666051	709073	709073	23375124	23375124	7445940	18913357	15929184	4461767	30
31	Net Income								11467417			11467417	31
32									18913357	18913357	15929184	15929184	32

Jose Ortega—Worksheet

the Adjustments columns, the amount in the Trial Balance columns was extended directly to the Adjusted Trial Balance columns. When an account balance was affected by an entry in the Adjustments columns, the balance entered in the Trial Balance columns was increased or decreased, as the case might be, by the amount of the adjusting entry.

For example, Accumulated Depreciation—Office Equipment was listed in the Trial Balance Credit column as $3,584.80. Since there was an entry of $1,792.40 in the Adjustments Credit column, the amount extended to the Adjusted Trial Balance Credit column was the total of $3,584.80 and $1,792.40, or $5,377.20.

A rule that can always be followed in combining figures in the Trial Balance columns and the Adjustments columns is that if there are debits in both columns or credits in both columns, the two amounts are added and the total is carried to the Adjusted Trial Balance columns. If there is a debit in one column and a credit in the other, the smaller amount is subtracted from the larger and the difference will be either a debit or a credit depending on whether the debit or the credit is the larger amount. If the debit is the larger amount, the amount carried to the Adjusted Trial Balance columns will be placed in the Debit Column. If the credit is the larger amount, the difference will be placed in the Adjusted Trial Balance Credit column. The Adjusted Trial Balance columns were totaled to prove the equality of the debits and credits.

Income Statement Columns. The fourth pair of amount columns in the work sheet was used to show the amounts that will be reported in the income statement. The amounts for legal fees revenue and collection fees revenue were extended to the Income Statement Credit column from the Adjusted Trial Balance Credit column. The amounts of the expenses were extended to the Income Statement Debit column from the Adjusted Trial Balance Debit column.

The Income Statement columns were totaled. The difference between the totals of these columns is the amount of the increase or the decrease in owner's equity due to net income or net loss during the accounting period. If the total of the credits exceeds the total of the debits, the difference represents the increase in owner's equity due to net income; if the total of the debits exceeds the total of the credits, the difference represents the decrease in owner's equity due to net loss.

Reference to the Income Statement columns of Ortega's work sheet will show that the total of the credits amounted to $189,133.57 and the total of the debits amounted to $74,459.40. The difference of $114,674.17 represented the amount of the net income for the year.

Balance Sheet Columns. The fifth pair of amount columns of the work sheet was used to show the amounts that will be reported in the balance sheet. The amounts were extended to the Balance Sheet Debit and Credit columns from the Adjusted Trial Balance columns. The Balance Sheet columns were totaled. The difference between the totals of these columns also is the amount of the net income or the net loss for the accounting period. If the total of the debits exceeds the total of the credits, the difference represents a net income for the accounting period; if the total of the credits exceeds the total of the debits, the difference represents a net loss for the period. The difference should be the same as the difference between the totals of the Income Statement columns.

Reference to the Balance Sheet columns of the work sheet will show that the total of the debits amounted to $159,291.84 and the total of the credits amounted to $44,617.67. The difference, amounting to $114,674.17, was the amount of the net income for the year.

Completing the Work Sheet. The difference between the totals of the Income Statement columns and the totals of the Balance Sheet columns should be entered on the next horizontal line below the column totals. If the difference represents net income, it should be so designated and entered in the Income Statement Debit and in the Balance Sheet Credit columns. If, instead, a net loss has been the result, the amount should be so designated and entered in the Income Statement Credit and in the Balance Sheet Debit columns. After the net income (or net loss) has been entered, a double line is ruled immediately below the totals.

Proving the Work Sheet. The fact that the difference between the Income Statement columns and the difference between the Balance Sheet columns are the same amount is not a coincidence. This occurs because an excess of revenue over expenses results in net income. Likewise, an excess of expenses over revenue results in a net loss. It is also true, but not quite so obvious, that if there is a net income, it will result in an increase in assets in the Balance Sheet columns in the form of additional cash, accounts receivable, or other assets. Sometimes cash received is used to pay liabilities, so that the assets at the end of the period may not have increased in total, but the liabilities have decreased. The increase in owner's equity, however, which results from profitable operations has not yet been entered in the permanent owner's equity account at the time the work sheet is prepared. The balance of the owner's capital account is the amount of owner's equity at the beginning of the period, because the day by day changes are entered in the temporary owner's equity accounts—the revenue and expense accounts.

When the amount of the net income is added to the Income Statement Debit column, the total of expenses and net income is equal to the revenue items in the Income Statement Credit column; and when the amount of net income is added to the Balance Sheet Credit column, the total assets equal the total liabilities and owner's equity, which is the accounting equation presented on page 5. After the temporary accounts are closed at the end of the period and the net amount of income for the period has been transferred to the owner's capital account, that account includes the net income for the period.

BUILDING YOUR ACCOUNTING KNOWLEDGE

1. In what three ways does an end-of-period work sheet assist the accountant?
2. Explain the purpose of each of the two adjustments on Ortega's work sheet.
3. State the rule for combining figures in the Trial Balance columns and the Adjustment columns.
4. What is the difference called if the total of the Income Statement Debit column is greater than the total of the Income Statement Credit column?
5. Why must the difference between the totals of the Income Statement columns and the totals of the balance sheet columns always be the same?

APPLYING ACCOUNTING CONCEPTS

Exercise 7-1. **(a)** The unadjusted trial balance of Michael O'Toole and Elizabeth Lowry, attorneys at law, on December 31, 1987, includes an automobile purchased one year ago at a cost of $12,600. The automobile is being depreciated over a period of three years. One third of the cost of the automobile will be charged to Depreciation Expense in 1987.

(b) The unadjusted trial balance also includes office furniture and equipment in the amount of $31,500. No purchases of office furniture and equipment have been made in 1987. The depreciation rate used by O'Toole and Lowry is 20 percent.

Using the journal paper provided, prepare the entries to enter depreciation expense in the year 1987. Total and rule the journal as a means of proof.

Exercise 7-2. **(a)** The unadjusted trial balance of Dr. Allen Nagle on December 31, 1987, shows that the balance in the account Accumulated Depreciation—Automobile on December 31, 1987, was $12,250. The automobile was purchased 2½ years ago at a cost of $14,700 and is being depreciated over a period of three years.

(b) The total amount of medical equipment in the medical equipment account in the unadjusted trial balance is $43,350. This includes medical equipment purchased three years ago at a cost of $40,850 and an additional piece of medical equipment purchased on December 5 at a cost of $2,500. Dr. Nagle follows the practice of not taking depreciation on equipment that has been owned for less than a month. The equipment is being depreciated over a period of five years or 20 percent a year.

Using the journal paper provided, prepare the entries to enter depreciation expense in the year 1987. Total and rule the journal as a means of proof.

Exercise 7-3. (a) The unadjusted trial balance on December 31, 1987, of Jean Sheridan, an architect, includes office furniture and equipment in the amount of $27,500. On July 1, a new desk was purchased at a cost of $550 and this amount is included in the figure of $27,500. One half year's depreciation should be taken on the desk. The office furniture and equipment is being depreciated over a period of five years or 20 percent a year. All office furniture and equipment except the desk has been in use for the entire year.

Using the journal paper provided, prepare the entry to enter depreciation expense for the year 1987. Do not make a separate entry to enter depreciation of the desk purchased on July 1.

(b) The unadjusted trial balance of Leon Holtman, an engineer, includes engineering equipment in the amount of $35,700. Of this amount, $4,000 of the equipment is fully depreciated, but is still in use. No further depreciation can be taken on this equipment. The engineering equipment has all been in use for the entire year. The equipment is being depreciated over a period of five years or 20 percent a year.

Using the journal paper provided, prepare an entry to enter depreciation expense for the year 1987.

Report No. 7-1

Complete Report No. 7-1 in the study assignments and submit your working papers to the instructor for approval.

THE FINANCIAL STATEMENTS

The financial statements usually consist of (1) an income statement and (2) a balance sheet.

The Income Statement

An **income statement** is a formal statement of the results of the operation of an enterprise during an accounting period. Other titles sometimes used for this statement include **profit and loss statement**, **income and expense statement**, **revenue and expense statement**, **operating statement**, and **report of earnings**. Whatever the title, the purpose of the statement or report is to show the types and amounts of revenue and expenses that the business had during the period involved, and the resulting net income or net loss for this accounting period.

Importance of the Income Statement. The income statement is generally considered to be one of the most important financial statements of a business. A business cannot exist indefinitely unless it has profit or net income. The income statement is essentially a "report card" of the enterprise. The statement provides a basis for judging the overall effectiveness of the management. Decisions as to whether to continue a business, to expand it, or to contract it are often based upon the results as reported in the income statement. Actual and potential creditors are interested in income statements because one of the best reasons for extending credit or for making a loan is that the business is profitable.

Various government agencies are interested in income statements of businesses for a variety of reasons. Regulatory bodies are concerned with the earnings of the enterprises they regulate, because a part of the regulation usually relates to the prices, rates, or fares that may be charged. If the enterprise is either exceptionally profitable or unprofitable, some change in the allowed prices or rates may be needed. Income tax authorities, both federal and local, have an interest in business income statements. Net income determination for tax purposes differs somewhat from the calculation of net income for other purposes; but, for a variety of reasons, the tax authorities are interested in both sets of calculations.

Form of the Income Statement. The form of the income statement depends in part upon the type of enterprise. For a professional practice, the professional revenue is listed first, the professional expenses are listed next, and the total of the professional expenses is subtracted from the professional revenue to determine the net professional income. The amounts of any revenue from other sources, such as dividend revenue from investments, are added to, and the amounts of any other expenses, such as interest on a loan from the bank, are subtracted from, the net professional income to arrive at the final amount of net income or net loss.

It is essential that the income statement be properly headed. The name of the business (or of the individual if the enterprise is a professional practice or if the business is operated in the owner's name) should be shown first. The name of the statement is placed on the second line, and the period of time that the statement covers appears on the third line. An income statement always covers a period of time, and if the period is a year, it may be stated, for example, "For the Year Ended December 31, 19--."

The income statement presented to the owner (or owners) of an enterprise and to potential creditors or other interested parties is usually typewritten. The income statement for Ortega for the year ended December 31, 1987, is shown at the top of page 233. The information needed to prepare the statement was obtained from the work sheet shown on page 227.

JOSE ORTEGA, ATTORNEY AT LAW
Income Statement
For the Year Ended December 31, 1987

Professional revenue:		
Legal fees revenue		$184,638.00
Collection fees revenue		4,495.57
Total professional revenue		$189,133.57
Professional expenses:		
Automobile expense	$ 4,051.57	
Charitable contributions expense	1,195.00	
Depreciation expense	7,090.73	
Law library expense	5,920.87	
Miscellaneous expense	792.91	
Office supplies expense	4,066.43	
Payroll taxes expense	2,985.45	
Rent expense	14,400.00	
Salary expense	32,635.40	
Telephone expense	1,321.04	
Total professional expenses		74,459.40
Net income		$114,674.17

Jose Ortega, Attorney at Law—Income Statement

The Balance Sheet

A formal statement of the assets, liabilities, and owner's equity in an enterprise at a specified date is known as a balance sheet. The title of the statement had its origin in the equality of the elements; that is, in the balance between the sum of the assets and the sum of the liabilities and owner's equity. Sometimes the balance sheet is called a statement of financial condition or a statement of financial position.

Importance of the Balance Sheet. The balance sheet of a business is of considerable interest to various parties for several reasons. The owner or owners of a business are interested in the kinds and amounts of assets and liabilities and the amount of the owner's equity or capital element.

Persons considering buying an ownership interest in a business are greatly interested in the character and amount of the assets and liabilities, though this interest is probably secondary to their concern about the future earnings possibilities.

Form of the Balance Sheet. Traditionally, balance sheets have been presented either in **account form** or in **report form**. When the account form is followed, the assets are listed on the left side of the page (or in the left of two facing pages) and the liabilities and owner's equity on the right. This form is similar to the debit-side and credit-side arrangement of the standard ledger account. When the report form of the balance sheet is followed, the assets, liabilities, and owner's equity elements are listed underneath each other. This arrangement is usually preferable when the statement is typed on letter-size paper (8½" × 11").

The balance sheet of Jose Ortega, Attorney at Law, as of December 31, 1987, in account form is reproduced on pages 234 and 235. The data for the preparation of the statement were secured from the work sheet shown on page 227.

Whichever form is used, it is essential that the statement have the proper heading. This means that three things must be shown: **(1)** the name of the business (or name of the individual if the business or professional practice is carried on in the name of an individual); followed on the next line by **(2)** the name of the statement—usually just "Balance Sheet"; and **(3)** the date

JOSE ORTEGA,
Balance
December

Assets			
Current assets:			
Cash		$67,578.06	
Petty cash		100.00	
Clients' trust account		4,000.00	
Advances on behalf of clients		775.00	
Total current assets			$72,453.06
Long-term assets:			
Automobile	$15,895.00		
Less accumulated depreciation—automobile	13,245.83	$ 2,649.17	
Office equipment	$10,042.96		
Less accumulated depreciation—office equipment	5,377.20	4,665.76	
Total long-term assets			7,314.93
Total assets			$79,767.99

Jose Ortega, Attorney at Law—Balance Sheet *(Left Side)*

(month, day, and year) on the third line. Sometimes the expression "As of Close of Business December 31, 1987" (or whatever date is involved) is included. It must be remembered that a balance sheet relates to a particular moment of time. This is in contrast to the income statement which always refers to a certain period of time.

Classification of Data in the Balance Sheet. The purpose of the balance sheet and of all other financial statements and reports is to convey as much information as possible. This aim is furthered by some classification of the data being reported. It has become almost universal practice to classify both assets and liabilities in the balance sheet as either (1) current or (2) noncurrent or long-term.

Current Assets. Current assets include cash and all other assets that may be reasonably expected to be realized in cash or sold or consumed during the normal operating cycle of the business. In a professional practice, the current assets may include cash and receivables, such as advances on behalf of clients.

Long-Term Assets. Property that is used in the operation of a professional practice may include such assets as land, buildings, office equipment, professional equipment, and automobiles. Such assets are called long-term assets because they have a useful life that is comparatively long. Of these assets, only land is really permanent.

ATTORNEY AT LAW
Sheet
31, 1987

Liabilities			
Current liabilities:			
Liability for trust funds		$ 4,000.00	
Employees income tax payable		397.00	
FICA tax payable		453.08	
FUTA tax payable		122.92	
State unemployment tax payable		107.06	
Total current liabilities			$ 5,080.06
Owner's Equity			
Jose Ortega, capital:			
Capital, January 1		$20,914.58	
Net income	$114,674.17		
Less withdrawals	60,900.82	53,773.35	
Capital, December 31			74,687.93
Total liabilities and owner's equity			$79,767.99

Jose Ortega, Attorney at Law—Balance Sheet *(Right Side)*

Reference to the balance sheet of Jose Ortega will show that the long-term assets consist of office equipment and an automobile. In each case, the amount of the accumulated depreciation is shown as a deduction from the cost of the depreciable asset. The difference between the cost of the asset and the accumulated depreciation is the book value of the asset. The book value represents the undepreciated amount of the asset. In future periods, the book value of a specific asset will decrease as depreciation expense is realized and the amount of accumulated depreciation increases.

Current Liabilities. Current liabilities include those obligations that will be due in a short time and paid with monies provided by the current assets. As of December 31, Ortega's current liabilities consisted of liability for trust funds, employees income tax payable, FICA tax payable, FUTA tax payable, and state unemployment tax payable.

Long-Term Liabilities. Long-term liabilities, sometimes called fixed liabilities, include those obligations that will not be due for a relatively long time. The most common of the long-term liabilities is Mortgages Payable.

A mortgage payable is a debt or an obligation that is secured by a mortgage, which provides for the conveyance of certain property upon failure to pay the debt at maturity. When the debt is paid, the mortgage becomes void. A mortgage payable differs little from an account payable or a note payable except that the creditor holds the mortgage as security for the payment of the debt. Usually debts secured by mortgages run for a longer period of time than ordinary notes payable or accounts payable. A mortgage payable should be classified as a long-term liability if the maturity date extends beyond the normal operating cycle of the business (usually a year). Ortega has no long-term liabilities.

Owner's Equity. As previously explained, accounts relating to the owner's equity element may be either permanent or temporary owner's equity accounts. The permanent owner's equity accounts used in recording the operations of a particular enterprise depend upon the type of organization; that is, whether the enterprise is organized as a sole proprietorship, as a partnership, or as a corporation.

In the case of a sole proprietorship, one or more accounts representing the owner's interest or equity in the assets may be kept. Reference to the chart of accounts shown on page 124 of Chapter 5 will show that the following accounts are classified as owner's equity accounts:

Jose Ortega, Capital, Account No. 500
Jose Ortega, Drawing, Account No. 510
Expense and Revenue Summary, Account No. 520

Account No. 500 reflects the amount of Ortega's equity. It may be increased by additional investments or by the practice of not withdrawing cash or other assets in an amount as large as the net income of the enterprise. It may be decreased by withdrawals in excess of the amount of the net income or by sustaining a net loss during one or more accounting periods. Usually there will be no changes in the balance of this account during the accounting period, in which case the balance represents the owner's investment in the business as of the beginning of the accounting period and until the books are closed at the end of the accounting period.

Account No. 510 is Ortega's drawing account. This account is debited for any withdrawals of cash or other property for personal use. It is a temporary account in which is kept a record of the owner's personal drawings during the accounting period. Ordinarily such drawings are made in anticipation of earnings rather than as withdrawals of capital. The balance of the account, as shown by the trial balance at the close of an accounting period, represents the total amount of the owner's drawings during the period.

Reference to the work sheet shown on page 227 will reveal that the balance of Ortega's drawing account is listed in the Balance Sheet Debit column. This is because there is no provision on a work sheet for making deductions from owner's equity except by listing them in the Debit column. Since the balance of the owner's capital account is listed in the Balance Sheet Credit column, the listing of the balance of the owner's drawing account in the Debit column is equivalent to deducting the amount from the balance of the owner's capital account.

Account No. 520 is used only at the close of the accounting period for the purpose of summarizing the temporary owner's equity accounts. Sometimes this account is referred to as a **clearing account**. No entries should appear in the account before the books are closed at the end of the accounting period.

The owner's equity section of Ortega's balance sheet is arranged to show the major changes that took place during the year in the owner's equity element of the law practice. Ortega's interest in the practice amounted to $20,914.58 at the beginning of the year. The interest was increased $114,674.17 as the result of profitable operations and decreased $60,900.82 as the result of withdrawals during the year. Thus the owner's equity increased by $53,773.35 because withdrawals were less than the income for the period. Ortega's anticipation of income was less than the amount actually earned. The owner's equity element on December 31 amounted to $74,687.93.

BUILDING YOUR ACCOUNTING KNOWLEDGE

1. Why is an income statement important?
2. Explain the two forms of the balance sheet.
3. What items are usually included in current assets?
4. Why would a mortgage payable usually not be included among the current liabilities?

APPLYING ACCOUNTING CONCEPTS

Exercise 7-4. Sonya Reeves and Patrick Reilly are attorneys engaged in the practice of law. The books have been closed as of December 31, 19--. The following is an alphabetical list of the assets and liabilities of the firm:

Account	Debit Balance	Credit Balance
Accum. Depr.—Automobile		$ 4,000.00
Accum. Depr.—Building		80,040.00
Accum. Depr.—Office Equipment		18,000.00
Advances on Behalf of Clients	$ 650.00	
Automobile	12,000.00	
Building	400,000.00	
Cash	78,637.50	
Clients' Trust Account	9,500.00	
Employees Income Tax Payable		351.00
FICA Tax Payable		562.50
FUTA Tax Payable		20.00
Land	35,000.00	
Liability for Trust Funds		9,500.00
Mortgage Payable (due in 12 years)		246,000.00
Office Equipment	30,000.00	
Petty Cash	100.00	
State Unemployment Tax Payable		37.50
	$565,887.50	$358,511.00

Required: **(1)** Using the paper provided, classify the assets and liabilities of the law firm under the following headings: Current Assets, Long-Term Assets, Current Liabilities, and Long-Term Liabilities. Subtract the accumulated depreciation accounts from the assets with which they are related and place the answer in the first column to the right. **(2)** Total each classification where necessary and total the classifications to obtain the total assets and the total liabilities. **(3)** Determine the total owner's equity on December 31, 19--.

Exercise 7-5. Karen Friedman and Janet Kreutser are psychiatrists who conduct a practice called the Millersburg Clinic. Net income of the clinic for the current year ended December 31, 19--, was $206,714.00. On January 1 of the current year the capital of the partners was as follows:

Karen Friedman	$78,014.36
Janet Kreutser	$69,437.29

During the year the partners made withdrawals as follows:

Karen Friedman	$80,549.00
Janet Kreutser	$56,834.14

Partnership net income or net loss is shared in the ratio of Friedman 60%, Kreutser 40%.

Required: Using the paper provided, prepare the owners' equity section of the balance sheet which would be prepared as of December 31, 19--.

Exercise 7-6. Mark Preston is a civil engineer who began his practice on January 2, 19--, with an investment of $75,000. Preston has two employees, an assistant engineer whose salary is $2,000 a month and a secretary-bookkeeper whose salary is $1,400 a month. The following is an adjusted trial balance of Preston's accounts as of December 31, the end of the first year of the practice. An income statement prepared for the year ended December 31, 19--, showed that the net income for the year was $38,956.56.

Required: Using the paper provided, prepare a classified balance sheet as of December 31, 19-- in report form for Mark Preston, Civil Engineer.

MARK PRESTON, CIVIL ENGINEER
Adjusted Trial Balance
December 31, 19--

Account	Acct. No.	Debit Balance	Credit Balance
Cash	100	58,864.24	
Petty Cash	105	100.00	
Automobile	200	13,500.00	
Accum. Depr.—Automobile	205		4,500.00
Engineering Equipment	210	8,200.40	
Accum. Depr.—Engineering Equipment	215		1,640.08
Office Equipment	220	10,475.00	
Accum. Depr.—Office Equipment	225		2,095.00
Employees Income Tax Payable	400		438.00
FICA Tax Payable	410		510.00
Mark Preston, Capital	600		75,000.00
Mark Preston, Drawing	605	32,000.00	
Professional Fees	700		110,860.00
Automobile Expense	800	2,463.80	
Charitable Contributions Expense	805	520.00	
Miscellaneous Expense	810	537.08	
Office Supplies Expense	815	684.22	
Payroll Taxes Expense	820	3,550.00	
Rent Expense	825	21,600.00	
Salary Expense	830	40,800.00	
Telephone Expense	835	1,748.34	
		195,043.08	195,043.08

Report No. 7-2

Complete Report No. 7-2 in the study assignments and submit your working papers to the instructor for approval.

MASTERY PROBLEMS

Problem 7-A Adjusting Entries in a Work Sheet

Sumio Mitsui and Carmen Aguilar have formed a partnership for the practice of civil engineering. They employ ten engineers and drafters, a secretary, and a secretary-bookkeeper. The partners share profits and losses equally. The Trial Balance columns of the work sheet for the current year ended December 31 are shown below.

SUMIO MITSUI AND CARMEN AGUILAR, CIVIL ENGINEERS
Work Sheet
For the Year Ended December 31, 19--

ACCOUNT	ACCT. NO.	TRIAL BALANCE Debit	Credit
Cash	100	105,804.30	
Petty Cash Fund	110	75.00	
Office Equipment	200	40,518.42	
Accum. Depr.—Office Equipment	205		24,311.05
Professional Equipment	210	60,687.11	
Accum. Depr.—Professional Equipment	215		22,757.67
Automotive Equipment	220	135,742.87	
Accum. Depr.—Automotive Equipment	225		81,445.72
Employees Income Tax Payable	300		4,440.00
FICA Tax Payable	310		2,250.00
FUTA Tax Payable	320		
State Unemployment Tax Payable	330		
Sumio Mitsui, Capital	400		50,129.40
Sumio Mitsui, Drawing	405	48,329.17	
Carmen Aguilar, Capital	410		53,430.38
Carmen Aguilar, Drawing	415	45,773.92	
Expense and Revenue Summary	420		
Professional Fees	500		715,800.00
Automotive Expense	600	10,625.91	
Charitable Contributions Expense	605	3,420.00	
Depreciation Expense	610		
Insurance Expense	615	25,600.00	
Miscellaneous Expense	620	2,557.32	
Payroll Taxes Expense	625	29,940.00	
Rent Expense	630	72,000.00	
Salary Expense	635	360,000.00	
Stationery, Supplies, & Blueprint Expense	640	10,370.48	
Telephone Expense	645	3,119.72	
		954,564.22	954,564.22

Required: Prepare a ten-column work sheet using the work sheet paper provided. Make the necessary entries in the Adjustments columns to enter the following:

Depreciation:
Office equipment, 20% a year, $8,103.68
Professional equipment, 12½% a year, $7,585.89
Automotive equipment, 20% a year, $27,148.57

Note: Mastery problems 7-B and 8-A are based on the work sheet for Mitsui and Aguilar. If these problems are to be solved, the work sheet should be retained for reference until they are solved, at which time the solutions of all three problems may be submitted to the instructor.

Problem 7-B Financial Statements

Refer to the work sheet for Mitsui and Aguilar (based on Problem 7-A) and from it prepare the following financial statements:

(1) An income statement for the year ended December 31.
(2) A balance sheet in account form as of December 31.

The income statement may be typewritten or handwritten. If it is typewritten, use plain bond paper 8½" × 11"; if it is handwritten, use the ruled paper provided.

The balance sheet may be typewritten or handwritten. If it is typewritten, use plain bond paper 8½" × 11"; if it is handwritten, use the ruled paper provided.

CHALLENGE PROBLEM 7

Benjamin Cohen and Judith Goldman are attorneys who started a law practice on January 2, 19--. They share profits and losses equally. They employ a secretary-bookkeeper and a secretary. The trial balance taken on December 31, 19-- is given below:

Cohen and Goldman, Attorneys at Law
Trial Balance
December 31, 19--

Account	No.	Debit	Credit
Cash	100	30,804.60	
Clients' Trust Account	110	950.87	
Advances on Behalf of Clients	120	450.00	
Office Supplies	130	2,286.94	
Prepaid Insurance	140	10,426.38	
Automobile	200	12,249.47	
Accum. Depr.—Automobile	205		
Building	210	80,667.19	
Accum. Depr.—Building	215		
Land	220	30,000.00	
Office Equipment	230	5,229.04	
Accum. Depr.—Office Equipment	235		
Liability for Trust Funds	300		950.87
Employees Income Tax Payable	310		398.00
FICA Tax Payable	320		465.00
Mortgage Payable	340		52,567.25
Benjamin Cohen, Capital	500		82,319.19
Benjamin Cohen, Drawing	505	30,420.36	
Judith Goldman, Capital	510		83,604.79
Judith Goldman, Drawing	515	28,847.50	
Legal Fees Revenue	600		68,017.00
Collection Fees Revenue	610		1,385.42
Expense & Revenue Summary	615		
Automobile Expense	700	1,740.18	
Depreciation Expense	705		
Insurance Expense	710		
Interest Expense	715	5,395.86	
Law Library Expense	720	7,148.09	
Miscellaneous Expense	725	532.27	
Office Supplies Expense	730		
Payroll Taxes Expense	735	2,839.00	
Salary Expense	740	37,200.00	
Telephone Expense	745	2,519.77	
		289,707.52	289,707.52

Required: (1) Complete the work sheet provided, making the required adjustments for depreciation expense for the year from the information provided below:

Depreciation:
Automobile—three year life.
Building—20 year life.
Office equipment—5 year life.

The amount of office supplies on hand on December 31 was $225.45. (Make the adjusting entry for the difference in the balance in Account 130, Office Supplies, and the amount on hand on December 31.)

One third of the prepaid insurance has expired and is now an expense. **(2)** Prepare an income statement for the year ended December 31, 19--. It may be typewritten or handwritten. If it is typewritten, use plain bond paper 8½″ × 11″; if it is handwritten, use the ruled paper provided. **(3)** Prepare a balance sheet in report form as of December 31, 19--. It may be typewritten or handwritten. If it is typewritten, use plain bond paper 8½″ × 11″; if it is handwritten, use the ruled paper provided.

Note: Challenge Problem 8 is based on the work sheet for Cohen and Goldman. If Challenge Problem 8 is to be solved, the work sheet should be retained for reference until Challenge Problem 8 is solved, at which time the solutions for both problems may be submitted to the instructor.

EXPANDING YOUR BUSINESS VOCABULARY

What is the meaning of each of the following terms:

account form **(p. 234)**
adjusted trial balance **(p. 226)**
balance sheet **(p. 233)**
book value **(p. 236)**
clearing account **(p. 237)**
current assets **(p. 235)**
current liabilities **(p. 236)**
end-of-period adjustments **(p. 225)**
fixed liabilities **(p. 236)**
income and expense statement **(p. 231)**
income statement **(p. 231)**
long-term assets **(p. 235)**
long-term liabilities **(p. 236)**
mortgage **(p. 236)**
mortgage payable **(p. 236)**
operating statement **(p. 231)**
periodic summary **(p. 224)**
profit and loss statement **(p. 231)**
report form **(p. 234)**
report of earnings **(p. 231)**
revenue and expense statement **(p. 231)**
statement of financial condition **(p. 233)**
statement of financial position **(p. 233)**
work sheet **(p. 225)**

8

Adjusting and Closing Accounts at End of Accounting Period

CHAPTER OBJECTIVES

Careful study of this chapter should enable you to:

- Explain and perform the steps in the accounting cycle that are needed to: (1) Journalize and post the adjusting entries and update the ledger account balances. (2) Journalize and post the closing entries and update the ledger account balances. (3) Take a post-closing trial balance.

As explained in the preceding chapter, the adjustment of certain accounts at the end of the accounting period is required because of changes that have occurred during the period that are not reflected in the accounts. Since the purpose of the temporary owner's equity accounts is to assemble information relating to a specified period of time, at the end of the period the balances of these accounts must be removed to allow the accounts to be ready to perform their function in the following period. Accounts of this type must be "closed."

ADJUSTING ENTRIES

In preparing the work sheet for Jose Ortega, Attorney at Law (reproduced on page 227), adjustments were made to accomplish the following purposes:

1. To record the estimated amount of depreciation of the automobile for the year.
2. To record the estimated amount of depreciation of the office equipment for the year.

Note that each of the adjusting entries affects both the balance sheet and the income statement. If an adjusting entry increases an expense, as when depreciation expense is recorded in entries (a), and (b), then the balance sheet accounts Accumulated Depreciation — Automobile and Accumulated Depreciation — Office Equipment are also increased. It should also be noted that adjusting entries for accumulated depreciation do not affect cash because the long-term asset has already been paid for. Depreciation, as explained in Chapter 5, is simply a way of allocating the original cost of the asset to the periods in which it is used up.

The effect of these adjustments was reflected in the financial statements reproduced on pages 233 and 234–235. To bring the ledger into agreement with the financial statements, the adjustments should be recorded in the proper accounts. It is customary, therefore, at the end of each accounting period to journalize the adjustments and to post them to the accounts.

Journalizing the Adjusting Entries

Adjusting entries should be recorded in the general journal. A portion of a page of a general journal showing Ortega's adjusting entries is reproduced below. Since the heading "Adjusting Entries" explains the nature of the entries, a separate explanation of each adjusting entry is unnecessary. The information needed in journalizing the adjustments was obtained from the Adjustments columns in the work sheet shown on page 227. The account numbers were not entered in the Posting Reference column at the time of journalizing; they were entered as the posting was completed.

GENERAL JOURNAL PAGE 13

	DATE		DESCRIPTION	POST. REF.	DEBIT	CREDIT	
1	Dec.	31	Adjusting Entries				1
2			Depreciation Expense	705	5 298 33		2
3			Accum. Depr. - Automobile	205		5 298 33	3
4			Depreciation Expense	705	1 792 40		4
5			Accum. Depr. - Office Equip.	215		1 792 40	5
6					7 090 73	7 090 73	6

Jose Ortega, Attorney At Law — Adjusting Entries

Posting the Adjusting Entries

The adjusting entries should be posted individually to the proper general ledger accounts. The accounts of Ortega that were affected by the adjusting entries are reproduced on this page. The entries in the accounts for December transactions that were posted prior to posting the adjusting entries are the same as appeared in the accounts reproduced on pages 144–149. The number of the general journal page on which the adjusting entries were recorded was entered in the Posting Reference column of the general ledger accounts affected, and the account numbers were entered in the Posting Reference column of the general journal as the posting was completed. This provided a cross-reference in both books.

ACCOUNT *Accumulated Depreciation - Automobile* ACCOUNT NO. 205

DATE		ITEM	POST. REF.	DEBIT	CREDIT	BALANCE DEBIT	BALANCE CREDIT
1987 Dec.	1	Balance	✓				7947 50
	31		GJ13		5298 33		13245 83

ACCOUNT *Accumulated Depreciation - Office Equipment* ACCOUNT NO. 215

DATE		ITEM	POST. REF.	DEBIT	CREDIT	BALANCE DEBIT	BALANCE CREDIT
1987 Dec.	1	Balance	✓				3584 80
	31		GJ13		1792 40		5377 20

ACCOUNT *Depreciation Expense* ACCOUNT NO. 705

DATE		ITEM	POST. REF.	DEBIT	CREDIT	BALANCE DEBIT	BALANCE CREDIT
1987 Dec.	31		GJ13	5298 33			
	31		GJ13	1792 40		7090 73	

Jose Ortega, Attorney at Law — General Ledger Accounts After Posting Adjusting Entries

BUILDING YOUR ACCOUNTING KNOWLEDGE

1. What is the purpose of each of the adjusting entries made by Jose Ortega?
2. Why do adjusting entries for accumulated depreciation not affect cash?
3. Where is the information obtained that is needed in journalizing the adjustments?
4. In the posting process, how is a cross-reference provided both to the general journal and to the general ledger?

APPLYING ACCOUNTING CONCEPTS

Exercise 8-1. The adjustment debit column of the work sheet for the year ended December 31, 1987 of the Stimson Machine Company contains the following amounts of depreciation expense:

(a) Automotive equipment........$25,661.46
(b) Machinery and equipment........$62,560.15
(c) Office equipment........$10,093.24

Using the journal paper provided, prepare the entries to record depreciation expense for the year 1987. Head the entries "Adjusting Entries." Total the entries as a means of proof.

Exercise 8-2. Refer to Exercise 8-1 and post the journal entries to the ledger accounts using the paper provided.

On January 1, 1987, the balances in the accumulated depreciation accounts of the long-term assets in Exercise 8-1 were as follows:

Automotive equipment........$ 38,492.18
Machinery and equipment........$187,680.45
Office equipment........$ 20,186.48

Exercise 8-3. Refer to Exercise 8-2. Assume that the cost of the long-term assets of the Stimson Machine Company was as follows on December 31, 1987:

Automotive equipment........$ 76,984.37
Machinery and equipment........$500,484.22
Office equipment........$ 50,466.18

Using the paper provided, state the book value of each of the long-term assets as of December 31, 1987 and the total book value of the long-term assets.

REPORT NO. 8-1

Complete Report No. 8-1 in the study assignments and submit your working papers to the instructor for approval.

CLOSING PROCEDURE

After the adjusting entries have been posted, all of the temporary owner's equity accounts should be closed. This means that the accountant must remove ("close out") (1) the balance of every account that enters into the calculation of the net income (or net loss) for the accounting period and (2) the balance of the owner's drawing account. The purpose of the closing procedure is to transfer the balances of the temporary owner's equity accounts to the permanent owner's equity account. This could be accomplished simply by debiting or crediting each account involved, with an offsetting credit or debit to the permanent owner's equity account. However, it is considered better practice to transfer the balances of all accounts that enter into the net income or net loss determination to a summarizing account called **Expense and Revenue Summary** (sometimes called **Income Summary**, **Profit and Loss Summary**, or just **Profit and Loss**. Then the resulting balance of the expense and revenue summary account (which will be the amount of the net income or net loss for the period) is transferred to the permanent owner's equity account.

The final step in the closing procedure is to transfer the balance of the owner's drawing account to the permanent owner's equity account. After this is done, only the asset accounts, the liability accounts, and the permanent owner's equity account have balances. If there has been no error, the sum of the balances of the asset accounts (less balances of any contra accounts) will be equal to the sum of the balances of the liability accounts plus the balance of the permanent owner's equity account. The accounts will agree exactly with what is shown by the balance sheet as of the close of the period. Reference to the balance sheet of Jose Ortega reproduced on pages 234 and 235 will show that the assets, liabilities, and owner's equity as of December 31 may be expressed in equation form as follows:

ASSETS	= LIABILITIES	+ OWNER'S EQUITY
$79,767.99	$5,080.06	$74,687.93

Journalizing the Closing Entries

Closing entries, like adjusting entries should be recorded in a general journal. A portion of a page of a general journal showing the closing entries for Ortega is reproduced on page 249. Since the heading "Closing Entries" explains the nature of the entries, a separate explanation of each closing entry is not necessary. The information required in preparing the closing entries was obtained from the work sheet illustrated on page 227.

The first closing entry was made to close the revenue accounts, Legal Fees Revenue and Collection Fees Revenue. Since these accounts have credit bal-

GENERAL JOURNAL PAGE 14

	DATE		DESCRIPTION	POST. REF.	DEBIT	CREDIT	
1	Dec.	31	Closing Entries				1
2			Legal Fees Revenue	600	184638 00		2
3			Collection Fees Revenue	610	4495 57		3
4			Expense and Revenue Summary	520		189133 57	4
5			Expense and Revenue Summary	520	74459 40		5
6			Automobile Expense	700		4051 57	6
7			Charitable Contributions Expense	703		1195 00	7
8			Depreciation Expense	705		7090 73	8
9			Law Library Expense	708		5920 87	9
10			Miscellaneous Expense	710		792 91	10
11			Office Supplies Expense	713		4066 43	11
12			Payroll Taxes Expense	715		2985 45	12
13			Rent Expense	718		14400 00	13
14			Salary Expense	720		32635 40	14
15			Telephone Expense	725		1321 04	15
16			Expense and Revenue Summary	520	114674 17		16
17			Jose Ortega, Capital	500		114674 17	17
18			Jose Ortega, Capital	500	60900 82		18
19			Jose Ortega, Drawing	510		60900 82	19
20					439167 96	439167 96	20
21							21
22							22
23							23
24							24
25							25
26							26

Jose Ortega, Attorney at Law — Closing Entries

ances, each account must be debited for the amount of its balance in order to close it. The debits to these two accounts are offset by a credit of $189,133.57 to Expense and Revenue Summary.

The second closing entry was made to close the expense accounts. Since these accounts have debit balances, each account must be credited for the amount of its balance in order to close it. The credits to these accounts are offset by a debit of $74,459.40 to Expense and Revenue Summary.

The posting of the first two closing entries causes the expense and revenue summary account to have a credit balance of $114,674.17, the net income for the year. The account has now served its purpose and must be closed. The third closing entry closes the expense and revenue summary account by debiting that account and crediting Jose Ortega for $114,674.17.

The final closing entry was made to close the Jose Ortega drawing account. Since this account has a debit balance, it must be credited to close it. The offsetting entry is a debit of $60,900.82 to Jose Ortega, Capital.

The account numbers shown in the posting reference column were not entered at the time the closing entries were made—they were entered as the posting was completed.

Posting the Closing Entries

Closing entries should be posted in the usual manner. Proper cross-references are provided by using the Posting Reference columns of the general journal and the ledger accounts. After all the closing entries have been posted, the accounts affected appear as shown below and on pages 251 to 253. The income statement accounts now have zero balances.

ACCOUNT *Jose Ortega, Capital* ACCOUNT NO. 500

DATE		ITEM	POST. REF.	DEBIT	CREDIT	BALANCE DEBIT	BALANCE CREDIT
1987 Dec.	1	Balance	✓				20914 58
	31		GJ14		114674 17		
	31		GJ14	60900 82			74687 93

ACCOUNT *Jose Ortega, Drawing* ACCOUNT NO. 510

DATE		ITEM	POST. REF.	DEBIT	CREDIT	BALANCE DEBIT	BALANCE CREDIT
1987 Dec.	1	Balance	✓			55647 18	
	16		CP23	2000 00			
	28		CP23	235 30			
	30		CP23	3000 00			
	31		CP24	18 34		60900 82	
	31		GJ14		60900 82	- 0 -	- 0 -

ACCOUNT *Expense and Revenue Summary* ACCOUNT NO. 520

DATE		ITEM	POST. REF.	DEBIT	CREDIT	BALANCE DEBIT	BALANCE CREDIT
1987 Dec.	31		GJ14		189133 57		
	31		GJ14	74459 40			
	31		GJ14	114674 17		- 0 -	- 0 -

Jose Ortega, Attorney at Law—Partial General Ledger *(continued)*

ACCOUNT *Legal Fees Revenue* ACCOUNT NO. 600

DATE		ITEM	POST. REF.	DEBIT	CREDIT	BALANCE DEBIT	BALANCE CREDIT
1987 Dec.	1	Balance	✓				165428 00
	31		CR25		19210 00		184638 00
	31		GJ14	184638 00		-0-	-0-

ACCOUNT *Collection Fees Revenue* ACCOUNT NO. 610

DATE		ITEM	POST. REF.	DEBIT	CREDIT	BALANCE DEBIT	BALANCE CREDIT
1987 Dec.	1	Balance	✓				4219 52
	31		CR25		276 05		4495 57
	31		GJ14	4495 57		-0-	-0-

ACCOUNT *Automobile Expense* ACCOUNT NO. 700

DATE		ITEM	POST. REF.	DEBIT	CREDIT	BALANCE DEBIT	BALANCE CREDIT
1987 Dec.	1	Balance	✓			3947 03	
	4		CP23	84 37			
	31		CP24	20 17		4051 57	
	31		GJ14		4051 57	-0-	-0-

ACCOUNT *Charitable Contributions Expense* ACCOUNT NO. 703

DATE		ITEM	POST. REF.	DEBIT	CREDIT	BALANCE DEBIT	BALANCE CREDIT
1987 Dec.	1	Balance	✓			1125 00	
	11		CP23	50 00			
	31		CP24	20 00		1195 00	
	31		GJ14		1195 00	-0-	-0-

ACCOUNT *Depreciation Expense* ACCOUNT NO. 705

DATE		ITEM	POST. REF.	DEBIT	CREDIT	BALANCE DEBIT	BALANCE CREDIT
1987 Dec.	31		GJ13	5298 33			
	31		GJ14	1792 40		7090 73	
	31		GJ14		7090 73	-0-	-0-

Jose Ortega, Attorney at Law — Partial General Ledger *(continued)*

ACCOUNT *Law Library Expense* ACCOUNT NO. 708

Date		Item	Post. Ref.	Debit	Credit	Balance Debit	Balance Credit
1987 Dec.	1	Balance	✓			4685 00	
	10		CP23	1235 87		5920 87	
	31		GJ14		5920 87	-0-	-0-

ACCOUNT *Miscellaneous Expense* ACCOUNT NO. 710

Date		Item	Post. Ref.	Debit	Credit	Balance Debit	Balance Credit
1987 Dec.	1	Balance	✓			627 35	
	2		CP23	61 30			
	14		CP23	100 00			
	31		CP24	4 26		792 91	
	31		GJ14		792 91	-0-	-0-

ACCOUNT *Office Supplies Expense* ACCOUNT NO. 713

Date		Item	Post. Ref.	Debit	Credit	Balance Debit	Balance Credit
1987 Dec.	1	Balance	✓			3932 66	
	17		CP23	123 35			
	31		CP24	10 42		4066 43	
	31		GJ14		4066 43	-0-	-0-

ACCOUNT *Payroll Taxes Expense* ACCOUNT NO. 715

Date		Item	Post. Ref.	Debit	Credit	Balance Debit	Balance Credit
1987 Dec.	1	Balance	✓			2711 13	
	31		GJ12	226 54			
	31		GJ12	47 78		2985 45	
	31		GJ14		2985 45	-0-	-0-

Jose Ortega, Attorney at Law — Partial General Ledger *(continued)*

ACCOUNT *Rent Expense* ACCOUNT NO. 718

DATE		ITEM	POST. REF.	DEBIT	CREDIT	BALANCE DEBIT	BALANCE CREDIT
1987 Dec.	1	Balance	✓			13200 00	
	1		CP23	1200 00		14400 00	
	31		GJ14		14400 00	-0-	-0-

ACCOUNT *Salary Expense* ACCOUNT NO. 720

DATE		ITEM	POST. REF.	DEBIT	CREDIT	BALANCE DEBIT	BALANCE CREDIT
1987 Dec.	1	Balance	✓			29615 00	
	31		CP24	3020 40		32635 40	
	31		GJ14		32635 40	-0-	-0-

ACCOUNT *Telephone Expense* ACCOUNT NO. 725

DATE		ITEM	POST. REF.	DEBIT	CREDIT	BALANCE DEBIT	BALANCE CREDIT
1987 Dec.	1	Balance	✓			1245 86	
	1		CP23	75 18		1321 04	
	31		GJ14		1321 04	-0-	-0-

Jose Ortega, Attorney at Law — Partial General Ledger *(concluded)*

After the income statement accounts have been closed, the accounts still open are the balance sheet accounts; that is, the asset, liability, and permanent owner's equity accounts. If a new general ledger is to be opened in which to record the transactions of the new year, the balances of the open accounts which have debit balances should be entered in the Debit Balance columns. The balances of the open accounts which have credit balances should be entered in the Credit Balance columns. The date will be January 1, even though the new ledger may be opened a few days after January 1.

If the old general ledger is to be used for the new year, the December 31 balances of the open accounts automatically become the balances on January 1. The number of the new year should be entered when the first entry is made in the new year.

Trial Balance After Closing

A trial balance of the general ledger accounts that remain open after the temporary owner's equity accounts have been closed is usually referred to as a post-closing trial balance. The purpose of the post-closing trial balance is to prove that the general ledger is in balance at the beginning of a new accounting period. It is advisable to know that such is the case before any transactions for the new accounting period are recorded.

The post-closing trial balance should contain the same accounts and amounts that appear in the Balance Sheet columns of the work sheet, except that (1) the owner's drawing account is omitted because it has been closed and (2) the owner's capital account has been adjusted for the amount of the net income (or net loss) and the amount of the owner's drawings.

A post-closing trial balance of Ortega's general ledger is shown below. Some accountants advocate that the post-closing trial balance should be dated as of the close of the old accounting period, while others advocate that it should be dated as of the beginning of the new accounting period. In this illustration the trial balance is dated December 31, the end of the period.

Jose Ortega, Attorney at Law
Post-Closing Trial Balance
December 31, 1987

Account	No.	Debit	Credit
Cash	100	67,578.06	
Petty Cash Fund	110	100.00	
Clients' Trust Account	120	4,000.00	
Advances on Behalf of Clients	130	775.00	
Automobile	200	15,895.00	
Accumulated Depreciation—Automobile	205		13,245.83
Office Equipment	210	10,042.96	
Accumulated Depreciation—Office Equipment	215		5,377.20
Liability for Trust Funds	300		4,000.00
Employees Income Tax Payable	310		397.00
FICA Tax Payable	320		453.08
FUTA Tax Payable	330		122.92
State Unemployment Tax Payable	340		107.06
Jose Ortega, Capital	500		74,687.93
		98,391.02	98,391.02

Jose Ortega, Attorney at Law—Post-Closing Trial Balance

The Accounting Cycle

The steps involved in handling the effect of all transactions and events completed during an accounting period, beginning with entries in the books of original entry and ending with the post-closing trial balance, are known as the accounting cycle. The following is a list of the steps in the accounting cycle.

1 Journalizing the transactions.
2 Posting to the ledger accounts.
3 Taking a trial balance.
4 Determining the needed adjustments.
5 Completing an end-of-period work sheet.
6 Preparing an income statement and a balance sheet.
7 Journalizing and posting the adjusting and closing entries.
8 Taking a post-closing trial balance.

In visualizing the accounting cycle, it is important to realize that steps 3 through 8 in the foregoing list are performed as of the last day of the accounting period. This does not mean that they necessarily are done on the last day. The accountant or bookkeeper may not be able to do any of these things until the first few days of the next period. Nevertheless, the work sheet, statements, and entries are prepared or recorded as of the closing date. While the journalizing of transactions in the new period proceeds in regular fashion, it is not usual to post to the general ledger any entries relating to the new period until the steps relating to the period just ended have been completed.

Income and Self-Employment Taxes

An unincorporated business or professional practice is not subject to income taxes. The owner — not the business or practice — is subject to income taxes. The amounts of business or professional revenue and expenses must be reported in the owner's personal income tax return regardless of the amount of money or other property the owner has actually withdrawn from the enterprise during the year. In the case of a sole proprietorship or a partnership, there is no legal distinction between the enterprise and the owner.

To bring a large class of self-employed individuals into the Social Security program, the law requires all self-employed persons (except those specifically exempted) to pay a self-employment tax. The rate is about 4.3 percent more than the prevailing FICA rate, but the base of the self-employment income tax is the same as the base for the FICA tax. If it is assumed that the combined FICA tax rate is 7.5 percent, the self-employment tax would be about 12 percent on the assumed base of $47,000. The actual rate and base of the tax may be changed by Congress at any time. In general, self-employment income means the net income of a professional practice or business conducted by an individual or a partner's distributive share of the net income of a partnership whether or not any cash is distributed. Earnings of less than $400 from self-employment are ignored for purposes of self-employment tax.

A taxable year for the purpose of the tax on self-employment income is the same as the taxpayer's taxable year for federal income tax purposes. The self-employment tax is reported along with the regular federal income tax. For calendar-year taxpayers, the tax return and full or final payment is due on April 15 following the close of the year. Like the personal income tax, the self-employment tax is treated as a personal expense of the owner. If the taxes are paid with business funds, the amount should be charged to the owners' drawing account.

BUILDING YOUR ACCOUNTING KNOWLEDGE

1. Where is the information obtained that is needed in journalizing the closing entries?
2. Explain the function of each of the four closing entries made by Jose Ortega.
3. What is the purpose of a post-closing trial balance?

APPLYING ACCOUNTING CONCEPTS

Exercise 8-4. After the revenue and expense accounts of the R. J. Williams Company were closed as of December 31, 19--, the expense and revenue summary account had a debit balance of $15,834.26. On December 31, 19-- the capital account of the owner, Robert J. Williams, had a credit balance of $60,589.47. Williams drawing account had a debit balance of $30,293.81. Using the journal paper provided, prepare the journal entries to complete the closing of the books of the R. J. Williams Company. Total the entries as a means of proof.

Exercise 8-5. Using the ledger accounts provided, post the journal entries made in Exercise 8-4.

Exercise 8-6. Linda Ashbrook is a self-employed financial planner. If it is assumed that the Social Security tax rate for self-employed persons is 12 percent on a base of $47,000, what would Ashbrook's Social Security tax payment, if any, amount to under each of the following conditions:

Ashbrook's net income is (a) $42,097.48
(b) $53,476.89
(c) $ 378.06

Use the ruled paper provided.

REPORT NO. 8-2

Complete Report No. 8-2 in the study assignments and submit your working papers to the instructor for approval.

MASTERY PROBLEMS

Problem 8-A Adjusting and closing entries

Refer to the work sheet for Mitsui and Aguilar (based on Problem 7A) and draft the general journal entries required: **(1)** to adjust the general ledger accounts so they will be in agreement with the financial statements. **(2)** To close the temporary owners' equity accounts on December 31. Use the general journal paper provided.

Problem 8-B Complete accounting cycle

Linda Jackson and Dennis Hoffman for several years have been partners in an advertising agency. The accounting records consist of a cash receipts journal, a cash payments journal, a general journal, and a general ledger. The November 30 balances have been entered in the accounts.

The trial balance as of November 30 is shown on page 258 and includes all of the accounts in the general ledger, some of which do not have balances as of November 30.

The firm employs seven persons, two artists, two persons in the advertising media department, two secretaries, and an accountant.

The partners share profits and losses equally.

Required: **(1)** Journalize the December transactions. **(2)** Post the journal entries to the ledger accounts. **(3)** Take a trial balance of the general ledger accounts and enter the figures in the first two columns of the ten-column work sheet provided. **(4)** Complete the ten-column work sheet making the required adjustments from the information given below.

Depreciation:
Automobiles, 33.3% a year, $7,950.66
Office and professional equipment, 20% a year, $14,518.81, based on the balance at the beginning of the year. No depreciation is taken this year on the purchase of December 22.

(5) Prepare an income statement for the year ending December 31 and a balance sheet in report form as of December 31. **(6)** Record the adjusting entries in the general journal and post. **(7)** Record the closing entries in the general journal and post. The page numbers of the general journal begin with No. 15. **(8)** Take a post-closing trial balance.

The Jackson and Hoffman Advertising Agency
Trial Balance
November 30, 19--

Account	No.	Debit	Credit
Cash	100	102,909.48	
Government Notes	110	35,000.00	
Petty Cash	120	100.00	
Automobiles	200	23,875.87	
Accumulated Depreciation—Automobiles	205		11,926.00
Office and Professional Equipment	210	72,594.06	
Accumulated Depreciation—Office and Professional Equipment	215		43,556.44
Employees Income Tax Payable	400		1,350.00
FICA Tax Payable	410		1,675.00
FUTA Tax Payable	420		
State Unemployment Tax Payable	430		
Linda Jackson, Capital	600		35,368.02
Linda Jackson, Drawing	610	64,682.73	
Dennis Hoffman, Capital	620		38,553.61
Dennis Hoffman, Drawing	630	58,326.47	
Expense and Revenue Summary	640		
Agency Fees	700		463,475.00
Interest Income	710		2,100.00
Automobile Expense	800	6,742.48	
Charitable Contributions Expense	805	6,850.00	
Depreciation Expense	810		
Electricity Expense	815	4,378.30	
Insurance Expense	820	3,745.00	
Miscellaneous Expense	825	640.18	
Payroll Taxes Expense	830	10,995.64	
Rent Expense	835	55,000.00	
Repairs and Maintenance Expense	840	7,029.86	
Salary Expense	845	123,741.85	
Stationery, Artists, and Media Supplies Expense	850	8,213.69	
Telephone Expense	855	4,762.35	
Travel and Entertainment Expense	860	8,416.11	
		598,004.07	598,004.07

NARRATIVE OF TRANSACTIONS FOR DECEMBER

Dec. 1 Paid the Ziegler Realty Co. $5,000 for rent of the office for the month of December. Check No. 845.

1 Received $8,450 from Thomas R. Spencer Co. for work completed.

Dec. 2 Paid the Bell Telephone Co. bill, $470.82. Check No. 846.

3 Paid the following payroll taxes based on salaries paid during the month of November by sending Check No. 847 in the amount of $3,025 to the Graham National Bank. Since the amount is in excess of $3,000, it must be deposited within three business days following the end of the month.

Employees income tax withheld from salaries		$1,350.00
FICA tax:		
Withheld from employees salaries	$837.50	
Imposed on employer	837.50	1,675.00
Total		$3,025.00

A Federal Tax Deposit, Form 8109, was filled out and sent with the check.

4 Paid the Franklin Gas and Electric Co. for electricity used during the month of November, $390.18. Check No. 848.

4 Paid for gasoline and oil used in the company cars during November, $209.47, Check No. 849.

7 Received $4,980 from the Warndorf Manufacturing Company for work completed.

8 Paid the Keen Art Supply Co. for artists supplies, $320.94. Check No. 850.

9 Reimbursed Hoffman for expenses incurred in attending a professional meeting, $498.37. Check No. 851.

10 Received fourth quarter interest on the government notes, $700. Debit Cash and credit Interest Income.

14 Paid the Schwartz Insurance Agency $7,350 for a one-year professional liability insurance policy. Check No. 852.

15 Paid salaries for first half of the month, $5,583.33 less employees withholding tax, $675, and FICA tax payable, $418.75. Checks No. 853–859 inclusive were issued for the net amounts payable to the employees.

16 Paid the South Hills Country Club $110.80 for entertainment of a client. Check No. 860.

16 Paid the Acme Cleaning Co. $720 for office cleaning services rendered during November. Check No. 861.

17 Received $11,500 from the O'Connor Supply Co. for work completed.

18 Purchased four new tires for one of the company cars, $251.96. Check No. 862.

Dec. 21 Received a check for $40.80 from the Keen Art Supply Co. The company advised that there had been an overcharge on the invoice paid on December 8. In the cash receipts journal, debit Cash and credit Stationery, Artists, and Media Supplies Expense, Account No. 850.

21 Paid the Ankenbauer Stationery Co. $220.42 for stationery and supplies. Check No. 863.

22 Received $7,500 from Oswego Home Builders in payment for work completed.

22 Paid the Grant and Pendleton Furniture Co. for a professional drawing table, $304.50. Check No. 864.

22 Paid the Toerner Stationery Co. $258.46 for office supplies. Check No. 865.

23 Linda Jackson invested an additional $5,000 in the agency. Debit Cash and credit Linda Jackson, Capital.

23 Paid the balance due on the pledge to the United Fund, $500. Check No. 866.

24 Received $10,000 from the Butler Machine Tool Co. for work completed.

28 Paid the Graham National Bank $30 for annual rental of a safe deposit box for the use of the partnership. Check No. 867. Debit Miscellaneous Expense, Account No. 825.

28 Paid the Higgins Office Equipment Co. $53.75 for typewriter repairs. Check No. 868.

30 Jackson withdrew $4,000 for personal use. Check No. 869.

30 Hoffman withdrew $3,500 for personal use. Check No. 870.

31 Paid salaries for the second half of the month $5,683.52, less employees withholding tax, $696, and FICA tax payable, $426.26. Checks No. 871–877 inclusive were issued for the net amounts payable to the employees.

31 Issued Check No. 878 to replenish the petty cash fund. A statement of petty cash payments for December follows:

Dennis Hoffman, Drawing	$20.00
Automobile Expense	12.50
Charitable Contributions Expense	5.00
Miscellaneous Expense	10.30
Stationery, Artists, and Media Supplies Expense	7.36
Travel and Entertainment Expense	42.60
Total payments	$97.76

31 Made an entry in the general journal for the employer's portion of the FICA tax for the month of December, $845.01.

CHALLENGE PROBLEM 8

Refer to the work sheet for Cohen and Goldman (based on Challenge Problem 7) and draft the general journal entries required: **(1)** To adjust the general ledger accounts so they will be in agreement with the financial statements. **(2)** To close the temporary owners' equity accounts on December 31. (The expense and revenue summary account is No. 520.)

EXPANDING YOUR BUSINESS VOCABULARY

What is the meaning of each of the following terms:

accounting cycle **(p. 255)**
adjusting entries **(p. 245)**
adjustments **(p. 245)**
closing entries **(p. 248)**
Expense and Revenue Summary **(p. 248)**
Income Summary **(p. 248)**
post-closing trial balance **(p. 254)**
Profit and Loss **(p. 248)**
Profit and Loss Summary **(p. 248)**
self-employment income **(p. 255)**
self-employment tax **(p. 255)**

INDEX

A

G

H

I

J

K

L

M

S

T

U

V

W

Z